THE DARK HEART OF RUSSIA

30 EXPERTS JOURNEY THROUGH
RUSSIA'S HIDDEN CULTURE

JONATHAN FINK
Editor

GIBSON SQUARE

Editor, Jonathan Fink

This first edition published by Gibson Square in 2026.

email: rights@gibsonsquare.com
website: gibsonsquare.com

All rights reserved. No part of this publication may be reproduced, stored in a retrieval system, or transmitted, in any form or by any means, electronic, mechanical, photocopying, recording or otherwise without the prior consent of the publisher. A catalogue record for this book is available from the Library of Congress and the British Library.

Papers used by Gibson Square are natural, recyclable products made from wood grown in sustainable forests; inks used are vegetable based. Manufacturing conforms to ISO 14001, and is accredited to FSC and PEFC chain of custody schemes. Colour-printing is through a certified CarbonNeutral® company that offsets its CO2 emissions.

Copyright © Silicon Curtain/Jonathan Fink 2022-2026 © Ilya Ponomarev 2026. Silicon Curtain/Jonathan Fink 2022-2026 © Ilya Ponomarev 2026. The interviews were conducted from 2022 to 2026 and were included courtesy of the Silicon Curtain podcast (youtube.com/@SiliconCurtain), edited for brevity and their core message. The publishers urge any copyright holder to come forward.

CONTENTS

Acknowledgements 5
The Dark Heart of Russia—*Jonathan Fink, Editor* 7

Section 1: Russia

1. *Dissent*—Ilya Ponomarev 15
2. *I Thought I Knew*—Bill Browder 21
3. *A Cult of Humiliation*—Peter Pomerantsev 28
4. *Calibre*—Garry Kasparov 34
5. *What Does the Ukraine Invasion Say about Russia?*—Owen Matthews 40
6. *Soft Power and Russia*—Simon Smith 49
7. *A Solution?*—David Satter 54

Section 2: Military Might

8. *A Refusal to Yield*—General David H. Petraeus 58
9. *Permanent Threat*—General Sir Richard Shirreff 63
10. *A Question of Morale*—General Mark Hertling 69
11. *The Russian Federation Will Disappear*—General Ben Hodges 75
12. *The New Iron Curtain*—Anders Puck Nielsen 84
13. *The Real Story of NATO Enlargement*—John Lough 88

Section 3: Putin

14. *Tunnel Vision*—Fiona Hill 95
15. *Opportunism*—Mark Galeotti 101
16. *The Godfather*—Luke Harding 109
17. *Petro-tyranny*—Alexander Etkind 114
18. *A Hundred-Year-Old Zombie*—Yuri Felshtinsky 127
19. *Moscow Rules*—Keir Giles 133

Section 4: Action

20. *Useful Idiots*—John Sweeney 145

21.	*Sanctions*—Timothy Ash	150
22.	*Grey-Zone Aggression*—Elisabeth Braw	157
23.	*Splintering Russia*—James Nixey	162
24.	*War Crimes*—Kateryna Busol	165

Section 5: Ukrainian Views

25.	*Absence of a Russian Nation*—Volodymyr Yermolenko	175
26.	*The Interest of Democracy*—Olena Halushka	182
27.	*Pleasure in Destruction*—Anna Danylchuk	186
28.	*Hundred Per Cent Evil*—Sasha Dovzhyk	191
29.	*Envy*—Olga Tokariuk	197
30.	*The Nobel Peace Prize*—Oleksandra Romantsova	203

Notes	206
Index	207

ACKNOWLEDGEMENTS

I would, in particular, like to thank: Alexander Etkind, Anders Puck Nielsen, Anna Danylchuk, Bill Browder, David Satter, Elisabeth Braw, Fiona Hill, Garry Kasparov, General Ben Hodges, General David H. Petraeus, General Mark Hertling, General Sir Richard Shirreff, Ilya Ponomarev, James Nixey, John Lough, John Sweeney, Kateryna Busol, Keir Giles, Luke Harding, Mark Galeotti, Olga Tokariuk, Oleksandra Romantsova, Olena Halushka, Owen Matthews, Peter Pomerantsev, Sasha Dovzhyk, Simon Smith, Timothy Ash, Volodymyr Yermolenko, Yuri Felshtinsky. A small selection from over a thousand interviews was made for the topic of this volume, but I extend my warm and special thanks to all contributors to the Silicon Curtain podcast and sharing their expertise with the podcast's expanding audience.

In addition, I am beyond grateful to Alan Scadding for being an inspiring teacher of Russian history; he introduced me to the Holodomor decades before it was recognised as a genocide. Also to Michael Falchikov and Lara Ryazanova-Clarke who inspired me at the University of Edinburgh. And to those who have helped support and mentor me in the growth of the Silicon Curtain podcast—David Satter (bis!), Ben Hodges and Edward Lucas, as well as all the friends who have been a great support and inspiration—Deane Joyce, Joseph Lindsley, Jason Jay Smart, Operator Starsky, Anna Danylchuk (bis!), Konstantin Samoilov, and many, many others, and of course my family for their support and forbearance well beyond what is sometimes reasonable.

THE DARK HEART OF RUSSIA
Jonathan Fink

When the missiles started falling on Kyiv and across Ukraine on the evening of Thursday February 24th, 2022, I knew in a flash what I had to do. It was clear that the global order was teetering as a result of the events unfolding on the Russian-Ukrainian border. The only precedent of one country seeking to swallow another whole since the Second World War was Saddam Hussein's 1990 invasion of mini-state Kuwait. But this was an attempt on an entirely different scale and by a state in a different league from Iraq. There would be immense consequences for us all, potentially life changing ones. The Kremlin, unlike Saddam, would not be routed and it had sizeable energy and ostensibly highly-trained military resources at its disposal, apart from being one of the nuclear powers in the world.

I could not remain on the sidelines as a very personal echo resonated that night. My father's family escaped from Vienna after Austria's *Anschluss* to Nazi Germany, just before the brutal aggression in Europe that would eventually engulf the entire world in combat. The Nazis may have benefited from nations being 'caught in the headlights' in the 1930s by being poorly informed but the Kremlin should not have that advantage almost a century later. As Russian ordnance killed and terrorised Ukrainians, I worked through the night to compile a list of guests for a new video podcast devoted to unmasking the mechanics, deceitful narratives, hidden pathways and impact of Russian propaganda. This tissue of systematic lies had done so much to ensure we did not intervene after Russia's surreptitious 2014 invasion of Crimea and Donbas. I wanted to map out the game plan of Russia's truthless myths and manipulations for all to see and help thwart its intentions.

In fact, Russian Active Measures against the West and its institutions had been escalating from 2016. Ever since, I had thought about what to do as Russia's sly, duplicitous poison of disinformation was increasingly spreading, supported through figures of influence in the West—targeted voices that included politicians, activists, journalists and geopolitical analysts. The Kremlin's narratives percolated through to Western media coverage without being countered and they were lulling us all to sleep. That Thursday evening, as people were being bombed and killed, all reasons to procrastinate had gone at a stroke.

I could not have predicted the impact my podcast aired on YouTube was to have—which I baptised Silicon Curtain. It has grown to become one of the largest and most influential podcasts globally focusing on Ukraine and Russia, with over 2 million views a month and nearly 1,000 interviews recorded. Based on deeply researched interviews, often on topics ignored by national news cycles, where the format does not allow time for long-form interviews, it focuses on Russia's brazen criminality and Ukraine's defence of freedom.

At the time few thought such a podcast was viable, or could be popular. But it quickly gained a following among Western experts, politicians, diplomats, analysts, activists, and Ukrainians alike. Its growing transnational following has made it one of the largest podcasts focusing on Russia and Russian imperialism, with a great variety of authorities participating, including household names such as Garry Kasparov and Bill Browder to General David H Petraeus and Fiona Hill. In addition, as well as being an incubator of exciting new voices, it now helps to fundraise for Ukrainian humanitarian volunteers and defenders.

Why Silicon Curtain? In today's world—unlike the twentieth century—there is no physical barrier that contains totalitarian propaganda, no Iron Curtain. When Moscow's state doctrine was Communism, the USSR's self-imposed 'ideological' border created a sharp demarcation between tyranny and freedom, and the traditional media acted as gatekeeper. But no such border line exists in the twenty-first century. Today's silicon-based media will pipe in messages and narratives they receive from anywhere, regardless of the source. Propaganda, that is, intentionally disingenuous misrepresentations of the truth and plain lies, are channelled to us under the guise of truth. Silicon Curtain aims to step into this void through its investigations of propagandistic methods, distinguishing falsehoods and weaponised information and counter the spread of Russia's ceaseless barrage of memes and misinformation aimed at tricking us and manipulating our actions. Importantly, Silicon Curtain has since inspired others to launch their video projects and cater for a burgeoning need to understand these geopolitical events in a way that cannot be provided by non-silicon-based mainstream media.

The core idea for the podcast has an even older pedigree, and dates from well before the internet was in general use. In 1992, just before commencing Russian studies at Edinburgh University, I made my first visit to Russia. The country fascinated me, but not in a romanticised way. In the grand sweep of history, I felt democracy and tolerance in the West were the exceptions rather than the rule; Russia shone a light on those, because of its long totalitarian culture despite its seeming engagement with Western thinking. The country exposed the mechanics of raw power, the trauma and brutality of human history, and provided a model through which I wanted to understand the West's democratic culture and legal foundations better.

I spent 6 weeks at Moscow State University, a gargantuan, Stalin era building that dominates the Moscow skyline, with a red star, the size of a double-decker bus perched atop its central tower. Perhaps the most potent symbol of Soviet power and ambition, and the crushing weight of a regime that has only just crumbled along with the USSR. This vast edifice appeared like a giant stranded whale of a building washed up on the tide of history. Orwellian in its scale and ambition. Soviet power had just collapsed spectacularly the year before, after the failed August 1991 coup during which the freshly elected President of Russia Boris Yeltsin famously climbed on a tank to denounce the coup.

We used to break out onto the roof of one of the wings of the building, sit on a cooling tower, and drink beer and smoke most evenings, in the hot and dusty summers that Moscow can experience. It was at this point it occurred to me that the Russians I met and interacted with, had little awareness they and Communism had lost the Cold War in a moral or political sense. Its power had gone, they were impoverished, and the empire had crumbled. Yes. But above all, they were acutely aware of the loss of empire—the humiliating loss of power and status in the world. It was also clear that this process had not consciously been initiated or embraced by them as a people. Like almost everything else in Russian history, it had been thrust upon them. It happened because it had not been prevented, as it had been in 1956 and 1968. Russia had simply been too weak to retain control of its empire.

What if one day they were no longer weak, I wondered not for the first time? They were painfully aware of the economic collapse precipitated by the disintegration of the Soviet system and loss of satellite territories. The idea 'we can repeat' (можно повторить) occurred to me then, maybe not this exact formulation, but the idea that if Russians had lost an empire through weakness, could they try to regain it, if their economic and military strength returned? That seemed absurd in 1992, as we sat amid the ruins of a bankrupt system.

After that first visit, I spent considerable time in Russia in the 1990s, from the first emergence of a market economy to the financial crash of 1998. I spent my weekends walking the streets and parks of the city, considering the conversations I was having with Russian friends and acquaintances, and collecting 'historical myths' in a notebook. All nations, especially ones with an imperial past, have a rich seam of historical myth that is woven into people's national and historical identities. But in Russia the sheer scale and variety of these myths was bewildering, and the 'active' relevance they seemed to have for people in the present—not just as historical curiosities and stories. How people framed Russian history, the recently collapsed Soviet Union, and Russia's role as an empire in history was fascinating.

I felt that, underneath, these myriads of explanations were informed by something peculiar. There seemed to be consistency between the myths people would refer to that did not feel entirely natural. Even when these stories were adapted and told in different ways, according to the level of education of the teller, the core narratives and 'intent' behind the stories created the curious impression that much of this new mythology was artificial, and not the result of organic storytelling and mythmaking. They seemed institutionally manufactured and potentially on a scale that left little to chance. Was it an echo of Soviet narrative brainwashing, or was it still actively happening?

The implication was Orwellian. The warped stories that served authoritarian and imperialist narratives with their associated goals, seemed to withstand the chaotic 90s. As early as 1996-97, Russia was showing signs of reverting to more statist, interventionist and intolerant policies, with the same contempt for the life of the individual, and treatment of humans as 'resources' to be expended at the whim of a ruler and their clique, with no concept of rights, rule of law or sanctity of individual life. There was a consumerist veneer placed over everything, a compelling 21st century facade of bling consumer civilisation, but underneath, nothing had really changed. Almost no one in Russia wanted to prise open that Pandora's Box of historical trauma anymore, and deal directly with the horrors it contained. So instead of being purged, they merely had been put to sleep—a political permafrost, ready to be dug up, when perhaps they would prove to be useful to figures in power once more.

The twisted tale of Russia, its 'dark and tortured heart', and what a threat it represents to our values, that I witnessed remained etched on my mind. There was no room for warnings, when life in the West offers so much that is 'light', so many distractions, and Russia—imperfect as it might be— seemed to incline towards modelling itself after the West? The Cold War was over, we were disarming rapidly, Londongrad was in full swing, and history had been relegated to the niche labelled 'instructive entertainment'. As

Fukuyama had written, history, at any rate Communist history, had come to an end.

In Russia, the economic collapse of 1998 provoked an outpouring of loathing and anger among the population—but it was not against the West or outsiders at that point. It was aimed at their own leaders, as well as the greed of oligarchs and emergent gangsterism. This unholy trinity had, in most people's opinion, led to Russia's tragic weakness and instability. The economic injustices of the time were undoubtedly real, but this deep well of grievance and resentment was to provide a fertile source for future regimes to manipulate. Instead of religion, grievance, it would turn out, was the opium of the people.

The commonly felt anger was amplified through narratives that promised simplistic solutions to complex problems, and their implied criticism of those who can't even get the basics right. This style of argument is something we have now all become familiar with in the West, but it was omnipresent in 1990s Russia: criticism was easy, seeking solutions and personal responsibility a rarity. Russians' economic grievance was spun into stories of historical humiliation, skilfully amplified through the media, books and films, keeping violence and loathing on the boil.

In many ways, Ukrainian identity is a perfect foil to understanding Russia's imperial identity. Ukraine is a post-colonial nation, rediscovering its past, its voice and its strength. The last great renaissance of its identity and culture in the 1920s was violently 'executed' by the Soviets in the 1930s (the *Rozstriliane vidrodzhennya*), but now it is undergoing another one. Ukraine seems to get stronger, the more pressure is applied to it, in terms of culture, innovation and commitment of reforms and freedoms. Even after years of full-scale war, Ukraine is inventive, humane and democratic (if at times wildly) in spirit. Its establishment is not afraid to examine, and confront, the darkest phases of its history, in order to prevent their repetition of the past.

Russia is the opposite—under duress, its leaders revert to stolid authoritarian models, with the strongman persona and nationalistic politics so beloved in tyrannies. The Russian blossoming of identity and political culture at the end of the USSR that I had been hoping for (half-expecting, given Russia's rich 19th and early 20th century culture) never came. Its identity returned to an imperial one—with added Soviet death-cult characteristics through the excessive veneration of the Great Patriotic War (Second World War). Not everyone agreed with the imperial mythologisation of history, but the liberal classes in Russia failed to rise to the occasion to create together a credible and powerful alternative narrative and identity. They once more became beholden to power, or, at any rate, never managed to escape from it.

From the early 2000s, a person's material existence and status emanated from the state and could be withdrawn at any moment from any individual who set their will against the state or sought to challenge the power projected by Putin and his clique. Once more, its population of 144 million became dependent on the state for resources, subsidised energy, power, prestige and position. Russians' passivity and extraordinary tolerance for extreme violence increased as well as their rejection of freedom and self-determination as dangerous, 'non-native' ideas. As in Soviet Russia, conformity and compliance were once again demanded by the Kremlin with one key difference. The messianic tone, and the moralising that had characterised Soviet communism was gone as well as the rituals and incantations that underpinned its cult of proletarian unity. In the new order, might is right, money accrues to the powerful, and the state defines what's right, not the law. It was Marxism, shorn of its idea

That did not mean that the Kremlin had no interest in being Messianic, quite the contrary. It wanted to propagate its kleptocratic mould to leaders around the world in the same way that the Politburo sought to convert nations to Communism. This was the new big idea, a new playbook to seek out aspiring autocrats and kleptocrats around the world: to support populist leaders willing to say anything to achieve power (even if it undermines democracy itself), treat the population as marionettes and cash cows, and their political office as an unfettered means to riches. This approach became Russia's new global ideology—kleptocratism: bolstering thievocracy around the world in the Kremlin's image. Russia leading like a comet with a tail of like-minded global leaders in its wake.

Arguably, from 2010-2014 Ukraine was the proud poster child of Russia's new ideology. During this period, Ukraine's President Viktor Yanukovych, nurtured and propped up by Russia, eviscerated Ukraine's nascent democratic institutions, stripped the army and bureaucracy of effective people and resources, planted Moscow's agents throughout the system, and—following in the kleptocratic footsteps of Vladimir Putin—extracted an estimated personal fortune of $32 billion from his country's economy[1] before he was forced to flee by his compatriots—who both wanted democracy and transparency, and who lacked the passivity of Russia's population.

Over the Yanukovych years Ukraine's resistance created an effective template of resistance to Russian propaganda for other nations to follow.

They had found an effective method of countering the Kremlin's insidious interference (through seeding greed amongst its leaders and undermining belief in the rule of law) in their country. From 2014, the country had gone from strength to strength in foiling Russia's playbook. The significance of what Ukraine had achieved in beating Russian imperial aggression had to be replicated everywhere: because the Moscow playbook is now everywhere.

After preparing and conducting over a thousand podcasts from 2022 to 2026, it struck me that the interviews also represented a unique insight into Russia's *modus operandi* and—equally important—how effective Ukraine has been in countering Russia's insidious nature in the media on the one hand and brutality on the battlefield on the other. Although the many guests have their own points of view, differing on important points, there was nonetheless a consensus of understanding that transcended each individual interview. Few, if anyone, moreover, will have been able to listen to them all and this book is meant to reflect through the many different voices that consensus. It is in this sense a blueprint of Russia's soul drawn by many architects and a source book on how Ukraine is successfully dealing with it.

At the same time, an anthology such as this one exemplifies the freedom at stake in Ukraine. This book (or the podcast) with its richness of many different voices could never exist in Russia or any other kleptocracy. In such cultures, there is room for one view only; the government's, or else. I myself have gone from fascination with Russia (always a species of horrified fascination), to learning the language, and now to my commitment to help dismantle the Russian state's imperial project. In this book you will find a range of opinions and nuances by leading experts.

This is also the beauty of the freedom that lies at heart of this book: at Silicon Curtain, we prepare each interview not to frame the interviewee or indoctrinate, browbeat or trick the audience to follow the government, but to hear, understand and listen to what the expert thinks by allowing them to set their views out clearly, and without interruption or manipulation for the viewer. This genuine freedom to think is reflected in our audience. It covers a broad political spectrum from the left, the centre to Reaganite Republicans and MAGA supporters.

Section 1
Russia

1. DISSENT
Ilya Ponomarev

Ilya Ponomarev is physicist turned oil executive who worked for Yukos and Schlumberger and helped found internet media such as gazeta.ru before his life turned into a political thriller. A Russian Duma member who abstained on the anti-gay propaganda law and cast the sole vote against Crimea's annexation in 2014, he was forced into exile. He now lives in Ukraine and fights as a Ukrainian soldier while also running a Russian opposition TV channel—Fevralskoye Utro (February morning).[2]

Saying 'no' to Vladimir Putin in public is not a difference of opinion. It is an act of open challenge, and so I consciously chose to abandon the safety of parliamentary immunity and to challenge the dictatorship. The invasion of Crimea, the promise to bring home 'our land', was practically unopposed in the State Duma. The vote was an extraordinary piece of stage-managed patriotism, the deputies applauding their Tsar who stood at the podium, in a frenzy of approval—445 green lights on the electronic board indicating votes in favour. Only one red light signalling dissent—my vote.

Within months, my face was on a giant billboard in central Moscow, branded a 'national traitor' and my parliamentary safety revoked. Criminal charges appeared. My bank accounts were frozen. I was asked to leave Russia, refused, and in a couple of months prohibited from returning from a business trip. I was stuck firstly in the United States, but then went for Kyiv, which became my permanent home in 2016. When flights home suddenly looked like one-way tickets to a penal colony in Siberia, I preferred to take an open fight.

This vote marked something bigger: the formal, televised start of a twelve plus-year war of imperial aggression against Ukraine—and the end of any serious illusion that modern Russia, as wired by Putin, could peacefully coexist with any free, democratic neighbours. The Russian tanks that rolled towards Kyiv in 2022 were not an aberration, or a random snap decision, but were the logical continuation of that Duma vote in 2014.

They were also, whether Europe likes it or not, a warning that if Ukraine falls, the front line moves west. But it seems that this realisation has barely begun to register, the lessons were not learnt, either from history, or from 25 years of extraordinary aggression by Putin. We must look at today's Russia as eerily similar to 1930s Germany: a dictatorship, locked in an imperial war, fuelled by propaganda, drifting towards outright fascism.

I never wanted to become a moralising dissident sitting safely in exile, speaking at the conferences and shaking hands with world leaders. I was always a man of action, results-oriented pragmatist, an insider who watched the system radicalise itself from within. First as a left-leaning reformer who still believed the state could be nudged into modernity, then as an opposition MP who saw the screws tightened year after year, and finally as an exile stripped of citizenship. This is when I took a fundamentally different path from liberal Russian opposition, who largely have adopted the principle of peaceful protest, fought through words, media and op-eds. After 24 February 2022, I joined Kyiv's Territorial Defence Forces, took up a machine gun, and chose to fight against Putin and Putinism and Russian fascism. This is not the same as fighting against Russia.

We are not fighting a weak or merciful regime. But a malignant and murderous one. I keep a gun by the door of my Kyiv house and am permanently aware that Putin's secret services have already killed one former MP, Denis Voronenkov, on the streets of Kyiv, just ten minutes from my home.

For years, Western capitals told themselves Russia's aggression against Ukraine was about 'security concerns,' NATO enlargement, or some tragic, but explicable and rational misunderstanding between Moscow and Brussels that could be fixed with 'dialogue' and a cleverly worded communiqué. Some of those delusions linger in the 2025 peace process. But this has always been a comforting lie, to justify inaction and political cowardice.

In my own book, *Does Putin Have to Die?*, I argue that Russia can only become a democracy after losing this war, after its imperial project is defeated on the battlefield, not merely curtailed for time at the negotiating table. As long as the regime in Moscow can think of its Ukrainian adventure a success, there will be no genuine reform, no repentance, no democracy. Only preparation for the next war.

The story of the last decade is brutally simple. Making it out to be more complex and nuanced is another way to shift moral and political responsibility for dealing with it. A kleptocratic dictatorship, built on the ruins of the Soviet Union, decided that its own survival depended on keeping Ukraine within its imperial orbit, undermining and intimidating the European Union and NATO and convincing its own population that there is no alternative to rule by a small, corrupt clique in the Kremlin.

To achieve those goals, the Kremlin has used every tool it possesses—the full spectrum of aggression from conventional war through to hybrid war;

disinformation and energy blackmail; political assassinations and cyberattacks, as well as what it calls 'special operations' against neighbours it insists are not real countries. Ukraine is not the only victim. Georgia, Moldova, Syria, Chechnya, the Central African Republic, Libya—all bear the scars of Russian 'peacekeeping', provocations and mercenary adventurism. But Ukraine is the central theatre, the place where empire and freedom collided head-on and neither can back down without changing fundamentally. In Ukraine's case, it will cease to exist if it is conquered, and the Ukrainian political and national culture will become a people in exile for the first time.

Over the last fifteen years, I can trace the longer arc of Russian imperial aggression through my life. I worked in the technology sector and helped design laws meant to foster innovation and entrepreneurship. These same laws that would later be twisted to enrich the security-state oligarchs I was trying to outflank. I entered the Duma believing Russia could still be steered toward a European-style social market model. For a while, that illusion seemed almost plausible; there were debates, street protests, apparently independent media, even a sense that pressure from below might push the system to open and reform.

Then came the crackdown after the 2011-2012 protests, the 'foreign agents' law, the 'gay propaganda' bill—which I refused to support, one more lone vote—and finally Crimea. The annexation vote exposed the truth. In that moment, almost the entire political class publicly endorsed the destruction of a neighbouring country's borders, and embraced illegality and violence, in a parliament that liked to pretend it still had an opposition. I refused to collude.

When the full-scale invasion began, I did not just talk about resistance but tried to organise it. I joined Ukraine's Territorial Defence Forces and became a political representative for the Freedom of Russia Legion, a unit of Russian citizens fighting on Ukraine's side and conducting raids and sabotage across the border. I launched a Russian-language media project, *Utro Fevralya* (February Morning), broadcasting from Kyiv into Russia, covering underground resistance, partisan attacks, and acts of sabotage against the regime. The accompanying Telegram channel, *Rospartizan* (Russian Partisan), amplified reports of arson at enlistment offices and attacks on infrastructure—and, controversially, published how-to material on resistance activity.

I announced a clandestine group called the National Republican Army had begun a campaign of armed struggle, claiming responsibility for the car bomb that killed Darya Dugina, daughter of the ultranationalist ideologue

Alexander Dugin, and for other partisan attacks. I believe that the occupier should never feel safe. Not in occupied Ukraine. Not in Russia itself. As the war escalated, so did my conviction that the only way to stop Putin's aggression was to make it dangerous, costly, and ultimately impossible for the aggressor.

From Brussels or Berlin, it is tempting to see all this as a regional tragedy, something that will be 'managed' with sanctions, ceasefires, and 'security guarantees,' while gas still flows and trade resumes. From Kyiv, or from the trenches near Kupiansk or Avdiivka, or from Russian exile communities in Warsaw and Tbilisi, the view is different. From there, you see what Ukraine represents, not only to Russia, but to Europe and the wider free world. For the Kremlin, Ukraine is a threat precisely because it proves that a Slavic, post-Soviet society can choose another path, the path of wilful, vibrant and unrestrained freedom. Competitive elections, independent media, a messy, quarrelsome democracy with real political competition and genuine civic activism. That is intolerable to a regime that insists Russians are 'not ready' for freedom, that insists only a vertical of power can hold such a vast country together. If Ukraine succeeds, every time a Russian citizen looks across the border, they'll see a mirror of what their own country might have been or could yet become.

For decades, European governments treated Russia as just another business partner: a large, moody supplier of energy, a useful investment destination, a market to be nudged gently towards 'reform.' They treated Ukrainian warnings about imperial ambition as complaints from a difficult neighbour. One with its own problems and complication. One that was more restive and less reliable or stable as a business partner.

These illusions started to crumble as the 'limited war in the Donbas' gave way to the reality of a continental confrontation between a fascist imperial project and the values Europe claims to stand for. All the delusions of the West about Putin should have died, when mass graves were opened in Bucha and Izium, and when missiles fell on Kyiv, Lviv, Dnipro, Odesa, Kharkiv.

Ukraine is not a buffer. It is the frontline. If Ukraine wins, it proves that a determined, imperfect democracy, supported by allies, can resist and defeat a much larger aggressor. It shows that borders still matter, that war crimes still have consequences, that dictators cannot simply redraw the map by force. But we have not been principled or determined allies. Our support has been 'just enough' to keep Ukraine in the fight and almost always late in coming.

If Ukraine loses or is forced into a sham 'peace' that rewards aggression and leaves the regime in Moscow intact and triumphant, every authoritarian on the planet will draw the same conclusion: that the West is afraid of confrontation, addicted to Russian gas and Chinese trade, and willing to trade other people's freedom and blood for its own comfort.

We must understand what Ukraine represents, not only as a victim, but as an active agent reshaping the future of European defence and security, of values and freedom. A country that has refused to surrender. An army that has humiliated a supposedly superior invader. A society that has organised itself from the ground up to survive under bombardment, and a political space in which exiled Russians, Belarusians, Chechens and others are learning to fight not just against dictatorships, but for a better future, fighting in the hope of an end to Russian imperialism, expansion and aggression.

Ukrainians fight because they still have hope and the conviction that Ukraine has the right to exist as a free, sovereign country; that Russian imperial aggression is criminal; that the Kremlin's propaganda about 'Nazis in Kyiv' is a grotesque inversion of reality; and that Europeans who look away are not neutral—they are simply outsourcing their own defence to Ukrainian people sheltering under the bombs night after night for four years.

They are also written in the conviction that the Russian people are not doomed to eternal dictatorship. The same society that produced Putin, Dugin and Prigozhin also produced dissidents, journalists, soldiers and politicians who refused to go along with creeping authoritarianism—and some who chose to stand with Ukraine at the cost of their own safety. I've said that we must be prepared to capture the Kremlin. There is no other way.

Just as Germany needed to lose a catastrophic war, confront its own guilt, and build a new state from the ruins of the old, Russia will only become a genuine democracy after a decisive defeat in Ukraine and the collapse of Putinism. This is not a comfortable argument for anyone.

The Free World needs to rearm and learn how to defend itself. I am now deeply involved in assisting Ukrainian defence industry to spread the lessons we have learned so hard at the battlefield to become available to our allies. And still we need to be proactive and remember: the only way to stop the next war in Europe is not a mere 'containment' and 'deterrence'—it is to dismantle Putinism.

It is a harsh vision of justice to ask Ukrainians to pay an enormous price to liberate their neighbour's future. It asks Europeans to reject 'peace at any price' and to sustain support for Ukraine through long, exhausting years of war and reconstruction. And it asks Russians to accept that real change begins with a defeat, that their own propaganda has taught them to fear and deny. The question now is not whether we like the choices in front of us, but whether we are honest about them.

2. I THOUGHT I KNEW
Bill Browder

Bill Browder is the CEO and co-founder of Hermitage Capital Management (HMC), which was the largest foreign portfolio investor in Russia. Through shareholder rights activism, Browder took on large Russian companies such as Gazprom, Surgutneftegaz, Unified Energy Systems, and Sidanco. On 13 November, 2005, he was refused entry to Russia and declared a threat to national security. He lobbied for the Magnitsky legislation globally (Sergei Magnitsky was a tax lawyer who was tortured and killed in Russian custody for his HMC work on 16 November 2009) and is the author of Red Notice *(2015) and* Freezing Order *(2022).*[3]

I moved to Russia full time in 1996. This was the period when Yeltsin had just begun his second term as president. That period in Russia can, I think, best be described as a time of total chaos and anarchy. There was, I guess, free speech. But at the root there were no rules, there were no property rights. As a result, you ended up in a position where 22 oligarchs controlled 40% of the Russian GDP, and, if you were to add on maybe the next 100 oligarchs, you would get up to something like 75% of the GDP of the whole of Russia, with everybody else living in destitution and poverty.

Yeltsin, the Russian President at the time, was a drunkard; he was unhealthy; he had a heart condition. He was unable to manage the situation. He needed to pass the baton to someone else who needed to do two things. First, they needed to pardon him on day one so that he would not be held responsible for any crimes he had committed. Then secondly, they had to remain president for long enough for that pardon to take effect. Yeltsin ended up picking three guys before he picked Putin, but none of them satisfied one or other of these two criteria. He picked Putin as some kind of last chance choice.

Putin became president and his big pitch to the Russian people to get them to rally round him was to say he was going to end the power of the oligarchs so that the average Russian wasn't living in poverty. That sounded like a pretty good idea to me and anybody else who was in Russia at the time, because what was happening to the average person was just so fantastically unfair. We all made the mistake of putting our hopes into the situation.

The richest man in the world

Putin has this totally empty face. In a way you can attribute anything you want to him. You can say, oh, he's a reformer, oh he's a nasty villain—you can say pretty much anything you want about him and anything is true, because he doesn't give you any information on which to make any judgments. Most people were optimistic. He started out tentatively, because the oligarchs had all the power; they had stolen the power from the president.

He spoke a little English. He wasn't drunk. He had a series of policies such as reforming the tax code and the land code. You would have said this guy is a technocratic reformer going through a list and getting stuff done. He's not charismatic at all. He was a tiny little man who didn't inspire any kind of enthusiasm. At the same time, he was a breath of fresh air after the chaos of the Yeltsin era. Then, in the third year of his presidency, in 2003, he arrested the richest oligarch in Russia, Mikhail Khodorkovsky, who was the owner of oil company Yukos. This was unexpected, because the prevailing view was that the oligarchs were untouchable, the oligarchs were more powerful than the president. And suddenly, the president is arresting this guy who is in theory more powerful than the president himself. Not only that, but he puts him on trial, and he allows the television cameras to film the richest man in Russia sitting in a cage in a courtroom. Everybody said, oh, he'll be out in a week, but he wasn't out in a week; oh, he'll be out in a month, but he wasn't out in a month.

There was one pivotal moment, where Khodorkovsky spoke out in a public forum, and he challenged Putin on camera. He challenged Putin, saying there's real corruption in Russia. Not that Khodorkovsky was not corrupt himself, but he had cleaned up his act. So there, on camera, he declares that there's terrible corruption going on in Rosneft, a state-owned Russian company which had bought some other Russian oil assets at hugely inflated prices. Khodorkovsky pointed this out in a meeting with other oligarchs and Putin said, 'you know, people in glass houses shouldn't throw stones'. Putin likes to rule by symbolism. If you look at Russia on a map, it's the largest country in the world. It crosses 11 time zones. It extends from Asia to Europe, and there's just no way that anyone can micromanage that country. The only way that Putin can enforce any kind of discipline is by example. Khodorkovsky's main crime was not simply being rich, but also the fact that he talked back to Putin. It wasn't the court which sentenced him, it was Putin.

After that the oligarchs said, oh my God, the game's changed. They went to Putin and said, okay, what do we have to do so we don't get arrested? And Putin said, 50%. And that was the moment that everything changed in

Russia, and that was the moment that Putin became the richest man in the world.

Turning point

When Putin first came to power, our interests were aligned. He was fighting the same guys I was fighting. The oligarchs were stealing power at the same time as they were stealing money from me. When I was publicising the corruption scandals in these big companies I was investing in, Putin would step in as well. (I should point out, though, that I've never met him. I have not had a conversation with him then nor since.) We would get articles in the *Wall Street Journal* or in *Kommersant*—one of the big Russian business newspapers—and there would be a scandal. Putin would do something about that scandal along the lines of, 'the enemy of my enemy is my friend'.

After he'd made his deal with the oligarchs, I'm carrying on with my anti-corruption exposés; but now these are no longer in his interests. In 2005, I was expelled from the country and declared a threat to national security. In 2007, my offices in Moscow were raided by 25 Russian police officers, and at that point I hired a young lawyer named Sergei Magnitsky to investigate why the offices were raided.

Magnitsky discovers that the purpose of the office raids was to gather financial documents that belong to me and my companies, and to use those documents to orchestrate a very complex fraud in which they stole $230 million of taxes that my firm had paid to the Russian government. Magnitsky exposed the fraud. Sergei was then arrested by the same people he had testified against, was put in pre-trial detention, tortured for 358 days and murdered in Russian police custody on November 16th, 2009, at the age of 37, leaving a wife and two children.

Magnitsky's murder was a turning point in my life. Before that, I was a full-time fund manager in Russia, and then, suddenly, one of my people had been tortured and killed because he worked for me. That affected me profoundly. I decided to give up my life as a businessman and to devote all my time, energy and resources to going after the people who killed Sergei Magnitsky and making sure they face justice. I've done an unforgivable thing in getting legislation passed—the Magnitsky Act, named after my murdered lawyer—which freezes the assets of human rights violators and corrupt officials.

For a person who values money more than human life, that's unforgivable. Putin has made it a top priority in foreign policy to try and repeal the Magnitsky Act. They've gone after me personally in every way that they could. I've been threatened with death on multiple occasions. I've been threatened with kidnapping. They've issued eight Interpol arrest warrants. I was arrested once in Madrid and once in Geneva. They tried to get me extradited from the UK. It's been a constant game of cat and mouse. I've got to be lucky every day. They only have to be lucky once.

I'm very far from being the only one who's been persecuted in this way. For instance, the situation with Mikheil Saakashvili is almost indescribable.

Saakashvili was president of Georgia. Putin invaded Georgia and Saakashvili resisted: he fought back hard. At the time, Putin said to the president of France, 'We're going to hang this guy. We're going to hang this guy by the balls'. In 2012, Saakashvili lost in a democratic process and stepped down, which is very unusual in that part of the world. About nine years later, he returns to Georgia and they arrest him, they put him in jail, they torture him, they poison him in prison.

If you look at him now, it's shocking. He looks like a prisoner in a concentration camp. You can see the bones sticking out in his chest. Forensic doctors have detected poison, arsenic and various other heavy metals, with which they've poisoned him. He's suffering from dementia at just over 50 years of age. The government of Georgia is a pro-Russian government under Russian control. Bidzina Ivanishvili, who made his money in Russia, was sympathetic to Putin and he became president of Georgia.

Putin is a man who likes to send messages, and this is a message—if you are a head of state and you stand up to me, we're going to come after you, no matter how long it takes. The same message was sent by assassinating opposition leader Boris Nemtsov outside the walls of the Kremlin.

Putin's ethos

The problem with the Cold War is that it never really ended. When Nazi Germany collapsed and Japan collapsed at the end of the Second World War, they collapsed completely. And we could replace all those systems with something new. But when the Cold War ended, the whole apparatus of the KGB stayed intact, and that's the apparatus that they're using to spread murder, fear, death all over the world, particularly in neighbouring countries. Putinism and KGBism need to be defeated firmly so that whatever comes next is no threat to neighbouring countries and to the stability of the world.

When I first got to Moscow in 1996, there were two groups. There were the run of the mill criminals wearing leather jackets and gold chains and driving around in their souped-up Mercedes, and then there was the state apparatus. But when Putin took over, there was a merger between organised crime and the state.

For many years afterwards, people continued to refer to the Russian state and organised crime as two distinct entities, but they're absolutely the same. It's hard to imagine that you could have a government meeting about tax policy and in the next meeting about which poisons to use to kill enemies: the same people would be ordering assassinations and talking about interest rate policy.

It's particularly hard for heads of state—Barack Obama, George Bush, Tony Blair, Boris Johnson—to imagine there is a murderer. They focused on how to create incentives for Russia to work more cooperatively. They tried their personal charm. But you can't use charm with a criminal. All the criminal is thinking is, 'What a sucker'. Putin would enjoy himself when a new head of state would come in and try to charm him into behaving himself, because that just gave him an extra year or two of leeway.

The crucial thing to understand about the way Vladimir Putin acts is that he doesn't care about his country. Putin went into public service, not because he's interested in serving the public, but to steal money. And that's not unusual. It's not like he's like some particularly evil Russian who went into public service to steal money. Everybody who goes to work in the government in Russia from the lowest traffic cop right up to the president, goes into it to steal money.

What prompted the war?

Putin was particularly good at stealing money. He stole unbelievable amounts of money, hundreds of billions of dollars. After a while, he had stolen so much money that he had put himself in the most impossible position. He can never step down.

Unlike Saakashvili, who could lose in a democratic election and go and do something else, Putin can never step down. He's killed so many people. He's arrested so many people, taken hostage so many people, stolen so much money, committed so many crimes that, should he step down, he would lose all his money and he'd probably die. There is only one way forward, and that is to stay in power until the end of his natural life. The war in Ukraine was life or death for him. He'd been around for 22 years. Sooner or later something was going to happen. He didn't want to wait to find out.

It had already happened to leaders in some of the neighbouring countries. For instance, in Belarus they had a fake election, and Lukashenko won by a landslide. The Belarusian people rose up, and Lukashenko would probably have been toppled if Putin hadn't sent his own people in to save him. And then a popular uprising succeeded in Kazakhstan. One weekend they raised the price of the liquefied petroleum gas for cars, which they use to fuel their cars, and suddenly the government buildings, the presidential palace, everything was aflame. The dictator there had been around for even longer than Putin and he was deposed.

You create an enemy to redirect people's anger away from you towards foreigners, somebody external, and then you start a war. Putin started thinking it would be a quick war. He'd swoop in and up would go his approval ratings. It hasn't worked out, but he has no choice now. If he shows any sign of weakness at any point, the Russian people will come for him. They can't stand a weak leader. In a dictatorship, a 'strong man' country like Russia, you've got to be the strongest, most vicious person out there.

Putin continues to escalate and escalate and maybe he defeats the Ukrainians, or maybe the Ukrainians fight him and destroy him. But there's no conceivable situation in which he says, 'Okay, I've had enough. Let's negotiate'. This is a huge, huge misconception on the part of pretty much all Western governments. Somebody interested in the national interests of their country would do that. But he doesn't care about Russia. He'll throw 5 million able bodied men into the meat grinder, if that's what it takes to stay in power. He'll burn through every dollar of savings that Russia has in order to stay in power.

Western governments don't want to give Ukraine enough weapons to defeat Putin because he's so unpredictable. They just want to move the situation to a negotiation. That's simply not going to happen. Putin is counting on Western hesitancy. He's counting on disunity emerging. And he's counting on the fact that as democracies, when the economic pain reaches a certain pitch, people demand peace. They're not willing to fight at any price. His big bet is that Donald Trump will stop supporting Ukraine. That's what he's banking on.

If we don't tool up our economy to match the stockpiles that Russia has, then there is the threat that Russia might physically outlast our supply systems.

A Viking kingdom

Putin hasn't just dominated Russia for over 20 years. He's been degrading and destroying every institution. It is unprecedented for a nuclear power, a complex post-industrial society, to have the political sophistication of a Viking warlord kingdom. All free press has been destroyed. All the courts report to the Kremlin. There are no independent political parties, just the ruling party and fake opposition parties. Nobody can challenge or succeed Putin because Putin is worried about being overthrown.

Another monster that Putin created—not only during this war, but all through his tenure—is extreme nationalism. He put Yevgeny Prigozhin, the head of Wagner, out there and lets him thump his chest and make all sorts of public statements. Prigozhin's extremism, and other extremists' statements, they're all part of the plan, it's all by design so that he can say, look, 'Here's the alternative. You should be happy with me'.

Putin has killed 140,000, at this point, of his own young men in a war that never had any purpose; not to mention all the Ukrainians he's killed and all the damage he's done to Ukraine. I don't think you can get any worse than that. This is just his way of trying to convince the Emmanuel Macrons of the world that they need to appease him.

There's no independent political voice tolerated in Russia. Putin destroys anybody who has any ability to challenge him. Back in the day when the stakes weren't so high for him, he'd allow Alexei Navalny to make his movies and Boris Nemtsov to write his reports and give speeches. Nemtsov would organise a demonstration and 500 people would show up and Putin tolerated it. He became more scared as the crowds became more responsive and Nemtsov, for example back in 2015, was going to organise a demonstration where perhaps 100,000 people were going to show up. He felt like the threat was too great, and so he killed him. That's the same thing he tried to do with Navalny, with Novichok. There are only three types of opposition leaders in Russia—those who are dead, those who are in prison, and those in exile.

The West needs a strategic idea of the kind of Russia we want to emerge. We need to give Ukraine more so that they can triumph, but equally we should be supporting the Russians who could be leading Russia out of this mess. There's not that many of them. I know that Mikhail Khodorkovsky, who was the very first major political prisoner, has been working on that on a steady basis since he got out of jail with his public works. But to be honest it's a bit like changing the deckchairs on the Titanic. There are so many issues, including the boat sinking.

3. A CULT OF HUMILIATION
Peter Pomerantsev

Peter Pomerantsev was born into a Russian speaking Jewish family in Kyiv, in 1977. After his father, the broadcaster and poet Igor Pomerantsev, was arrested by the KGB he moved with his parents to West Germany and then London where Igor Pomerantsev worked for the BBC World Service. Peter is a journalist and TV producer and author of various books including How to Win an Information War (2024).[4]

My parents were political dissidents. In 1978 they were thrown out of the USSR. My father had been arrested for the heinous crime of giving censored books to his friends. I only went back to Ukraine when I was 22. It was the late 90s, and we had family there. I always felt at home in Kyiv, and Odesa, which is where most of my family is from.

But then I lived in Moscow from 2001. I wanted an adventure somewhere after university, and Moscow was one of the places that I could have that adventure. It was already brimming with evil. I was there for nine years, and I left for many reasons. Nine years is more than enough in one place, but it was already clear for me that it was heading towards dictatorship. You could see the signs.

I was very much an expat and a westerner. I could speak decent Russian, so I had an insight into society. But Russians could sense straight away that I had not grown up there, and I was quite naïve. The first years especially, I bought into the idea that Russia was moving towards being a democracy. My Russian friends in the arts, and in business, were telling me that I didn't get it. They were always hedging their bets. That's why so much money leaves Russia. They were always keen to get second passports, and always very keen to have a backup plan.

My Russian friends were the ones who always thought this could disappear in a second, and knew it was the Westerners who kept on believing in it, and who kept on investing in it. They would buy apartments, and then be in shock when thugs would turn up and take the apartment away. Westerners would rely on the rule of law, but the Russians always got it, and exploited it, and always had a plan B.

Even foreigners could tell by 2008. The invasion of Georgia was a massive wake-up call. Then the second arrest of Khodorkovsky. The second trial was just so perverse that you knew something was going on. Then Bill Browder's lawyer, who was incredibly intelligent, was horrifically, and obviously murdered within the prison system. They then put him on trial, even though he was dead, and posthumously prosecuted him. An empty chair. It was like something out of an absurdist satire about dictatorships.

The Pussy Riot trial as well. They were being put on trial for being witches, playing on medievalism. I remember writing about these things and often I'd get notes from readers saying, 'well, this can't be true'. When you live in Russia, you realise that Bulgakov and Gogol are realists. You live in a surreal space. It's a very literary culture. Games are played out with a lot of literary references. Literary references are one of the few common signifiers that pull this chaotic culture together.

From 2006 to 2010 I worked for a production company which made Western TV formats for Russian entertainment channels. Reality shows. They made stuff like Top Gear, Come Dine with Me, etc. Most of the networks that I worked with were pure entertainment networks. So, the state was pretty hands off with them. A lot of people were flooding into entertainment, because you could still have complete creative freedom there. You could do whatever you liked as long as you didn't touch politics. We were doing some subversive stuff, trying to mainstream LGBT people. Getting them on screen. Everybody was really into that kind of social change.

But the state was saying the news is ours in stages. First, they got rid of one channel, then another. There were still pockets of good current affairs programmes left, but slowly every one of those would be destroyed. That was the deal, and frankly, a lot of people were happy with the deal. They could make tons of money. It was a very cynical compromise, and the lines had become very blurred. Former dissidents were working with the Kremlin. The Kremlin was working with the reality show producers. Everything was mixed up socially, and people would go to the same bars.

Underneath this louche cynicism was a deep moral depravity. And beneath that a sort of lava of trauma just waiting to explode. I mean sadism and masochism and those sorts of things. It is quite misunderstood how traumatised, deeply confused, and even lost Russians are. People would try on new ideas, new identities in the way that other people would try on new clothes and styles. There was a sense of society being postmodern and posttruth. You could be anything and nothing at the same time. There was a horrible emptiness at the core of it.

I am not pitying them. Russia is strange, in that it is often both the perpetrator and the victim. Let's not start absolving the Russian state and

Russian political culture, and to a certain extent Russian society, for being an aggressor.

This is an empire that has never for a single moment wanted to be anything but an empire. Which considers it has a right to wipe out others. I funded myself by working as a consultant for various EU development programs, going to the regions a lot and drinking with people in regional businesses and administrations from the early 2000s. A few drinks in and they'd be like, 'Oh, we're taking it all back. This is all ours. Let's divide Europe together.'

Not for a moment did they stop thinking about the world as a dog-eat-dog place where 'might is right', and not for a moment did they relinquish their belief that it was their right to crush others. That never went away. Even in the early 1990s, when there were democratic aspirations, there weren't any serious aspirations to get over the legacy of being an empire.

It's what psychoanalysts would call secondary narcissism when you want things you don't need and that destroy you because there's some deep, deep lack of something. It could be attention, love, self-respect. We talk of Russia as living off empire building, but this is not 19th-century empire building like France or Britain, which is deeply embedded in a theory of rational self-interest. This is a self-destructive empire building, which is much weirder. It pulls everybody down to your own level, sucking them into the vortex of your own hell.

Government propaganda only works when it reverberates with people's traumas and desires: often unspoken desires. Famously, every Hitler or Goebbels speech starts with the idea that the whole world, especially the Jews, have conspired against Germany and forced it into the war. It's the same with Russia.

The main Russian line is, 'We have no choice. We were forced into this by the great conspiracy.' There are several things to think about here. Erich Fromm, the great German psychoanalyst, talks about the victim narrative in German (Nazi) propaganda. Basically, this is the classic thing with bullies claiming victimhood. What they're expressing is what they want to do to you. They're preparing the ground. Saying, 'we are the victim, and we have been victimised. Therefore, I'm going to crush you.' It's classic among mass murderers as well. They were hurt. They were wounded. They had to go and kill all those women. This is about not taking responsibility.

When you live in Russia, you're humiliated all the time. You're humiliated by the state, by your teachers, by your husband. It's a culture that is built on humiliation, and which is deeply reflected in the literature. After you've spent your day being humiliated by bureaucrats, cops, your boss, etc, you come home full of resentment and then on TV, Putin is saying, 'it's Obama who was humiliating you all day'. It's a way of exporting internal tensions.

Every Putin speech—like every Hitler speech, and often many Trump speeches—has one rhythm. He starts off as the humiliated Russian everyman. He even does this with his body. He does this sort of face, the sad face of Putin. I'm a little boy and have been humiliated. We've been humiliated. And you're saying, 'Yes', I've been humiliated too. Through the speech, he'll grow and grow and grow. And in the end, he is the god of wrath and anger, humiliating others.

This is why, The Apprentice was a complete failure in Russia. They had a real oligarch—Potanin—a proper scary oligarch. The US producers came over and babysat the Russian production company through all the stages. It was very well made, very well edited, great music, great storylines. But a complete and utter failure.

Russians, think, you just make money. You don't make money by having a clever business idea and then selling it. You make money by extortion. Having connections in government corruption. Sleeping your way up. If you have a brilliant business idea, you end up in jail. Because the bad boys come and take it away from you. The ones that did well were stuff like Survivor. Put people on a desert island and torture them. Russians are like, 'this reflects our experience. The Gulag'. Anything based on getting people to survive in extreme conditions, the Russians knew that.

If you look at the Russian literature of the 1990s and 2000s, even the very good ones like Sorokin, they're very good at deconstructing the facets of Russian and Soviet culture. Sorokin is probably the most important Russian writer, and he has a book about a piece of shit walking around town. Literally. My reference to faeces is not facetious. All these writers are like doctors looking at a decomposed corpse and prodding it and making wry remarks about it. But none of those books have a capacity for imagining the future. I don't find the terms 'Russian liberals' and 'Russian opposition' very useful. There are different ones, all of them politically impotent.

Ukrainian literature is often full of sadness and despair, but the works of Serhiy Zhadan and Yurii Andrukhovych, always have a glimmer of the future. There's a sense of a journey to somewhere—it's not always clear where to—but there is a journey somewhere. There's a vision of somewhere that we're trying to get to, even when it's through tears. There's been no attempt within Russian literary criticism to understand the imperial structures and underlying patterns in high Russian culture. You always have good individual voices but imperialist narratives in the works of Tolstoy and Pushkin.

It's strange, because the American, British, and French intellectual classes spend a lot of time deconstructing evils that are encoded within our most glorious cultural works. It's good that we do that. I think that's the sign of a healthy society. In Russia, there is this tradition of deifying dead writers. It's the literary version of the death cult of Stalin and Lenin. Let us stop praying to corpses. There is absolutely nothing stopping a new generation of Russian thinkers getting to grips with the 'evil' of imperialism, or the prejudices that lead to evil.

Russian talk shows are an entertainment format, and many people will know they're being lied to. They'll listen to it and take away from it what they want to take away from it. Some of it may pander to their desires and ambitions, but the rest is almost like background noise. That's shocking, given what is being said on these programs just reeks of immorality and toxic attitudes. The programmes spew out ideas that even in the same sentence will contradict each other. But the conflicting narratives don't seem to necessarily jar for every Russian. No one is looking for ideological consistency in the first place. They've grown up with so many different belief systems and paradigms that being consistent isn't really something people value.

These kinds of shows are watched by around 30% of the population. Presenters have very high profiles. Ratings are dipping, which means they have to get more and more shocking. People watch it as dark entertainment and as a licence to hate. It allows you to articulate and express taboo feelings that in normal society, you need to hide. And suddenly it's okay to hate. To want to murder.

Then make it profitable for the people creating it. No one is really following every word. But there is a consistent worldview, which is a conspiratorial worldview. The conspiracy changes. The nature of the conspiracy changes. One day it's NATO. Then it's the British Secret Service, then it's the Jews, then it's someone else. But the conspiratorial worldview is there. One minute they talk about wanting to make peace, the next to make war. One minute we're invading Ukraine to get rid of Nazis, the next it's because of NATO. It's a way of absolving people from responsibility. We live in a dog-eat-dog world. Putin may be a son of a bitch, but he's our son of a bitch.

The point of these shows is to get the audience's attention. Shock jocks. If you know the American experience, then there is not much that is new about this. What is different about Russia is that it's sponsored by the state. Pushed by the state.

Putin has a problem though because a lot of the internal propaganda effort, until recently, has focused on promoting indifference to make sure people are apolitical, don't take action, don't believe in anything. Suddenly Putin needed to pivot. He wanted people to act. Follow through on their nationalistic feelings and go to fight on Ukrainian soil. It puts them in a very vulnerable place.

There are no signs of the war in Moscow. There are no posters. As if it doesn't exist. He's still trying to keep them in a stay-at-home state—drink your beer, watch TV shows. But he needs a certain amount to be mobilised. He's trying to instil a patriotic education, which is failing. Largely because people aren't attending these courses. The deal was, buy into television propaganda and get on with your personal life. It was a pyramid of corrupt mutual interest: make money through the system as long as you swear fealty when it matters. That was the deal. That's being replaced with something that is Stalinist, requires motivation and pulling together, and sacrifice. It's very unclear whether they're going to succeed.

What should Ukraine do?
Ukraine has developed extraordinary resilience techniques to counter Russian propaganda. But Russian narratives are still penetrating our media. Obviously, the Ukraine media are putting out stuff about atrocities being staged, but there is a bigger narrative: 'The inevitability of Russia; we must make peace with Russia because it's big and strong and forever. And whatever happens, we're going to have to bend the knee.'

It's not easy to cut yourself off from Russia. But we really need to cut Russia off, like an abusive partner or an abusive neighbour. It will be tough, but it's important. It will be expensive. But you can't stick around an unreliable and psychotic partner. Russia will carry on mounting information assaults because it's unlikely to suddenly become a liberal democracy. It's unlikely to stop attacking or trying to control and coerce its neighbours. It won't go away.

Depending on how well Ukrainians do, that'll be a lesson for China. We see Russia and China combining forces in information, to support each other's narratives. That doesn't mean they are allies, but rather partners of convenience. And we've seen them joined by Iran. I think that the authoritarian network will expand.

On the upside, we've seen democracies pull together for the first time. We are starting to realise our political values are worth fighting for. Poland and Estonia used to be as vulnerable as Ukraine. They're not the case anymore. We don't know what is going to happen in Russia, but we've got to make sure that it can't attack Ukraine and others again.

4. CALIBRE
Garry Kasparov

Garry Kasparov became the youngest world chess champion in 1985 and held the title. In the mid-2000s, he became one of Vladimir Putin's most high-profile Russian critics. He founded the United Civil Front, a movement aimed at resisting his country's slide into authoritarianism, helped build The Other Russia, a broad anti-Kremlin coalition, and intended to run for president in 2008 but withdrew after systematic obstruction. He fled from Moscow to New York in 2013. From exile he co-founded the Free Russia Forum in 2016. Russia designated him a 'foreign agent' in May 2022 and put him on the list of 'terrorists and extremists' in March 2024.

I drastically reduced the list of countries I visit: I don't expect any surprises in Warsaw, Bucharest, Tel Aviv, or Frankfurt. But in theory, being on Russia's terrorist list, and having been 'arrested in absentia' and tried on state treason, means I expect consequences. I don't care, because I don't believe the regime in Russia is legitimate. They hate me because I'm a soldier. Maybe even a junior officer on the other side. For me, people on the other side, Putin and his gang, are enemies. Whatever they say doesn't change an inch. It's too late to be scared—not that I haven't been scared. It shows that they pay attention to what we have been doing.

Many of my colleagues already made the list. Some of them have also been convicted in absentia. So, I'm in a good company. We recall the famous saying of the late Boris Nemtsov, one of the great Russian opposition leaders: 'at a time of authoritarianism, at a time when you cannot validate your popularity by elections or by any other democratically measured instruments, the only way to recognise that you are you are not redundant is if you are still relevant. It's the government's attacks on you. If they step up with attacks, you're doing something right.'

Obviously, Boris received the highest reward from the government, a bullet, which proved his point. It's a tragic irony. It's the same with Alexei Navalny. They killed him. It was not accidental. It was also a statement because he was killed on the night of the 15th to the 16th of February, the first day of the annual Munich Security Conference. The moment of the announcement, for me, was the best proof that it was intentional. Navalny was not in great health. They sent him to the middle of nowhere, a penal colony in Siberia, beyond Arctic Circle. They could easily have held this secret for the next three or four days. But no, they announced it almost at the opening of the conference. I think this was Putin's message to the West. I can kill Ukrainians. I can kill Syrians, and I can kill Navalny. What can you do to me? There were no consequences for Putin. It was another way for him to prove the total impotence of Western leadership. Unfortunately, he was right there would be no consequences for the murder of Navalny.

Putin labels his internal enemies as 'terrorists'. External enemies are labelled 'Nazis'. It's worth mentioning that the Nazi label has not been picked by accident, because the very foundation of Soviet propaganda was built on victory in the Second World War. With every year, with every decade passing, mythology has taken over. Today many Russians, even relatively educated ones, may struggle to say who was fighting whom in this war. Were the Americans and Great Britain allies of the USSR? It's all about the Soviet Union defeating mighty Germany. There were other battles—in Japan, Europe, but they were minor. The real battles took place here, in Russia. Even the most educated Russians will not be able to tell you the role of the American Lend-Lease in helping Russia to survive in the first two years of the war. Or the fact that most German warplanes fought in the West throughout the entire war.

Britain and America drew a lesson from the Second World War—'never again'. But in the Soviet Union, and in Putin's Russia, the lesson they learn is 'we can repeat'. That's why Putin looked for any plausible, or implausible justification for his attack on Ukraine and came up with the 'Nazis' label, despite the fact Ukraine is led by a Jewish president. Russian society has reached such a point of social and historical amnesia that the fact Ukraine (unlike Russia) is a vibrant democracy, means nothing to them. And of course, the rest of the world are Nazis, too, because they are opposing Putin.

Reality is perverted. Garry Kasparov is a terrorist and some of my colleagues are thieves. But everybody knows the terrorists and thieves are in the Kremlin. Neither Kafka nor Huxley could have imagined a world with this level of craziness, because the great writers of the past believed that abundance of information would be the best guarantee against dictators. They didn't know that modern dictators are adept at using technology to poison and brainwash our minds. Hitler's propaganda chief Doctor Goebbels must be green with envy in his coffin.

Russia's slide to authoritarianism didn't begin with Putin's appearance in the Kremlin. Russia was already moving in the wrong direction well before then. Under normal circumstances, you would not have had a KGB operative (one proud of his KGB origin), nominated and then elected to this position, without the support of a powerful administrative machine built by Boris Yeltsin. We missed our historical chance. The window of opportunity was very short in the early 90s. But after Yeltsin resolved his crisis with parliament by tanks shelling it, Russia headed in the wrong direction. The turning point came in 1994. Yeltsin was facing dire re-election prospects: his ratings were negative. Then he began a 'small victorious war' in Chechnya to boost patriotic feelings. Yeltsin was not a dictator, but he didn't see any other chance to revive his rule.

People often ask me, what's the difference between Russia and Ukraine? I point out that Ukraine is not a small country. It's the biggest European country, and it's not homogeneous. Western Ukraine is different from Eastern Ukraine. Crucially, they had elections at the same time as Russia, in 1994. The first Ukrainian president, Leonid Kravchuk, lost them and walked away. Ukrainians experienced something important unlike Russia—the peaceful transfer of power. They became a different people because the voter had determined who would rule the country. When, twenty years later, Putin tried to keep President Yanukovych in power in Ukraine in 2014, it led to the Maidan protests. Ukrainians resisted Russia's attempt to impose rulers on them but is paying an enormous price in blood for that. They're still fighting. Whether they're Russians, whether Ukrainians ethnically, whether they're Hungarians living in Ukraine or Greeks or Jews or Muslims, they're all fighting for their country called Ukraine, and they're willing to pay this price.

What's happening in Ukraine every day is hard to describe. Putin has been deliberately attacking civil infrastructure. They are not hiding it. Their goal to destroy Ukrainian infrastructure, energy, civil infrastructure, to make sure Ukrainians will not survive next winter. This is the way Putin is conducting the war. But you can also feel proud for the spirit of humanity that cannot be broken, even by the most vicious Russian dictator. When you fight a war, you must decide what is the goal of that war. For me it is very simple—Ukraine must win. For Russian opposition groups led by Mikhail Khodorkovsky and me, the key for Russian freedom is the Ukrainian flag flying in Sevastopol. Victory that includes full liberation of Ukrainian lands up to Sevastopol as well as reparations and bringing war criminals to justice.

The world's attention is divided—for example by Gaza. I didn't hear Western leaders repeat three simple words: 'Ukraine must win'. Instead, they say 'we stand with Ukraine for as long as it takes'. This sentence is very ambiguous. It could mean, we will stick with Ukraine as long as it takes for us to make a deal with Moscow. During the war, and as we speak, they're trying to find a compromise.

They don't appear to understand that this is a global war between freedom and tyranny. This war, unlike chess, has no tie. There's no compromise. You win or lose. And this is not just a war of Ukraine against Putin's invasion. It's a war conducted by Iranians, the Chinese, who are manipulating everything from behind the stage. Today the balance of power is very different, however. For the first time in history, as a result of NATO, Europe has an overwhelming advantage, both militarily and economically. European countries are not individually facing the Wehrmacht and Luftwaffe, Hitler and Stalin.

What we're missing is political will. Today business continues with Russia, because we do not consider ourselves at war. But Putin is at war with us. Putin is at war with the free world. The idea of Obama's was that you can walk away and there will be peace. It's geopolitics that there can be no vacuum of power. You walk away, somebody else comes in: Putin, Xi Jinping, the Taliban, Hezbollah, Hamas, Iran. We are retreating, because we don't want to recognise it's a war. Ukrainians demonstrated to us that it's a war.

Ukraine could have won the war already in September 2022 when Russians retreated in a panic—a stampede. With enough weapons, Ukrainians could probably have pushed Russians further across the Dnipro River. Russia was in disarray.

But the US tread water, and this delay gave Russia eight months to build massive defences. US General Mark Milley, Chairman of the Joint Chiefs of Staff, spoke on the Hill, testifying before the Congress, that giving Ukraine serious weapons, heavy weapons, would be a mistake, because the Ukrainian army would collapse in a couple of weeks, and these weapons would be seized by Russians. Ironic, that these comments came from someone who was partially responsible for leaving American weapons worth of tens of billions of dollars in the hands of the Taliban six months earlier. The US offered Zelenskyy, not military assistance, but extraction by helicopter. They didn't want to fight. When Ukraine survived the first onslaught, won the Battle of Kyiv, the free world was still trying to find a way to minimise the collateral damage to globalisation.

The biggest fear in Washington is the collapse of Russia. This fear led Bush 41, back in 1991 to deliver his infamous Chicken Kyiv speech. They used to live in a world where the Soviet Union was a factor, and collapse would bring God knows what. Today we know that for as long as the Russian Empire exists, it will be a problem. It's not just victory in this war, and the defeat of Vladimir Putin, but of the imperial concept as well. We must demonstrate this defeat to the Russian public, to my compatriots. The only way to do that, is to have a Ukrainian flag flying in Sevastopol. You must kill the imperial virus that has been poisoning the minds of Russians for centuries.

What is standing in the way of a decisive defeat of the Russian Empire? Some say, Russia can occupy Tallinn in three days. No—those are sovereign countries, and they have NATO, and weapons. It's Estonians and Finns that will head to Saint Petersburg in three days.

I'm not saying you should demand unconditional surrender from Russia, but you should say Ukraine must win. When it is argued Ukraine is not ready for NATO, it seems increasingly clear that NATO is not ready for Ukraine. But what is NATO? Why was it created in the first place? It was not built to fight the Taliban, but to fight the Russians—a Russian invasion of Europe. NATO had but one goal—to prevent a Soviet invasion.

The constant placing of red lines, not on Russia, but on Ukraine—and on how they use Western weapons—isn't accidental. It's informed by 'escalation' management. The best illustration of the horseshoe theory can be found in US politics. You have people on both sides of the aisle from Jeffrey Sachs to Tucker Carlson, who have found common cause in not wanting America to play a global role again. It beats Orwell and Kafka combined, when far left and far right align to abandon Ukraine and the ideals of freedom.

There is a theoretical risk of Russians using nuclear arms, but the problem is that the moment you make a concession based on a hypothetical blackmail works. If in Ukraine, it'll work in Lithuania, and work everywhere. You must be prepared to defend every inch of NATO territory, for the principle of deterrence to work. That's what advocates from the right or left ignore. Ukraine is the best opportunity to destroy Russia's threat without nukes, and without putting any American lives at risk.

There is another signal to the world. If you want to protect your borders, get nuclear arms. Thirty years ago, America forced Ukraine to give up its nukes, for so-called security guarantees. The memorandum. It was not binding. But Ukraine gave up the third largest nuclear arsenal in the world, which was bigger than Britain, France and China's nuclear arsenals combined. Ukraine received guarantees from America and Russia, that their borders would be intact, sovereign.

I've been promoting the idea of a Russian Taiwan. You must start thinking creatively about winning the war and replacing Putin's regime with a structure that could offer Russia a chance for the future, to make Russia an ally of the free world, part of Euro-Atlantic civilisation, opposing China and other dictators. But you need people of different calibre to have the vision for this, people who worked on global strategy, whether it was FDR, Truman, Eisenhower, Kennedy or Reagan. Today, we're dealing with people who shuffle papers around. They are talented at how to avoid making decisions. The next generation must recognise that the future can be shaped by people of a different calibre.

5. WHAT DOES THE UKRAINE INVASION SAY ABOUT RUSSIA?
Owen Matthews

Owen Matthews was born in Britain in a bilingual Russian-English family. From 2006 to 2012, he was Newsweek's Moscow Bureau Chief and regularly returned to Moscow until his last visit in 2022. He previously wrote Overreach: Inside Story of Putin's War Against Ukraine (2022) and Stalin's Children (2008).[5]

Seen from outside the Kremlin, Putin's invasion made no sense. That's the mystery. Why did he do it? It only starts to make sense when you begin to see it from the Russian point of view or, rather, from inside the Kremlin information bubble that Putin inhabited since the beginning of lockdown. The bubble of people around him and their worldview. As stated by Putin, he wanted to de-nazify Ukraine. Obviously, there are also Nazis in Russia and Poland and Germany. There is one ultra-nationalist member of the Supreme Rada out of 450 members of Ukraine's parliament. Ukraine is obviously not run by Nazis. Why do they claim that Ukraine is run by Nazis? Why do they think it needs to be de-nazified?

The second stated aim was to prevent NATO from using Ukraine to create a sort of anti-Russia. The West's project in Ukraine and Ukraine's own project to Westernise itself is described as an attack on Russia by the Kremlin insiders. But the idea that Ukraine was imminently about to join NATO was far-fetched indeed.

The third practical demand was to save the Russians, as the Kremlin describes it, from 'genocide'. What they mean is the Russian-speakers of eastern Ukraine. It's mystifying because even by the accounts the rebel Donbas republics—the Luhansk and Donetsk People's Republics—submitted to international bodies, including the UN and the OSCE, the actual number of people being killed in the fighting, by 2016 and by 2020, were a dozen civilians killed a year in Donbas—not anything approaching a genocide.

So why did he do it? And the first and most simple answer to the mystery is that he did it because he thought he could win.

He thought three things were going to happen that did not happen. The first is that he thought the level of support for Russian intervention in eastern Ukraine was much higher than it actually was. Had he done this full-scale military intervention back in 2014 when he occupied Crimea, he might have had a much better chance of annexing Donetsk and Luhansk. In the intervening eight years support for Russia in the eastern part of Ukraine fell dramatically, even more so for actually joining Russia. Even pro-Russian sympathy fell enormously. The second thing that he miscalculated was that he assumed Zelenskyy would cut and run just as his predecessor, Viktor Yanukovych, had done in 2014. Putin was convinced the Americans created the Maidan revolution at the beginning of 2014, so, his logic went, if the Americans can do it, then we can do it too.

Another miscalculation. They believed they could actually do their own pro-Moscow coup in Kyiv. They were convinced they could do that if they handed out enough money and corrupted enough people and pumped out enough propaganda. They didn't think the Ukrainians could fight, because the two times the Russian regular army had confronted the Ukrainian army in the field in 2014 and 2015, the Ukrainian army was completely destroyed and routed by the Russian army.

Lastly, they did not believe the West would support Ukraine. When he annexed Crimea, in February of 2014, the West came out with a chorus of disapproval. Angela Merkel said, this must not be allowed to stand, this must be reversed. Then, surprise, surprise, 15 months later, in spring of 2015, Angela Merkel signed a $10 billion gas pipeline deal with Gazprom.

Up until the crackdown on Bolotnaya protests in 2012, there were many liberal economists within the Russian regime. Putin would have heard a multiplicity of voices. Even if he ignored them, there would have been different sources of information. With Covid, he seems to have become ever more isolated and dependent on a small circle of advisors who themselves may be getting poor information or may have intense self-interest in terms of feeding Putin a simplified story or even a false story.

The story of the war is the story of the closing of Putin's mind. Over the last 20 years, the Kremlin has had all kinds of projects and ideas and initiatives. There was an attempt to make Russia the leader of world conservatism, in Communist International style. There are all kinds of things the Kremlin tried and abandoned, but all the way through, the people who were always there in the room were the KGB cronies; Putin's associates and colleagues from his very earliest days in the KGB in the 1970s. Specifically there were Nikolai Patrushev, who was, in fact, Putin's boss in the late 70s, and Alexander Bortnikov, the head of the FSB. These people were always hawks. The difference is that, pre-Covid, they had been surrounded for most of Putin's tenure with other people.

These others are called technocrats. They're called liberals. They're somewhat technocratic and, in fact, not at all liberal. But these people were recognisably post-Soviet. In other words, they were pragmatists. They were people who realised which side Russia's bread is buttered. All of Russia's prosperity and the much-vaunted stability of the Putin regime is 100% funded by Western money, which Russia receives from hydrocarbon exports. That is the source and origin of Russia's prosperity. But those pragmatists, by the beginning of 2020, had essentially left the room for various reasons. Putin found himself in a sort of black swan event. Covid comes along at just the moment when Putin is most vulnerable to his worst instincts and his most radically hawkish advisors. He was always isolated. He always had a very small number of interlocutors. But Covid just locks that in. He finds himself basically alone with his most paranoid, most aggressive and oldest advisors.

There are lots of dictatorships that have refrained from invading: North Korea, for example. The basis of the misunderstanding between Russia and the West over NATO is that what Russia says about NATO is fundamentally true, but trivial. When Russia says, America was giving military aid to Ukraine, they were. But it was peanuts. That infamous 2019 conversation between Donald Trump and Volodymyr Zelenskyy, how much money are they talking about in that conversation? That year, Ukraine actually got far more than they were expecting. $400 million. NATO gave $400 million in military aid to Kyiv. The US spends $2 billion a day on its own military. It's literally six hours of US military spending for a year. It's a rounding error.

What does that tell you about how important Ukraine is? There were military manoeuvres, NATO manoeuvres, all along Russia's borders every year. There have been throughout the Cold War and after the Cold War, though since 2007 they've been closer to Russia's borders. It's really interesting when you talk to Michael McFaul, former US ambassador to Moscow and Obama adviser, who was present every single time Putin spoke to Obama for four years. NATO expansion and NATO exercises were never mentioned.

The key point is everything that NATO has done with Ukraine appears provocative to Russia because they have no real sense of scale. The whole NATO story is actually very much in the eye of the beholder. The question that Russia crucially did not ask was, how likely is it that Georgia and Ukraine are ever going to join NATO? The answer, before Russia's invasion, was absolutely zero, for a very simple legal reason. The legal reason is that the

NATO charter does not allow any nation with disputed borders to join. Georgia, with its disputed territories Abkhazia and South Ossetia, could not legally have joined. Putin, by his actions, created the conditions, the things that he most feared. He made them true by acting.

A much more important factor for the Russians was something that has been famously described by the American deputy Ambassador George Kennan in his long telegram in 1946 about how Russians think, how the Soviets think, and that's a profound fear of encirclement and of Western aggression. The head of Putin's bodyguards, now head of the Russian National Guard, Viktor Zolotov, said to the *Ekho Muscovy* (Moscow echo) editor Alexei Venediktov a few years ago, 'Ukraine doesn't exist. Ukraine just happens to be where the border between Russia and America lies'.

For the Russians, strangely in terms of strategic thinking, Ukraine itself is just incidental. It's a pawn. The high elite say this very often, people like Bortnikov and Patrushev say repeatedly that for them this is really about a battle for survival, for Russia's survival against US aggression. They are profoundly convinced that this is a pre-emptive war of defence, that they are fighting against Western aggression. That may seem paranoid and crazy to us, but to people with that background and that mentality, there is a conviction that the West, and particularly America, is working actively to undermine their regime and to achieve regime change. The poisoning of Alexei Navalny in August of 2020 and the invasion of Ukraine are both part of the same project. They're both about defending Russia from American aggression. It's obviously not true. But the important thing to understand is that's how they think. That's a really important factor when you're thinking about practical ways to end the war.

The Russian elite even think of Europe as a proxy of American power. They don't give Ukraine agency, they don't give Europe agency. We're all sort of pawns in the big game. And that plays back to the idea that Russia sees itself as this global power. They talk about multipolarity, but it seems they still think of themselves in almost a bipolar world of them against the US, and that harks back to something far more atavistic, like a village pugilist who has to prove themselves to be the roughest, toughest guy in the village. You're going to want to take on the next toughest guy and give them a good drubbing so that everybody knows you're the toughest guy with the biggest stick. It has the sense of a playground bully about it.

Just as the problem with NATO is a fundamental failure of perspective, a fundamental sort of egotism (countries just as people can be egotistic). They're egocentric, they think that NATO, and Joe Biden, think about and see only Russia. Of course, it's not true. It's nonsense. Joe Biden's big election talking points when on the campaign trail were actually to disengage from Europe and to let Europe be responsible for its own defence. That was also a Trump policy. Neither of them was really bothered about Russia. Barack Obama famously said that Russia is a regional power. For Joe Biden the obvious strategic interest is China. That's America's peer. It's in no way Russia. No one cares about Russia.

We had two Jack Russell terriers. These are, like, seven kilo dogs that believe they are 70 kilo dogs. They just have no cognizance of the fact that they are a little dog, the size of a rugby ball that you can kick across the room. They think that they are like a gigantic Rottweiler and will attack enormous dogs, and the enormous dogs are actually very often completely terrified by this attack. That may seem flippant, but it's very illustrative. Russia honestly believes that it is the peer of America. If you look at various metrics such as relative GDP, for instance, Russia's GDP is 36 times smaller than the collective GDP of NATO. It's not three times smaller, it's 36 times smaller. This is a fundamental problem with Russia, not just in terms of Russian psychology, but in the way that psychology translates into a fundamental flaw in its strategic thinking. Putin's gas weapon failed because Putin thought they were much more important as a country than they actually are. They massively underestimated Europe's ability to just buy their gas from someone else. Gas prices are now back to what they were pre-war.

How the Lives of Ordinary Russians Changed

I was last in Russia in mid-October 2022. The English language Western correspondents left Moscow en masse at the beginning of the war, while the French, Germans, Poles and Italians all stayed. They left because of the fake news laws, they were afraid of being prosecuted. It's true that there is a climate of suspicion, a sort of despair and a sort of depression. But to say that there's any kind of serious crisis in Moscow—no, there really isn't. Moscow has ignored the war. It literally doesn't exist. I tune into people's conversations, eavesdropping, and nobody's talking about the war.

For a proportion of my friends, the war was totally disastrous. They fled; liberal political activists, several hundred thousand people fled, but those who stayed, their reaction has been one of total denial, wilful denial. If you really want to get your fix of propaganda, you can switch on the television and get the hysteria. But the people who do that are marginal. There's a vast majority of people who have too much to lose to leave, and they have no good reason to leave because they do their jobs, and they have got their houses, their nice cars, their jobs. Sure, they have problems, but it's not a crisis.

The fundamental change has been among two groups of people—liberal, politically active people on the one hand, and, on the other hand, pro-government people, propagandists, people who work for the Kremlin officials, foreign ministry people. For them the whole situation is completely and strikingly different because the government had done something that was utterly unpredictable and was utterly inexplicable. They had not predicted it.

There was no popular preparation. The people who run the television stations were not briefed on the fact that the Kremlin was about to launch a full-scale war. That level of operational security is just crazy. It took everyone who thought they were well-connected with the security services completely by surprise. Top-level government contacts said, don't worry, it's not going to happen. Everyone who thought they were connected suddenly realised they were not connected at all.

Only four people apart from Putin knew of the full extent of the plans. We're talking about the most powerful—at least on paper—men and women in Russia. The rest of the elite suddenly took fright, as they realised that a system that had formerly worked and had protected their interests (because the interest of any Russian bureaucrat is just to steal as much money as possible), a system that had formerly worked on what the Russians call a system of understandings—you are loyal, so you kick out some money to your Swiss bank accounts—suddenly that system has been hijacked by a bunch of 70-something-year-old KGB agents, and suddenly you just don't know what is going on anymore. Furthermore, you don't know what the bounds of acceptable discourse are anymore—can you meet with Owen Matthews, British journalist, is that still okay? People just got very paranoid and very confused.

It also sheds an interesting light on the system prior to the war, the so-called hybrid informational autocracy. The liberals had their little media outlets. They could think that they had a role in changing society, they had a sort of media playpen. The liberal media was not only tolerated, but, in a very weird way, actually encouraged by the Kremlin.

Dmitry Muratov wins a Nobel Peace Prize (2021) for his fantastic work at *Novaya Gazeta*. It's independent, but it was formally financed by Alexander Lebedev, the London-based former KGB colonel and oligarch. When Lebedev ran out of money, the Kremlin stepped in to find someone to finance their opposition. They found Sergey Adonyev, who's a very famous donor. He's a telecoms magnate. He does a lot of business with Russian-state owned defence conglomerate Rostec. I can't, for confidentiality reasons, tell you who asked Sergey Adonyev to step in and fund *Novaya Gazeta*, but there were people, at the very top of the state, who asked him, can you please fund this opposition newspaper? Some *Novaya Gazeta* journalists, including Anna Politkovskaya, were murdered. It was a paradoxical system. The space for independent media was extremely small, but it existed, and then it just suddenly imploded.

Journalist Alexei Venediktov is a very interesting example as well, because *Ekho Moskvy* is a famous liberal radio station and was one of the main drivers of glasnost in the 1980s. Then it was bought in early 2000 by Gazprom Media. So you have this weird hybrid—a liberal, notionally anti-government, notionally editorially independent news resource that is owned by Gazprom, which is owned by the state. So how does that even work? It's really simple, actually. The rules are that there are a few red lines that you cannot cross that allow you to operate in that media environment. *Ekho Moskvy* did not interview Alexei Navalny. That was their red line, in the case of Dmitry Muratov and *Novaya Gazeta*, it was that they didn't write about Putin's personal wealth. They wrote quite a lot about the corruption of key people, but not Putin.

Most Russians still get their information from television, but the numbers are falling. They're tuning out Solovyov, Simonyan and these inflammatory figures. Viewing figures for combative propaganda formats have been steadily declining throughout the war. One of the things people tend to forget is that if you are a consumer of Russian television propaganda, the tone and the timbre actually has not changed since the beginning of the war. They were always as crazy as this, even before the war.

For a couple of years, in 2016, 2018, I went on these shows myself, as a sort of weird masochistic exercise. It was partly for journalistic interest. It was quite interesting to see how the propaganda machine actually works. Journalistically, it provided a rather important opportunity to meet third-tier people like the heads of Duma committees, senators, Duma members, governors, that kind of person who were not really in the room where it happens, but who nonetheless might be in the building where it happens. They get the cafeteria gossip. I went on as a sort of Western whipping boy and got shouted at for an hour by Vladimir Zhirinovsky, amongst others, who said, we need to send you to the Gulag, Owen Matthews.

It's very well packaged. The storylines are remarkably consistent, they have high production values. It's put together by extremely talented, totally cynical people. In this kind of totalitarian environment, it's bizarre and crazy and decadent and frankly terrifying what modern Russia has become.

Vladislav Surkov invented the whole idea of sovereign democracy. He's been working since 2003. He was brought in to stem the tide of popular revolution, the colour revolutions, to stop that from ever happening in Russia. He was a playwright, a television producer and a PR manager. He was also a novelist. In some ways he's a classic 1990s person. He had a fundamentally consumerist and totally post-modern attitude to ideology; totally cynical, in the sense that he would basically use anything. His brief was to stop the youth of Russia being affected by nasty Western ideas that might make them come out on the streets. So he just created a sort of soup of everything, a bit of orthodoxy here, a bit of Soviet nostalgia there. Some like war films, some Soviet soap operas, it's all sort of mixed up together, and from that he concocted the Russian television media product, and did it extremely effectively.

Then in February of 2020, right at the beginning of lockdown, he quit the Kremlin. That sort of essentially post-modern, consumerist, pragmatic attitude to ideology was replaced by people who actually believed this crazy nonsense. The old KGB believers suddenly took charge.

What surprises and shocks me is how many people are willing to ride this burning death cart right off the edge of the cliff. But the regime has swept up this whole swathe of former liberals, through Surkov and Konstantin Ernst, who's the head of Channel One, right up to Dmitry Medvedev, the former prime minister and president, who was all about modernizing Russia. All these people are suddenly in a death cult.

We saw this in the takeover of NTV. You'd have expected such a vibrant television station to lose all its staff when it was basically gutted and taken over by the Kremlin. Actually, there were only a few headline figures who left and a few key journalists, while many at the lower tiers carried on working for the channel.

My intellectual friends went to all the meetings and risked arrest for supporting Navalny. They all just left. The people who stayed are essentially cynics, or powerless. The people who remain working for the Kremlin machine are by and large cynics. A few of them are idiots. A number of them are both cynics and idiots. People who are outside the Kremlin machine just don't have a vested interest. They simply see no reason to blow up their lives. All they want is for the whole thing to go away, either through victory or in some other way. The people who are left are in a state of profound denial or riding this out for their own benefit.

The main opposition to Putin and the main political threat comes not from Navalny, or from pro-Western liberals, but from the ultranationalists.

There's a much more substantial part of Russia which is essentially poor, provincial, good, bad, ugly, whatever. They have been told that their country is being attacked. So they support the war because they think it is a war of defence. The Kremlin has adopted positions that were formerly considered to be radical positions adopted by the far-right nationalist opposition that has now gone mainstream. Or, rather, the Kremlin has now moved there. In that sense, they've already opened this terrifying Pandora's box of ultra-nationalism, this extremely aggressive, bloodthirsty rhetoric. And that leaves the Kremlin in a very vulnerable position. Putin is not Hitler. He's Kaiser Wilhelm II, the idiot who leads his country into a disastrous and unwinnable war, which is followed by a humiliating defeat, a massive angry nationalist backlash, and economic collapse.

6. SOFT POWER AND RUSSIA
Simon Smith

Former ambassador Simon Smith had a 35-year career in the UK diplomatic service with postings in Moscow, Kyiv, the IAEA, and was Director, Russia, South Caucasus, and Central Asia, at the UK Foreign and Commonwealth Office. He currently chairs the Ukraine-Russia steering committee at Chatham House.[6]

How do Russian officials operate internationally?

Even while I was in Ukraine, explaining Ukraine and what was going on there to my colleagues in London, I felt there was still a little bit of a hangover from Yugoslavia. That meant people were thinking, gosh, this is a complex landscape of different ethnic communities with different backgrounds and different aspirations and different languages and so on and so on. I used to find it challenging just to have to keep on explaining repeatedly that this really was not the way to see what was going on in Ukraine. But understanding has moved on a lot in the eight years between the two Russian invasions of Ukraine, in 2014 and 2022.

Russian propaganda is about sowing that confusion, trying to ensure inaction on the part of the West by suggesting that things are much more complex than they really are.

In Britain we have been to some extent immunised against this kind of Russian propaganda. Obvious incidents such as the assassination of Litvinenko, the poisoning of Sergei Skripal and the downing of MH17, have led British consumers to have had a very clear dose of the absolutely wanton Russian effort to say to us, 'you think the explanation for this incident is one thing? But, you know what, we have another one. If that won't do, we have another one', and so on, and so on. Having been through those episodes, British readers and viewers were already at a point where they were saying, no, we're familiar with this, this is another situation in which the Russian machine will just start spewing out lies and diversionary alternative versions of what happened, and we're not falling for it.

There's one other big gap in what you might call the Russian attitude to soft power or soft influence. When I was heading up the Russia team in the Foreign Office, we had a bit of a joke that went across the directorate, to say if anyone could come up with a plausible and authentic Russian-language translation of the expression 'charm offensive', they would be given a big prize. It just seemed to be an element that was almost entirely and consistently absent in Russia's engagement with other countries. I think that over the last ten years, the world has hardened to this expectation that the Russians just don't do soft power; they don't do charm offensives. They simply do threats, aggression and confrontation.

Truth to tell, Medvedev up close and personal, is not a terribly interesting guy to talk to. In the days when I was working in the British embassy in Moscow and seeing a fair bit of the team around Putin who were crafting economic policy, we would definitely have associated Medvedev with the people who were looking around at the Russian economy, and saying there are things here we've got to fix, otherwise we're going to be in a hopeless mess. Medvedev wasn't one of the movers and shakers in that team, but he certainly came across as someone who was in line with the direction that they were taking.

The contradictions in the Russian stance are particularly apparent in reference to economic policy. There were several people in the early 2000s with whom I was talking; at that date there would still be people coming over to London for discussions on fiscal policy, economic policy and so on. Throughout the early 2000s up to the mid 2000s, we were still seeing people who were both influential and making earnest efforts to grow the Russian economy—in sustainable ways—that were compatible with the ways in which the rest of the global economy works. But what appeared to happen to a number of the policy makers, was some kind of conflict, that meant they either remained loyal to their principles, to the concepts in which they believed as an economist or as a practitioner in foreign relations or whatever, or they remained loyal to what appeared to be the political philosophy of their home country.

Timothy Snyder talks about this. There is a pre-emptive accommodation with an autocratic regime. You may not entirely give your soul over to it, but you don't believe that you personally can make a difference or change anything. And you don't necessarily have a set of principles which you adhere to, which set up red lines for you, so it becomes easy to get blurred in that world.

What is the West's biggest misconception?
If you're to negotiate about territory, then surely there needs to be some sort of genuine territorial dispute. But the boundaries of Ukraine are not in dispute. They were universally recognised in 1991, and that recognition was part of what was included as the basis on which Russia was acknowledged as

a member of the Security Council of the United Nations, in succession to the Soviet Union. There is no territorial issue in Ukraine.

There is to my mind no conceptual basis on which the award of territory to the Russian Federation makes sense. To be talking about ethnic communities in Ukraine, to be talking about one community preferring to be Russian, or another community preferring to be Ukrainian—that is simply not the case. I think that the advocacy for a territorial element to a peace deal in Ukraine is driven by a major misunderstanding of the whole concept of what ethnic Ukrainian or ethnic Russian means. It's a misunderstanding of the language issue. I'm still astonished when I speak to people who should know better, that if you are somebody who grew up speaking Russian in Ukraine, that must make you a sort of Russian-Ukrainian or Ukrainian-Russian. It's absurd.

One of the things that does need to be spelled out is that, if you are thinking of a territorial element as a solution to an end to the war that Russia has unleashed on Ukraine, you are almost certainly doing that based on a misunderstanding. There is a Russian-language community in Ukraine, and they do need to be taken seriously. Just as there is a Turkish-speaking community in Cyprus—one should be taken seriously. Of course, there'll be people who object on those grounds. There'll be people who object on hard-nosed, ultra pragmatic grounds, who'll say, yeah, we know it's terrible, we know it's unfair, and we know it's outrageous. We know it's an outrage against justice and reality and everything of that sort, but the thing here, the crucial thing here, is to stop the war. Because if we follow the path that you're advocating, then the war will go on forever, and tens of thousands of people will die, people who didn't need to die, and do you want that on your conscience, Mr. Smith? That's the ultra-pragmatic view.

But if you if you hand territory over to Russia, that is essentially a message that says you have won, you have scored success in your efforts over the last 20 years or so, not only with regard to Ukraine, but with regard to other countries in the neighbourhood, such as Moldova, Georgia and so on. We will officially give you a seal of approval for success in your policy of making your neighbours weaker, and, in a sense, rendering them failed states, because that suits your concept of security better than having strong and successful states in your neighbourhood. And that allows you to grab slices of their territory from which you can do what, exactly? Grab more, perhaps? Well, we think very probably that's the case.

That brings us back to Crimea. Not because I think that Crimea should be an exception, but because I am conscious that there are so many people out there in the landscape who do think that Crimea is different. There are people who would argue that even the 1954 transfer just showed that, well, this is a bit meaningless, and it doesn't really matter which side it belongs to.

There are many, many people—including a lot of people who understand Ukraine, who support Ukraine, who are outraged by Russian action in Ukraine—who would say, yes, but Crimea, come on, you know, it's always been Russian. To which I would answer, you surely wouldn't say, come on, India, it's always been British. It's not a question of moral outrage, it's a practical question. What do you think the Russians are going to do if you award them possession of Crimea as a great prize for this outrageous war that they've launched on Ukraine? You may think you're solving the problem, but in my view, you're doing something which will hugely increase the chances of Russia bringing this problem back to you again, in even greater measure.

We're still dealing with the ambiguity with which that Russian aggression in 2014 was met. There was some sort of superficial kicking out of diplomats and this, that and the other. But that would have been nothing more than a gnat sting to Putin. He could brush it off without a thought. Not only did that move not weaken his regime, but it also massively strengthened his popularity, both his invented popularity and genuine popularity. We know that Russians align behind a strong man. So, the move in 2014 massively consolidated his regime, and it made the West look incredibly weak, vacillating and so on, perhaps making the current conflict inevitable. Perhaps people are stuck in a mindset that this is as bad as it can get.

I rather fear that we're at another 2014 moment, where we're arming Ukraine to survive, to hold its own, but not be victorious. We probably do need to ask ourselves whether we have not lost confidence in our own deterrence? Nuclear deterrence is a policy into which, whether we have liked it or not, successive governments have invested a great deal. Not only a great deal of money, but also a great deal of confidence. Does it make sense to dismiss some of the fears about Putin using nuclear weapons?

In some ways, it is a little bit like 2014. It's a reluctance to understand that we're in a position that is very dire, and that reacting incrementally is not going to work.

But it's very difficult to change the mindset which says, look, we don't want to smash up the landscape irreparably. Let's just do it enough to keep Ukraine in the war and to keep Russia from being able to beat Ukraine. Putin has told us that he's at war with us, so we don't need to worry about whether we're a party to this conflict in that sense. But there is still this inhibition, the belief that says, it's about winning this war with the minimum necessary effort. So, let's be very incremental, let's tease out bit by bit the support we give to Ukraine.

In fact, a Russian defeat is by no means the least bad outcome from this war. A Russian defeat is probably better than any other outcome which sees Putin still pulling the switches in the Kremlin. Russia's been defeated plenty of times in its history through sheer incompetence, strategic misjudgements, an absolute dearth of equipment. You can go back and find many examples where Russia got an incredibly bloody nose and didn't tear the world down.

How do you see the future?

There are a lot of very level-headed, grounded people in, say, Latvia, Estonia, Lithuania, in Moldova. In some of the Eastern European countries, parliamentarians in those countries and members of their governments who are deeply concerned about whether they will be next in Russia's effort to weaken the European Union, and to undermine democratic structures in member states of the European Union.

When I was working in Russia and visiting a lot of the further flung subjects of the Russian Federation, the opinions you would hear there were that the guys in Moscow don't give two hoots about our livelihoods here, they're only interested in us because of the resources they can extract from us. There is no policy in Moscow that aims to enhance the integration of Russia and create a Russia where, in a sense, decentralisation and devolution can be respected and in which Russian resources are fairly allocated. Without nothing in Russia is really going to work. But that does rely on having an administration in Moscow that has got its head screwed on about how devolution and decentralisation work. But those concepts have not been anywhere near the front of the minds of Russian policymakers for several years.

The people who are sitting around in Moscow, anxious at the prospects of a fragmentation of the Russian Federation, to an extent, they're operating based on their own misplaced assumptions, their own lack of knowledge about the way in which the Russian regions work. It's all too easy to convince a Russian administrator in Moscow that, because the situation in Chechnya was so awful, that's the kind of thing you'll find throughout Russia. And it is nonsense; but it's what is there in the minds of those people who have been the administrators of Russia for the last 15 to 20 years. That and acute paranoia, the paranoia which was fostered by the KGB.

That is the class of people who are running the show, ill-informed paranoid bureaucrats. And I imagine that working in the Kremlin, that ancient giant fortress, after several years, imbues people with an even more intensely heightened sense of paranoia.

7. A SOLUTION?
David Satter

David Satter was the first American journalist to be expelled from Russia since the Cold War in December 2013. He was the Moscow correspondent of the Wall Street Journal and Financial Times, and then became a special correspondent on Soviet affairs for The Wall Street Journal and is currently a senior fellow at the Hudson Institute and a fellow of the Johns Hopkins University School of Advanced International Studies.[7]

It was clear after the Autumn 1999 apartment bombings, in which Putin and his henchmen murdered hundreds of their own people, that they didn't operate with any kind of moral restraint. A regime headed by a terrorist, that is afraid of its own people, is capable of practically any crime. They have a built-in justification; that the highest moral criterion is the interest of the state. Attacking a school full of hostages with flamethrowers and grenade launchers is a vital state interest. As for the lives of the hostages, well, that's collateral damage.

The Ukraine war is not ideologically driven. In Russia they have the saying 'information for fools.' It's something that they can pound into the heads of people, not that they believe it themselves. That's the crucial thing to grasp. Any theory of Russian greatness or restoration of the empire or resistance to the West, that's all just camouflage. What's involved here is personal interest. This is a small group of people able to manipulate an unthinking mass against its own real interests and use it as cannon fodder in order to preserve their hold on power. To an extent it was a miscalculation. The failure of the Russo-Japanese War led to the Russian Revolution of 1905. The defeat in the Crimean War in 1856 led ultimately to the emancipation of the serfs. There's plenty of precedent in Russian history for defeat in war leading to fundamental changes.

The problem is Russia needs a moral and psychological change. For that it needs the influence of the West. But the post-Cold War West is little equipped to exert that kind of influence. We've turned inward, obsessed with things like race and gender discrimination. Without commenting on how important or unimportant those issues are, they're not going to make it possible for the West to exert international influence. Authoritarian psychology can be weaned away only through the conviction that individual human life and individuals themselves have value.

Russia has never really reconciled itself to the horrors and crimes that were committed in the 1930s. Russia is going to have to revisit its past before it is transformed into understanding the value of an individual human life. All too often Russians regard the victims of totalitarianism as the inevitable cost of modernisation, as unavoidable as the weather. They don't understand human agency and moral responsibility.

One way to counteract that, of course, is to memorialise those whose lives were taken so pointlessly. There was a start during perestroika, when the idea of memorialisation, commemoration, honesty about history, were important. But they were important because they could be used as a political weapon against the old regime. Once the regime had fallen, interest in those issues diminished. Yeltsin showed no real interest in commemorating victims when it was not to his political advantage. In fact, Yeltsin was the party official who was responsible for the demolition of the house in Yekaterinburg where Tsar Nicholas II was murdered by Bolshevik assassins, along with the members of his family.

Few sites for the mass killings in the 1930s were admitted to—only a fraction of the real number. Rather than being memorialised, they were handed over to the church. Many of the victims were not believers, however. They were not Russian Orthodox, and the church itself was subordinate to the regime. Today church leaders are very much complicit in Putin's crimes, appropriating memory which glorifies the prerogatives of the state.

The core problem was that there was no rule of law after the breakup of the Soviet Union. The entire economic system changed from state ownership to private ownership without moral rules. This was a legacy of Soviet ideology, where law, morals, ethics, culture are all derivative. It was probably the largest peaceful transfer of property in world history, accomplished without the benefit of law.

What you got was gangsterism. It's unrealistic to think that those who use terror in order to seize power will ever give it up. A potential barrier was never created. On the one hand, you've got this criminal group who have the levers of power. On the other hand, you have a critical mass of people who seem perfectly happy to enslave themselves to power. In every country people accept a set of propositions uncritically and then apply them to every political situation. This simplifies the world. Soviet ideology, broken down to a few simple-to-understand precepts, engendered a feeling of superiority, paradoxical as that may be. Soviet citizens had the answers to every question.

They had a formula that could be applied to anything, whether it was art, music, literature, politics. The idea that some things are simply correct appeals not just to Russians, but in Russia this tendency was massively reinforced. In other words, if something is in the interests of the working class, then it's moral. There's no higher goal for society. The effect of that was to destroy any sense of right or wrong, irrespective of the political context.

What is really motivating the Ukrainians is the integrity of the nation and the desire not to have their national identity destroyed and not to be dominated by force. I wouldn't necessarily attribute all this to a defence of democracy so much as a defence of the Ukrainian nation—which is not the same thing. Ukraine's victory would be, potentially, a huge contribution to the development of a consciousness of right and wrong in Russia. Ukraine's Euromaidan saw hundreds of thousands of people in the streets. It was a spontaneous, democratic, self-organising protest. It led to the overthrow of a kleptocratic ruler, Viktor Yanukovych.

One of the most persistent narratives from the Soviet period is that Russians somehow are genetically incapable of creating a democratic society. A functioning, prosperous democracy in Ukraine would have a huge impact in Russia. The fates of Belarus, Ukraine and Russia are all intimately tied together in the sense that they were all parts of the Soviet Union. They are all recovering to one degree or another, in Belarus and Russia not very well, and in Ukraine partially. A successful democratic society in Ukraine would be very infectious.

Section 2
Military Might

8. A REFUSAL TO YIELD
General David H. Petraeus

General David Petraeus served over six consecutive commands, five of which were in combat, including command of the Surge in Iraq, US Central Command, and NATO/US Forces in Afghanistan. Afterwards, he served as Director of the CIA in Barack Obama's Administration. He is currently a Visiting Fellow/Lecturer at Yale University and author of Conflict: The Evolution of Warfare from 1945 to Ukraine (2023) with Andrew Roberts.[8]

It appears the Ukrainians may be recognising they cannot just launch right into the multiple defensive layers that the Russians have established, especially in the southern and south-eastern parts of the country. The counter-offensive is encountering very substantial mine fields, with anti-tank and anti-personnel mines, overwatched by Russian soldiers who have indirect fire capability that they can use when the Ukrainians are trying to breach those mine fields. That's very, very difficult. There are very substantial obstacles, and this is very challenging for a Ukrainian force that doesn't have the kind of air power that we in the US would put over such an operation. It has some limited capacity, using drones as forward observation platforms, and then linking to the Western-provided artillery and multiple-launch rocket systems.

Russians have adjusted tactically, to try and make the drones less effective by jamming them with electronic warfare and limiting their access to GPS signals. The challenge here is for a force that doesn't have the massive breaching capability that say a Western force or a US force would bring to bear with massive, armoured bulldozers and so forth, just ploughing through. But they're setting the conditions for their ultimate success by specifically targeting and attritting Russian logistical depots, and major ammunition and fuel depots in the south. They're going specifically after headquarters, they're going after their reserve force assembly areas, and they're going after the artillery pieces. They're going to pick away at all of this, and attrit it over time.

Russia has shown that it doesn't limit its activities to conventional warfare. Throughout this conflict the Russians stand accused of multiple war crimes against civilian objects, targeting energy, targeting fuel, light, heat, food, and specifically we've seen terrorist action, in destroying the Kakhovka dam, causing a vast environmental catastrophe.

Russians will resort to further scorched-earth or terrorist tactics if they are demonstratively losing on the battlefield. And again, the Russians keep rattling the nuclear sabre. They're reaching for anything that could possibly create concern among European countries, to try to drive a wedge between those who are just solidly with Ukraine and those that have some reservations. I don't think Putin will be able to show that the Russians can out-suffer the Ukrainians, the Europeans, and the Americans. But that is still his hope and that is his strategy. They're going after the infrastructure to turn out the lights and turn off the heat and cut off the water.

You must try and appreciate the incredible determination of the Ukrainian people, throughout the country, but especially in the capital. They refuse to allow the Russians to keep them from going about their daily existence, going to work, going to dinner, sitting out in the nice spring weather. They just will not give in. This is like London during the Blitz. It's not anywhere near as devastatingly destructive of the capital as the Blitzkrieg was of London, but it has its moments.

Among all the activities ongoing here, they are doing an archaeological dig, which happens to be underneath the American University. So even in the middle of a war, they refuse to give in to the Russians. The historical significance is very substantial because it seems to show that Kyiv came before other Russian cities, contrary to the grievance-filled, revisionist history that Putin puts forward. That is not just symbolically but substantively very significant, in undermining one of the reasons he has asserted for pursuing this war, all of which are flawed and inaccurate.

Ukrainians have continued to go about their daily activities. It is astonishing how capable, how resourceful they are, how skilled—especially in engineering, mechanical and IT fields. To see all of that being used to help the state rather than private companies, achieving highly impressive results in these areas.

The closer you are to Russia, for instance, if you're one of the Baltic states who have a border with Russia, the more substantially you are supporting the Ukrainian cause. If you have the luxury of a bit more distance, then you have the luxury perhaps to be a little less passionate. Although Germany has been very impressive, in that they are providing lethal weapons to another country for the first time in their post-World War Two history; it's fair to say that the translation of that policy declaration into action has taken a bit of time. Germany is a crucial player in Europe; what the Bundestag does and what it authorises really matters.

There are other elements that are not present as fully as we in the US would want, were we to be conducting combined arms operations. The Ukrainians don't have substantial expeditionary logistics, for example. That's a limiting factor. They have infantry fighting vehicles. They have heavy artillery, they have a variety of other arms and capabilities, but the question is, can they put it all together? Because they've not achieved that so far. They did it to a degree in the fall offensive in Kharkiv oblast, when they liberated that area, but their forces couldn't continue much farther. They really had the Russians moving and, on the run, but they couldn't press the attack because they didn't have sufficient follow-on forces. You can't train for this because there are no training areas in Europe that are large enough to deploy more than a battalion task force. And we're talking about brigades—nine additional armoured brigades, each of which has about 3,500 to 4,000 troops depending on how they're configured. Our entire training area in Germany where they have trained, that area is just not large enough.

You can do simulations, you can talk it through, you can rehearse it, without all the troops. You can do all these training tasks, but you then must do it. They're going to be learning on the job—on the job training, it's discovery and learning to a degree. I am impressed that the Ukrainians are a learning organisation. I saw this even before this latest invasion.

I was there just before Covid, after President Zelenskyy was elected. I made the effort to not only meet the Minister of Defence and the general staff, but I also then went out to the east, to Kharkiv, and then to the front line. On that trip, I came away feeling that these forces have really been transformed. The transformation has been dramatic, and it has accelerated.

Where can we do more?

The UK has been prominent in often being the one that first provides a particular capability. The shoulder-launched anti-tank guided missiles, and Storm Shadow; the first to commit to various other systems like tanks, the first Prime Minister to visit; that has been helpful because what you've seen is the UK essentially walking point for the Alliance, walking point for the US. The US then watches what the reaction is; we're testing this escalation dynamic just to see what Putin will do. In every case, Putin's threats have turned out to be hollow. They will continue to ring hollow, but he will also continue to issue them, trying to steer the Alliance into reducing or restricting or constraining what it provides to the Ukrainians.

The Ukrainians have shown a willingness to adopt very unconventional tactics. Tactics aimed at undermining the opponent. They are not necessarily intended to help retake ground directly or liberate Ukrainian soil. They're more intended to show the Russians that if they continue this, there is not only a price on the Russian Federation, but they will be forced to also divert resources. The operations in Belgorod, just to the east of Ukraine, clearly showed that the Russian defences of their own territory, even near the Ukrainian border, were inadequate. That showed the Russian people that their territory is not off limits, given what it is they are doing to Ukrainian civilian infrastructure. Again, they are reportedly focusing on legitimate military targets in accordance with the law of warfare. That it is an appropriate tactic and operational campaign, carrying out insurgency operations behind Russian lines on Ukrainian territory. That's got to be very challenging for the Russians because then nothing is secure.

It also gives us a premonitory peek at the state of Russia, the brittleness of its economy, its regime, its power structure. Should we, in fact, be preparing for some kind of collapse or even disintegration of the Russian Federation itself? This is obviously not a subject that is discussed openly in Washington circles and elsewhere. The fact is, there is that kind of discussion going on. There are concerns. This is not something we would necessarily welcome. We've seen what happens when these large countries that are held together by strong central governments collapse, and the outcomes are not always all that positive.

We've seen it with the Arab Spring. There must be various contingency plans, to the extent that you have any capacity to influence what might happen. We must be very cautious and, frankly, intellectually humble and policy wise, about what we might be able to influence given our experience of the last 20 or more years. Of course, Russia is a nuclear power, and that must be a very prominent feature in these discussions. Russia has the largest nuclear arsenal in the world. There must be a concern that they could resort to the use of tactical nuclear weapons in some way or another.

There have been very serious warnings about that, including from President Xi of China and Prime Minister Modi of India, both of whom have repeatedly cautioned Putin not to consider such an escalation.

It seems that we've always been a little bit behind the Ukrainian requests, behind the demands they've had; we have dithered and strung out the supply of weapons since February 2022. However, it's significant the way in which the US has kept the Alliance together. It has prevented Russia from driving wedges between Europe and North America. It's prevented Russia from driving wedges between individual European countries and the global south. Other very prominent countries have not joined in, although in some cases they have aided Russia in various ways.

It is fair to say there has been over-caution about the provision of certain systems which the Ukrainians have requested. The initial answer is always no, then there's reconsideration, and then, over time, eventually it's approved. We've seen this repeatedly, most recently with the commitment of Western aircraft and the decision to provide F16s.

There have been implications. It means that the Ukrainians have not had capabilities quite as soon as they otherwise would have had. In some cases, the reluctance had to do with concerns about potential Russian escalation or something along those lines. In other cases, the Alliance has been shown to be overly cautious, because the Russian response has not been significant.

We can't say the Ukrainians will retake a hundred percent of their territory, but certainly they've survived. They retain their independence. There could be perhaps a negotiated resolution. There would need to be incentives for Ukraine, a Marshall-like reconstruction plan, a security guarantee, a pass on NATO membership, continued armed ammunition, material support, et cetera. On the Russian side, a negotiated peace would stop the horrific losses that they have been sustaining, which are now many, many times the 15,000 or so they sustained in nearly 10 years in Afghanistan.

I think that we can see a possibility of Russian morale eroding, of their spirit eroding—we'll just have to see how it plays out.

9. A PERMANENT THREAT
General Sir Richard Shirreff

General Sir Richard Shirreff served in the British Army and commanded operations at every combat level. His last post was NATO's Deputy Supreme Allied Commander Europe (2011-2014). He is an honorary Fellow of Exeter College, Oxford, and author of War With Russia: An Urgent Warning from Senior Military Command (2016).[9]

This is the most dangerous moment in Europe since World War Two. We have to recognise that there will never be peace in Europe while Putin or a Putin lookalike, ultra-nationalist, hellbent on rebuilding a Russian empire, is in power in the Kremlin.

Russian leaders, to carry sway with their people, need to have strength to stay on top of the pyramid. Think back to 2014, March the 14th, the day that Crimea was incorporated into the Russian Federation, and the mass crowds in Red Square waving banners. Putin's popularity ratings have never been higher. Conversely, if Russia suffers a major defeat or a catastrophic defeat—which is what the loss of Crimea would amount to—that will really shake Putin's position to its foundations.

Reality is predictable. I predicted that Russia would attack Ukraine. I said it would go on to attack the Baltic states. It has not come to that yet because Russia has found itself so bogged down in Ukraine. What I don't think anybody could have conceived of, was the depth of genocide, massacre, mass use of rape as a weapon of war, and the sort of depravity and ghastly violence that we've seen Russia visit upon Ukraine and the Ukrainian people, Ukrainian cities, Ukrainian women and children. They are a stark historical reminder of the Red Army's taking of Berlin, where you heard the same stories of mass rape, terror, and murder as they marauded their way across Europe.

The stories of 1945 and the way in which the Red Army behaved in its subjugation of Nazism, are the stuff of history now, and I don't think anybody could have conceived that, in this increasingly closely connected world, hard on the heels of the World Cup in Moscow and with Russians living in London, that we could see Russia do quite what it has done in Ukraine. We must recognise that this is fundamentally a form of genocide. Putin wants to wipe Ukraine off the map as a state. To crush it, politically and militarily, by raping its women and destroying and massacring its people. This is sanctioned from the very top. But this is not just one man's effort. These crimes have been committed and enabled by many, many millions of people.

What finally pushed America into agreeing to send M1 Abrams tanks? Initially America was reluctant. Firstly, let's dispel any idea that the M1 Abrams tank is not suitable for the steppes of eastern Ukraine. It's a superb tank, and it's absolutely suitable for that terrain. The challenge with the M1 Abrams is that it's logistically very demanding, in common with many large American machines. It's a hell of a gas guzzler. You must think about tanks in context. The tank is not just the machine—it's the logistics, it's the recovery, it's the repair, it's the spares, it's the fuel, and it's the combined arms capability that goes with it.

There are some 2000 Leopard 2s across Europe. Of course it makes sense for the Leopard to be deployed. It would also make sense for Britain to send many more Challenger 2s. The key thing is international pressure. The loss of reputation for Germany has been catastrophic. Many of us were thinking that Germany's reluctance and procrastination was all about pushing for a negotiated ceasefire by not letting Ukraine have the offensive capability required to retake Ukrainian territory and to defeat the Russians. This was a way of Germany undermining what is effectively the NATO strategy of giving Ukraine the tools it needs to do the job. It appears that this is not the case. One could be cynical and say they don't want Russia to lose decisively because they want to hold the door open to normalise economic relations after the conflict.

There is a deep pacifism in Germany, because of the history of the 20th century. It goes even further, though. The so-called 'Russia Understanders' have played a significant part in German politics since the end of the World War Two. The cynicism of economic self-interest and appeasement, ignoring the reality of the threat posed by Russia, is very strong.

But equally, Germany has not been alone in ignoring the threat from Russia. Many other nations adopted a similar stance. London(grad) needs to look at itself. A lot of lawyers, bankers, accountants and other professionals in London have benefited. Investment managers have benefited hugely from Russian money. I can remember speaking engagements with many of them who really did not like being told that Russia was a serious threat.

What is needed to win?
There are massive challenges for Ukraine. Abrams. Bradleys, French vehicles, this incredible variety of machinery that's being sent. It's a logistic and training nightmare, this Noah's Ark of vehicles and equipment, guns and artillery

pieces and the plethora of ammunition is a massive challenge for the Ukrainians. Training not only the crews of the vehicles, the tanks, the armoured personnel carriers, but also training the fitters, the mechanics, the recovery experts, to ensure they have the logistical capability and the means to support all this hardware. It's a classic case of where there's a will, there's a way. The Ukrainians have shown us that where there's a will, there is absolutely a way.

Their military capability says to me that they understand the importance of combined arms. For the uninitiated, this is about the complex orchestra of different weapons and different capabilities. The traditional combined arms capabilities of tanks, armoured infantry fighting vehicles, self-propelled artillery, armoured engineers, air defence, attack aviation and air logistics all coming together in a combined way under a single commander in order to produce a synergistic effect in which the vulnerabilities of one weapon system, for example, the vulnerabilities of a tank, in built up or forested areas, are offset by the strength of another capability.

On top of that, 21st century conflict requires new combined arms warfare. Cyber, drones and satellite intelligence capabilities, which are now providing capability in the form of precision down to really quite a low level, which was previously the preserve of special forces or strategic level commanders, that requires training. You don't do this unless they've done some serious training, working together, drilling, endless drills and establishing an understanding of the science of war, to ensure that when you need to, you can deliver it. That's what militaries do. Endless training.

Russia does huge annual drills. They do massive set piece engagements, potentially with tens of thousands of troops. There is a huge difference between the way NATO, the US and the UK train and the way Russia trains.

An obvious insight into the lack of Russian training has been the Russian performance in this war. It's quite clear that they have no real understanding of the integration of combined arms. Just think back to those Russian tank columns in built-up areas advancing on Kyiv and being destroyed by well-sited, courageous Ukrainian anti-tank missile carriers. This is something the British Army does very well, training as realistically as you possibly can and making the environment as realistic as possible through what is called force on force. Then, of course, you debrief in detail afterwards to see where you've gone wrong and ensure to get it better next time.

We know that the Russian vertical system does not encourage criticism. Juniors are not encouraged to criticise their seniors or even their peers. What you see in Russia is the legacy of a very highly centralised Soviet command

and control system, where subordinates are afraid to make decisions because if they get it wrong, it's the salt mines or it's Siberia or the firing squad.

The converse is the way the Ukrainians have espoused the notion of what is called mission command, which is empowering subordinates to use their initiative, ensuring that they understand the commander's intent at a high level, but also at a tactical level, ensuring that they have the resources they need to use their initiative to get on with it. A junior NCO guarding or observing on the ground, way forward, can see things much more clearly than any general sitting in a remote headquarters. Empowerment of initiative through mission command is a fundamental enabler of military success. The Russians simply don't have that. The Ukrainians have learned that, very successfully since 2014. If Ukraine is to recapture the territory it's lost, it must go on to the attack.

Putin is mobilising more manpower, scooping up young men, and not so young men, off the streets to put them into the battle, probably with very little training. You're going to see this mass human wave tactics that we've seen around Bakhmut and Soledar continue, with mass casualties for the Russians.

What Ukraine will be seeking to do is to unhinge the Russian decision-makers, because that is the art of war, to make the political leadership realise that they've lost. If Ukraine tries to attack across its whole front, which is over 1000km, it's going to get nowhere. It's got to concentrate force in a specific area, achieve a breakthrough and then go for it.

There are second and third lines of defence. One of the principles of defence is defence in depth, so that if your first line is broken, you've got some other means of soaking up an attack. It's extraordinary because it's reminiscent of the World War One, in the sense that this great trench line has not just been there since 24th of February 2022, it's been there since 2014.

Given the brutality of it, it's also reminiscent of the Titanic clash between the Soviet Union and Nazi Germany. There's a supreme irony here in that Putin and his armies and air forces and navy have been launching an unprovoked genocidal assault on a democratic, peaceful neighbour without cause, except that of subjugating Ukraine and rebuilding the Russian empire. Putin and his cohorts are describing the Zelenskyy regime as a Nazi regime, racist and antisemitic—which, of course, is supreme cynicism, but Putin has controlled the information space in Russia for the 23 years since he took power.

Despite the massive casualties that the Russians are taking—which must be having an impact on Russian families—all the indications are that Russians submit passively, which has been part of the Russian condition for centuries.

You either submit passively or you accept tacitly. Russians are conditioned to accept and to put up with things and almost take pride in suffering.

There's one contingent of the Russian population which is still in the country and is quite vociferous, and that is the extreme nationalists and the so-called community of military bloggers who are quasi-official. They are generally tolerated to spew their bile and hate.

They've been extraordinarily critical, not typically of Putin, but certainly critical of the army commanders. They're accusing the government of not going far enough, for not taking the gloves off; for not being brutal enough.

This highlights the longer-term threat that Europe and, indeed, the Western world faces from Russia, even if Putin is replaced. He's not going to be replaced by an olive-branch-bearing liberal seeking peace and accommodation with the West—even if Ukraine achieves its military objectives sufficiently to ensure that it can guarantee its security and sovereignty against Russia. We will continue to face a threat from Russia indefinitely.

There's a lot of wishful thinking around a Russian liberal opposition. I don't think Russia is ever going to change this mentality unless it goes through the sort of transformation Germany went through in 1945. We all know why Germany went through that. It was unconditional surrender, forced on it by the Allies. That is never going to happen in Russia. In a sense, Europe is chained to a lunatic as its neighbour for the foreseeable future. We must do everything we can to empower and support any form of liberal opposition. We must do everything we can to open the eyes of decent Russians as to what is being perpetrated in their name, through strategic communications—as was done so successfully towards the end of the Cold War with the BBC World Service, Radio Free Europe, Radio Liberty, et cetera.

We've got to be pragmatic and say this is what we're faced with for generations to come. Ukraine must become part of NATO. That also absolutely applies to Georgia and Moldova. We must assume that Russia will remain a threat in perpetuity. It is voracious because Russia has never been a sovereign state in the way that France has been a sovereign state or Britain, Italy, Germany. Russia has only ever existed as an empire and has only been able to survive through being voracious and gobbling up its neighbours. We must be prepared to deter Russia in the same way that we deterred the Soviet Union during the Cold War.

Not to stretch historical analogies too far, but there's a tactic that certainly Nazi Germany used and which you see very much on display in Russian propaganda. That is of aggressive victimhood—attacking while claiming you are the victim, flipping everything on its head in quite an absurd manner.

But that sense of victimhood is an incredibly powerful and toxic emotion. It plays into the minds of the Russian population. It plays on their insecurities, on the sense of encirclement; that Russia is a victim and is threatened by nefarious and dangerous outside forces bent on destroying the third Rome and the very foundations of Russia. That idea is baked in very deeply. It's not just Putin who came up with it; it goes back to the 19th century. We're bound to get this language of escalation coming from the Kremlin, and we're also bound to hear that language being repeated, as if through an echo chamber, by those who nominally are pacifist or maybe even Russian sympathisers.

The only way to avoid catastrophe is to be strong. It was Churchill who said, the Russians only understand strength. If you demonstrate any weakness, you're going to get walked over. The way to continue to live in peace is to be strong, to understand that we must protect ourselves. The way to protect our freedoms is through the old-fashioned way of deterrence, and that means, I'm afraid, investing in military capability, because that is the way you prevent escalation.

I always knew the Ukrainians were going to fight like tigers. But I assumed the Russians were going to be much more effective than they have been, and that the Russians would succeed in enforcing capitulation. The Ukrainians have given us a master class in the application of the principles of war, the concentration of force, security, economy of force, ensuring that when you fight, you have thought about it, and you fight on your own terms, and you don't match enemy strength with your strength. You look for enemy vulnerability and enemy weakness, and that's where you apply your strength. They've done that superbly.

In Cromwell's words, the Ukrainians know what they are fighting for, and they love what they know, which is how Cromwell described his soldiers of the New Model Army. The Russians don't know what they're fighting for.

Where does NATO need to improve?

There is a lack of strategy, as to what NATO and the West will be faced with subsequently. The fundamental is to start putting in place the long-term deterrence against whatever happens in Russia, all of which could continue to pose a threat. The only way we're going to deter is through being militarily strong and accepting that we must be prepared for the worst case. Frankly, it's not a question of thinking at all. And nobody is saying wake up, smell the coffee. We face a dangerous generation now and we need to look to our own defences. I've heard no senior politician say anything like that, recognising what needs to be done, in terms of UK defence. It's not just the UK, of course, it's right across the alliance.

10 A QUESTION OF MORALE
General Mark Hertling

Lieutenant General Mark Hertling is a decorated US Army veteran. His last posting was as the Commanding General of US Army Europe.[10]

The Russians have always had elements of a kleptocracy. All dictatorships have that, whether it's a kleptocracy for money or kleptocracy for power. This was both. What is interesting is that the culture, over the 20-plus year reign he has now had as leader of Russia, has really burrowed into all organisations and institutions.

I had dealings with two chiefs of Russian ground forces. One told me that he couldn't get anything done. The second one, six months after being appointed, was court martialled by Putin for accepting bribes. Back in 2011, my counterpart in Ukraine was a guy named Hennadiy Vorobyov, chief of their ground forces. He approached me one day and said one of his primary functions was to get rid of the Soviet-trained officers inside his army because they were destroying it.

During the last ten years of my career as a general officer, from 2003 to 2013, I spent three years in Iraq, but the rest of the time was in Europe reading intelligence bulletins. Up until about 2011, I was connecting with my Russian counterparts, inviting their soldiers to go to our NCO school at Grafenwoehr, conducting an exercise that was called Torgau, which was the place where the Americans and the Russians linked up on the Elbe River in World War II. And we would have a celebratory exercise every year. I watched the Russian troops, I observed Russian senior leadership, generals and colonels, and I would issue reports back to my headquarters in Washington and at European Command saying, these guys aren't that good. In fact, they're pretty bad in most cases.

Travelling to Russia one time, I had the opportunity to watch a training demonstration, where I was able to talk to a couple of the soldiers and found out an entire tank platoon had fired one round of ammunition prior to conducting this demonstration. During the demonstration, there were no targets, but there were a lot of tanks firing at very short distances. I talked to a Russian pilot and found out the limited number of hours they flew. All of that was because of graft. They are a force that has very large quantities, but very poor quality.

The chickens are coming home to roost, and violence is increasingly more apparent on Russian soil. We see the emergence of private armies. Some of the major oligarchs and industrialists are creating their own private armies. This surely cannot be a good sign for the cohesion of Russian society and indeed for any kind of peaceful succession when Putin finally leaves. Unfortunately, we in the United States are experiencing a small fraction of that. It started out with Blackwater, and it continues with various state militias. Now we even have some members of the state government saying that they should have their own little army outside of the National Guard. This is somewhat of an authoritarian approach—if the big army isn't working, then let's make smaller armies that we can control. None of those smaller armies have the professionalism that is required. You are establishing bands of paid murderers. It really damages the state as well.

Where is the Ukrainian military superior to the Russians?
There has been an increase in training Ukrainians at the battalion over 500 soldiers and above level on weapon systems and on combined arms operations. Ukraine has not previously received this kind of training. This is something new for them. They've received training from some of the more advanced NATO forces in Europe at different locations.

You see Russia being attacked in various sectors and having disorganised and dysfunctional communications. There is a constant increase in Putin's unwillingness to accept reality, not only as reported by journalists within Moscow, but also through some apparent indicators from his cabinet ministers and his subordinate leaders. You see very little improvement in the Russian military from the standpoint of soldier capability and leadership. They've had huge difficulty in conducting offensive operations, which tells me they're also going to have difficulty conducting counterattacks against Ukrainian forces. At the same time, the indicators on the Ukrainian side are that they are ready for offensive manoeuvres.

The Ukrainians could perhaps be forgiven for being a little overconfident. They pushed the Russians back from Kyiv. They took Kherson. The Kharkiv Oblast was an incredible advance. But one of the things I learned, unfortunately rather late in my career, is that you should never underestimate your enemy. No matter how poor you think they are, no matter how dysfunctional they appear or how lacking in equipment you believe them to be. Because they, the enemy, will always surprise you. Especially if you're overconfident and neglect an adequate analysis of what the enemy is doing.

Starting back in February 2022, I've pointed out where the Russian military is weak, based on my experience conducting exercises with Russian military forces back in the 2008 to 2011 time frame. In fact, in this campaign, the Ukrainian military understands some of their shortcomings; they have been through some tough battles. They have lost a lot of their soldiers and commanders who had trained in the Western way of war.

Even with the Western media and the pressure on Ukraine's partners to do something and to do something quickly, the Ukrainian military needs to be mindful that its resources aren't infinite. They have a duty of care to preserve the lives of their troops in a way that the Russians don't. The Russians have shown they really don't care about individual life. I could give you some personal vignettes about experiences that I've had both with Ukrainian forces and with Russian forces, and how they approach battlefield casualties. It is a night and day difference. Ukrainians understand the requirement to care for their soldiers, the trust that imbues in a force when you're a soldier and you know that if something happens to you, you're going to receive medical aid and be transported to the rear; that your next of kin, if you die, are going to be taken care of, and that you're always going to be remembered on a wall somewhere, like the one they have in Kyiv with the names of all those who have sacrificed their lives for this cause.

In the Russian military, there's a seeming lack of attention to both medical treatment for the wounded, and to caring for the dead and an understanding of how they have contributed to the motherland or the fatherland. It is a fascinating disconnect that runs counter to the kind of trust Clausewitz told us needs to be in existence between the government, the public and the military forces.

What is Putin's greatest military failing?
For a Russian general, it must be the worst nightmare to have someone like Putin meddling and micromanaging. It is, unfortunately, the disease of autocrats. They want everything their way because there is a narcissistic quality about them, but whenever someone speaks truth to power in Russia, they are immediately blocked. Putin is not a military man. He does not understand strategy, tactics or operations from a military standpoint. He is a spy. He's a KGB agent. He not only has a lack of willingness to listen to advisors, but he also combines that with a single-minded obsession with what he thinks can be done when all evidence points to the contrary.

As a military analyst I had to talk about military operations. But to talk about military operations, you first must determine what you think a politician's strategic objectives are. I wrote down what I thought were Putin's five major political objectives. I had to make an informed guess because they were never stated. There's a disconnect between how Putin was attempting to treat this so-called vassal state, as he considers it, saying, I want to subjugate the nation. So that was one political objective. I want to conduct regime change and to destroy their army. At the same time, another of his political objectives was to create divisiveness within NATO and within the United States. Putin saw some of our shortcomings as a nation and thought he could leverage them to his advantage. When you have those kinds of political objectives, you must attach the means and the ways that your military is going to need to accomplish those objectives. He never did that. In fact, in many cases, quite the opposite.

The Ukrainian military, however, has improved steadily and has worked on eliminating corruption, even though some of that still exists within government in Ukraine, whereas the Russian military has continued down that road to corruption, which takes us back to trust—when the soldiers can't trust the captains or the colonels or, especially the generals, then it's going to be a force that can't fight very well.

Ukraine has not had all the equipment in place to effectively deliver combined arms at the front line. They have had some elements go through combined arms operations. There are places like the UK where they are conducting basic training for new Ukrainian soldiers. In other places, like Poland, in Germany, in Bavaria, where they are trying to put battalions together. What may still be missing is the senior level staff training, the emphasis on courses of action development, military prep of the battlefield. As a NATO soldier, you want perfection. You want opportunities to practice multiple times. You want training events and exercises to help prove your abilities and be a little bit more confident. I don't think the time is available for Ukraine to do that.

Russia's reputation for toughness and for being superlative warriors was eroded in Syria, Chechnya, Georgia. They are just not that good against highly organised, disciplined and well-equipped opponents. Russia has not faced a major, large-scale manoeuvre offensive. Both sides will have challenges, but Ukraine has much better will and morale in their force, and certainly much better leadership. Some military analysts and the media continue to fall into the trap of underestimating them, but Ukraine has shown a very creative approach throughout the war and the Ukrainian army has developed into a very capable territorial force.

They have already shown themselves to be magnificent in striking very precise targets that contribute to logistics activities or force resupply. It's good to strike an ammo dump or a fuel dump. It's even better when the smoke from those fuel dumps burns on for a couple of days, because that's a signal to the Russian people that their government and their military is incapable of stopping these actions.

You would have thought that Russians would rally round after the attacks of drones on that wealthy suburb of Moscow, but it was quite the reverse. Z Patriots, the liberals, everyone was cheering on the fact that the apparatchiks and the thieves were being bombed. This shows the disunity in Russian society. There's not been a single instance where any Ukrainians celebrate an attack. When Irpin and Bucha, the wealthy suburbs of Kyiv, were attacked, nobody was rejoicing. There isn't the same envy in Ukrainian society. You've got a sense of unity. But what is being exposed are the fissures within Russian society, the contempt many Russians have for their fellow citizens. Ukrainians are very cleverly using strategies to expose that. Perhaps these divisions within Russian society are a foreshadowing of what could happen when they lose the war. You could see extraordinary division and chaos.

Putin and, to a lesser degree, Lukashenko, are both stuck on the horns of a dilemma because they're trying to desperately create forces to send to the front, but they know they can only take so many from Moscow or from Minsk, because as soon as they start taking the palace guards, the military that protect the dictators, then it weakens their ability to counter any protest. At the beginning of the war, every time there was a protest in either Saint Petersburg or Moscow, it was rapidly put down by the thugs wearing uniform. Those thugs must remain in place for the regime to survive.

What should we look out for?

What I'm really watching is the flow of logistics, together with the training of battalions and brigades within Ukraine, or outside of Ukraine, by NATO alliance forces. It's difficult. And it's exceedingly difficult to not only train the leading edge of the force, but also to pull the logisticians back to train them to support fast-moving operations. Let's use two of our favourite generals, Montgomery and Patton. Both outran their logistics in fast-moving operations. They had a very capable logistics supply chain, but their tactical brilliance outran their logistical support, and that's never a good thing. Another challenge of a fast-moving operation which we saw in Kharkiv, is that suddenly you might find you've got a vast number of Russian prisoners and a huge amount of Russian kit that you've suddenly come into possession of. That can create its own challenges,

I have read some research on Russian soldiers who returned from Afghanistan. It was like PTSD on steroids. I think Russia saw that with their veterans from Afghanistan and it caused some significant damage. It was on an incredible scale, and, in addition, it's a society that's not particularly tolerant to disability, mental illness and so on. Especially in terms of those coming back from a war that, truthfully, is not popular, that doesn't create a rush of civic pride or patriotism.

Ukraine, along with a few other countries, will be the linchpin of a very secure Europe in the future, because they have suffered so greatly under this invasion. They will be in that position, not only because of their ability to fight off the Russians, but also because of their magical culture and their wonderful people. A linchpin of progress within Europe in the coming decades.

11. THE RUSSIAN FEDERATION WILL DISAPPEAR

General Ben Hodges

Lieutenant-General Ben Hodges succeeded Mark Hertling as Commanding General of United States Army Europe in November 2014, and held that position for three years until retiring from the United States Army in January 2018. He was the Pershing Chair in Strategic Studies, at the Centre for European Policy Analysis, specialising in NATO, Transatlantic relationship and international security.[11]

Putin has made several fatal strategic mistakes that are certainly going to lead to the defeat of the Russians on the battlefield, and, I believe, to collapse of the Russian Federation in the coming years. They calculated the West would not stick together; that we would not really support Ukraine. He went ahead back in February, feeling confident that he could get away with what he had been doing in previous years.

The Ukrainians are defending their homeland, whereas most Russian soldiers who have been deployed into Ukraine are from ethnic regions well outside of Moscow. This is the traditional method of the old Russian Empire. The majority of those killed don't come from Moscow or Saint Petersburg, which is a way to shield the elites from having to deal with the reality of what is going on. I was not surprised that Ukrainian soldiers would do well. We were working with them starting in 2015. They are very tech savvy. What I did not anticipate was how the Ukrainian people would respond and would come together. On 24th February, Ukrainians were Googling how to make a Molotov cocktail. On 21st September, Russians were Googling for flights out of Russia.

We saw in the summer of 2022 that Russians fled in panic, whether it was drones or sabotage, that made a huge impact, as well as looking impressive on social media. That creates a psychological fear and a sense of loss in Russia. The image of people on the beach revealed either total arrogance or a simple 'not my problem' response. The next day, instead of rushing to the recruiter's office saying, how do I fight to protect what is the Holy Land of Crimea, there was a massive traffic jam on that bridge trying to get out of there. That was revealing. It also pulled away the curtain of invulnerability, the myth that they couldn't be hurt.

Ukrainians, especially the senior officers, were trained in the old Soviet system. This is part of the reason for the success of sinking the Moskva, the Black Sea Fleet's flagship, because the Ukrainian Navy knew every square inch of that ship, what its abilities were, that its radar could only operate in 180 degrees, not 360, meaning that, if they could distract the radar, which they did with the drones, there would be a blind spot. That comes from that sort of intimate knowledge.

They also understand that Russia's logistics system is not designed for sustained land operations outside of Russia. Ukrainian soldiers serving alongside British and American soldiers and other allies for the past several years in Iraq and Afghanistan, and then training with them, I don't want to overstate this, but they have evolved rapidly into a more Western style command and control. Junior leaders are expected to make decisions, unlike in the Soviet (and now the Russian) military system, which has a very centralised command and control.

One of the things I missed before February, that I had failed to anticipate, was the impact of corruption on Russian military performance. I overestimated their capabilities, and I did not appreciate the depth of corruption that shows up in lack of quality control of what the defence industry provides to the services. This has been a catastrophe for the Russian military forces and the government.

Everything that a soldier uses, wears, eats, drinks, everything he or she does, there's got to be a supply chain that provides it. Modern warfare requires enormous amounts of maintenance fuel. If you've got 100,000 soldiers, that's 100,000 soldiers that have got to eat 2 or 3 times a day. They must have ammunition. They need boots, socks, belt buckles, everything. Over a million bits of winter warfare equipment, clothing gone missing. I'm sceptical that much ever existed, but somebody probably got paid for it anyway. They're having to import winter uniforms from North Korea.

The bottom line is that the Russian logistics system was never designed to support sustained, large scale land operations outside of Russia. They never thought they would have to do it. They don't have the infrastructure. Ukrainians who know everything there is to know about the Russians, the weaknesses as well as the strengths, and have very cleverly targeted the logistics system, going after transport capabilities and artillery ammunition to defeat Russian forces.

Seizing various rail hubs has been a very important part of the operational design. The Ukrainians understand these hubs are necessary for resupply and for moving ammunition. The Russian army is an artillery army. It's not a tank army. Moving thousands of tons of heavy, high explosive artillery ammunition is no mean feat. So, the more you can destroy the rail connections or deny those to the Russians, the greater the burden it puts on their truck fleet, which has undergone severe attrition.

The deception of drawing the Russians down towards Kherson so the main attack could go up near Kharkiv. Many of us are going to be studying this for quite some time, the operational design of this campaign. The discipline that was required from the very top has impressed me very much. For deception to work, it had to be believable. I remember people being frustrated, good professional journalists as well as other observers of the conflict, saying where's the famous Kherson offensive? When's it going to start?

How did they manage to keep the surprise, the deception in play? Earlier in the year they did undertake immense purges of the administration, the security services and political circles. That was a gift to propagandists at the time, who could say, look, they're undemocratic, etc. But it becomes quite clear why those purges were necessary to root out Russian influence.

Long range precision fire is the number one modernisation priority for the United States Army, starting several years ago with General Milley as chairman of the Joint Chiefs. When he was Chief of the Army, he made precision, long-range fire the number one modernisation priority for the US Army because of what you can achieve at distance with a rocket that's GPS guided. I'd like to see us give them more of these launchers. Nonetheless, they have made very skilful use of the capability that comes with HIMARS or the MLRS and various other systems. I don't think there are any soldiers in the world that are faster or better than Ukrainians are at adapting to new technologies.

My criticism of the Biden administration is that they have self-deterred because they have been concerned the Russians would escalate. This is an exaggerated fear. The fact is, the sooner we can deliver things like ATACMS, which is a 300-kilometre range rocket that could be fired from HIMARS, the sooner we start getting Abrams tanks or German Leopards, those kinds of capabilities will accelerate the end of this war. We know from history that war is a test of will, and it's a test of logistics. The Ukrainian General Staff has impressed me with their knowledge and their skill of employing operational art. They seem to be agile enough to exploit opportunities when weaknesses are discovered.

The Black Sea Fleet is cowering under the cliffs of Crimea and Ukraine does not even have a navy. There's not been a day in the last seven months where the Russian Air Force, Land Forces or their Navy operated together. They never got the benefit of modern capabilities in an integrated way. I'm not defending tanks out of a personal love, but too many people were quick to say, that's it, no more tanks. Every video I saw of a Russian tank getting destroyed, it was improperly camouflaged or not camouflaged. It was sitting out in the open. It was unprotected by dismounted infantry. Every mistake you could imagine was made.

There's going to come a time when Russian forces will—what Clausewitz called the culminating point—run out of impetus, run out of resources, and run out of the will to fight for a variety of reasons. You want to identify it. As early as May 2022, Ukrainian strategists were already beginning to think about how they would do this. At some point they're going to come up against the Russian border. To force Russia to conclude a reasonable peace, they are going to have to occupy chunks of Russian territory, otherwise these places are going to be just lobbing missiles over, even if they've regained their territories. Belarus as well is just a puppet state of Putin's, economically, politically dependent. They're also lobbing missiles from their territory. At one point they were allowing troops to cross those borders. Somehow both these countries will have to be dealt with.

Belarus is a very interesting question. Lukashenko has, thus far, managed to sit on the fence, allowing Russia to use its airspace and bases for staging; but all the while none of the units of the Belarusian armed forces have gone into the fight. They're worse than the Russian forces in terms of quality. I believe they have about ten battle groups total. It's a huge country, but not with a huge population. Lukashenko is wary about letting his units go in there and get ground up, because protecting his own regime is their number one job for him.

How do you see the war unfold?
In the long run, the future potentially looks quite positive for Ukraine. They've shown their bravery, their resourcefulness, the quality of their IT services, their self-organisation and their superpower—being extremely resourceful.

There's not quite the same optimism for Russia, because they've squandered their hydrocarbon resources. The dependency they'd cleverly managed to build up among European and other countries is now shot. They've blown their own pipeline. Arms were their second largest export, and their equipment has been shown to be, frankly, not quite up to scratch. Everybody has seen the video of the Russian reactive armour tiles that are layered around the tanks; you open them up, and it's supposed to be an explosive inside. Instead, there's rubber. The reports about reliability of precision weapons, of 30% failure rates. This is atrocious.

I don't think that anybody will be too impressed or anxious to buy Russian equipment in future. There have been reports of high failure rates of some of the weapons that either don't hit the target, or don't detonate. Artillery that's being fired, they have had to pull things out of storage. Older systems and ammunition that have not been properly stored. Artillery ammunition is not like hammers. You can't just leave it on the shelf forever and then use it whenever you're ready. Typically, armies use their oldest ammunition for training so that you've got the newest ammunition for crises. The Russians obviously are deep into old ammunition now. The rate of fire exceeds all the normal planning figures.

It's not just about ammunition consumption. It's about the wear and tear on the howitzers themselves. After 2000 rounds, the tube must be replaced. These artillery pieces that the Russians and the Ukrainians are using are way, way beyond 2,000. Where are those being manufactured? If you don't replace them, at some point you're going to have structural failure in the breech. The rounds don't go as far, they're not as accurate, or you have an explosion, and it kills or injures the crew members. Part of the reason having sergeants in our formations is so important, is because they have experience and they can anticipate when a young private is going to make a mistake. You don't have sergeants in the Russian army who are on top of these kinds of things.

Even with the best, most modern equipment—such as the Russian Air Force had—if you're not trained, if you don't know how to employ it, then it doesn't matter how expensive or how technologically advanced your equipment is. Generals were getting killed at the beginning of the conflict because they were on a cell phone: you wipe out a headquarters in this vertical command and control system. When you start taking out headquarters, it's not just the guy that's making the decisions. It's the staff around him that are doing analysis, that are anticipating what needs to be done. Then you have junior leaders that are not accustomed to or are unwilling to make decisions.

I thought the Russians must have so much operational experience. It turns out that only about 5% of the military, including the Air Force and Navy, had operational experience, and very little of that was against anything like fighting against Ukrainians, except in the Donbas region. And the Ukrainians stopped them in the Donbas. What the Russians do well is mass. They are clearly willing to absorb any number of casualties as long as they can keep pounding away.

Is there a reluctance on the part of Ukraine's allies to allow them to strike targets with the missile systems, and especially in Belgorod, a strategic Russian military hub? This is one area where we've got the policy wrong, not providing ATACMS to Ukrainian forces which have the 300-kilometre range, out of a concern that they would use it against targets inside Russia. Of course they would. Of course they should. Ukrainians are being murdered every day by rockets, Iskander missiles, aircraft and drones that are being launched from inside Russia and inside Belarus. They could already be making Sevastopol untenable for the Black Sea Fleet as well as the other Russian airfields. And of course, the Kerch Bridge and the other logistics capabilities that the Russians need to continue to defend in southern Ukraine.

That's a lesson we haven't really learned from the Second World War. There were points in the beginning when we could have intervened. Potentially Hitler, as has been written in his diaries and interviews, would have fled with his tail between his legs when they retook the Rhineland, if the British had gone in. But there's a certain need to normalise the situation.

War of the future is going to be as in Ukraine that combination of who can rapidly assimilate new technologies and who can be cleverest about crowdsourcing. You're still going to need to address the industrial base. The amount of ammunition that was consumed in the last seven months is far more than we spent over the last 20 years in Iraq and Afghanistan. We have a challenge in all our countries. Air and missile defence have had to recalculate the requirement because the Russians clearly are targeting populations. The number of missile defence systems that we have is barely enough to protect critical infrastructure.

These attacks on Ukrainian cities and infrastructure are in effect about weaponising refugees, to get hundreds of thousands of Ukrainians heading into Central and Western Europe in search of places to live, not just during the winter. The Russians realise that they have no chance of winning on the battlefield; the only chance for the Russians is to drag this out in the hope that we all lose the will to continue supporting Ukraine. Life is becoming harder in Ukrainian cities as winter sets in and the supply of power and heat become uncertain. People in big cities cannot survive for long periods without heat. Russia's campaign to cripple Ukraine's power infrastructure could therefore trigger a new wave of immigration to Europe.

What is the endgame?
The combination of all these factors, battlefield losses, sanctions, defeat and corruption is going to lead to the breakup of the Russian Federation. There will always be a Russian state, but the Russian Federation, which is an

artificial rump of the Soviet Union, will disappear. Are we prepared for what that entails? We were not prepared for the breakup of the Soviet Union.

I don't think we have any kind of plan to deal with it and perhaps don't even appreciate the scale of the problem in dealing with Russia. In some ways, it's even more complex than perhaps dealing with Germany and Japan after the war. Geographically it's a much bigger problem. Justice will be meted out in The Hague; I have no doubt. It will take time. The UN will block anything because Russia and China will block anything coming out of the UN.

What the Russian Federation is doing is in violation of international law—using force to change borders, sham referenda, illegal annexation, murder of innocent civilians, targeting civilian areas with very expensive precision munitions. None of these are accidents. Threatening the lives of millions of people by blocking the shipment of grain and energy. All these things are part of the Russian way of war, not to mention undermining democracies around the world through malign influence. Nobody's saying that Ukraine is perfect or that Europe is perfect, or that the United States is perfect. But this conflict, which has been going on for about 30 years, starting with the breakaway of Transnistria, then the invasion of Georgia, then the invasion of Crimea, then support for Assad, and what started in February 2022.

It's a new 30 Year War. The argument somehow that this war is really the fault of the West, that we lied after the breakup of the Soviet Union, that NATO was encircling Russia is a total farce. The question is, why do all the nations that used to be Soviet republics or under the Warsaw Pact, go scrambling to join NATO and the EU as fast as they could? Because they know what it's like to be a part of the Russian Empire. The idea that somehow NATO is expanding is a completely wrong way to describe it. The safest part of Russia was always the part that touched NATO. You look at the geographical mass of Russia, and you can see that those NATO territories were a small minority of their geographic borders.

Many analysts seem uncomfortable with the idea of a decisive Ukrainian victory. It upends so many decades of their thinking about the power structures in the world. Maybe books and papers they've written will become redundant. 'All wars end in negotiation', I hear. The Russians will benefit from that sentiment. It would give them a chance to rebuild and regroup. It would also entail Ukraine forfeiting sovereign territory. In other words, Russia's war would be rewarded.

As Russia's position on the battlefield becomes more precarious, Putin may resort to more terroristic threats against nuclear facilities or other irresponsible actions. Over the last couple of centuries, a lot of work has been done to try and limit the destruction, the brutality and the targeting of civilians. It's a war crime to target civilian infrastructure that is not directly related to military requirements. Everything that the Russians are doing now is a violation of multiple articles of the Geneva Convention. I hate to even think about it, but the deportation of hundreds of thousands of Ukrainian kids that are being sent to Russia, is exactly what Stalin did. It's an element of genocide. Genocide is not just killing everybody. It's depopulating an area to change the demographic balance there, and this is what has been going on. Putin's objective from the beginning has been the destruction of Ukraine as a state and the idea of Ukraine as a state. It's hard to imagine Russia re-entering the community of responsible nations anytime soon.

If Russia were to cause a meltdown of the Zaporizhzhia nuclear power plant as part of their hybrid warfare, using a scorched earth policy to create a nuclear accident, that would be disastrous. The international community has got to be working 24/7, putting pressure on the Kremlin to make sure that nothing happens at Zaporizhzhia. The United States Army had to do a lot of soul searching and reform after Vietnam. Thousands of sergeants had been killed. We had to rebuild ourselves. It took a complete change of culture. We had the right leaders in place to be willing to do that. I don't know that Russia has enough senior people. But the culture of accepting responsibility for something that went wrong, that's what it's going to take. You can't fix something until you can identify why is it broken. That will require a serious cultural change. Otherwise, Russia will just build back what they have, what they started this with.

If Russia were to cause a meltdown of the Zaporizhzhia nuclear power plant as part of their hybrid warfare, using a scorched earth policy to create a nuclear accident, that would be disastrous. The international community has got to be working 24/7, putting pressure on the Kremlin to make sure that nothing happens at Zaporizhzhia. The United States Army had to do a lot of soul searching and reform after Vietnam. Thousands of sergeants had been killed. We had to rebuild ourselves. It took a complete change of culture. We had the right leaders in place to be willing to do that. I don't know that Russia has enough senior people. But the culture of accepting responsibility for something that went wrong, that's what it's going to take. You can't fix something until you can identify why is it broken. That will require a serious cultural change. Otherwise, Russia will just build back what they have, what they started this with.

The Chinese are watching all this. President Xi told his military—in 2027, be ready for Taiwan. That coincides with the end of what will be his third term. The conflict with China would be different in many ways from what is happening here. China is playing quite an interesting war of attrition. People argue that in some ways the US is playing an attrition game here by eking out supply of weaponry to destroy Russia. China is playing an even bigger and more cunning game. If Russia does collapse, and it may happen whether we like it or not, China could very well sweep up from the South. It could get exceedingly messy in years to come.

12. THE NEW IRON CURTAIN
Anders Puck Nielsen

Anders Puck Nielsen is a military analyst and naval captain at the Danish Defence Academy, specializing in Russia, Ukraine, and maritime operations.[12]

The demands that Russia came out with in 2021 didn't make sense. If what they were doing around Ukraine was just posturing, they were basically inviting a diplomatic defeat. My reading of it at the time was that there had to be some kind of bigger plan. Analysts had different opinions. Some thought, right up until the moment when war broke out, that Putin was winning. I did not see it that way. Russia was getting a more united NATO and stronger support for Ukraine, with more NATO engagement on the borders of Russia. Putin, I thought, he wants to fix this.

We fail to take leaders like this at their word. Hitler told us what he was going to do in *Mein Kampf*, but it was so outside the norms of normal diplomatic and political behaviour that it wasn't believed. Similarly, Putin's been telling us for quite some time what he intends to do. Autocrats are quite happy to tell us what they want to achieve and why they want to achieve it. However, they often lie about how they're going to achieve it.

Few people in the Russian administration were warned in advance. So, they didn't have a chance to do proper planning for the operation. In hindsight, it's easy to see that there were many mistakes made by the Russians. It did not work at all the way they had intended. Within a month, they had to totally revise their campaign plan. At the start of the invasion, the general assumption was that Russia would be doing well and that the Russian army was in a good shape after almost 15 years of reforms, and that the Ukrainians would have to deal with a modern and capable fighting force. But we've had to adjust that picture quite radically.

A lot of third-party analysts have been surprised by the Ukrainians. The general assumption was that the Ukrainian army would be very much the same as in 2014. This turned out not to be the case and the Ukrainians' success has contributed to the image that this is a failure for the Russians. Those working with the Ukrainians sensed this transformation. A lot of it had to do with, on the one hand, training, and, on the other hand, a burning conviction that something had to be done.

There was the simmering war in the Donbas, where Ukrainians were able to get experience of how to fight the Russians. The Russians were very generous in demonstrating all their equipment. So, the Ukrainians learned how to deal with the Russian army and how to prepare for the invasion we saw in February 2022. One of the most extraordinary things is the sheer number of Ukrainians who've been exposed to military experience by spending time on the front over the last eight years, and then returning to civilian life.

It's bizarre to think that a huge country like Ukraine was functioning with part of its territory in a state of almost perpetual warfare. How did the Russians not factor that in? They seem to have completely ignored their role in training and upskilling the Ukrainian army. The mistakes the Russians made were as much political as military. The isolation of Putin during Covid probably contributed to this. While Putin was getting annoyed that things were dragging out in the Donbas, and felt that it was not going anywhere, in fact, Ukraine was going somewhere, and at a very rapid pace.

There are several scenarios for how this war ends. One is a stalemate with the conflict frozen along North Korea lines. Another one, of course, is that Russia is defeated decisively and pushed back across the borders. But the end game here, when the invasion is over, is that this is a new Cold War. A new Cold War would be a good result, because that means we're not in a hot war. We're not going to be friends with Russia again. That's not going to happen in the coming decades. What Ukrainians are fighting about is where the new Iron Curtain in Europe is going to be. Most likely, a divided Ukraine with some part of Ukraine on one side and another part on the other side. It looks as if Russia is preparing for a long-term war.

The most useful assumption is to take on board the fact this is going to take a long time, and that we must equip Ukraine to fight and win this war in the long run. It's said that time isn't on Russia's side, but in fact it is in Russia's interests to have a stalemate, to have a war of attrition, a continued artillery duel, with a First World War style front line, because they don't have any consideration for how many men they throw at this, whereas on the Ukrainian side, every life is precious. It's a common assumption that the Russians are very good at suffering, that they can endure all kinds of things that Westerners can't.

What it comes down to is, if Russia is to win this war, then it'll be because the West loses its determination. If the West is determined and united, then Russia will lose. That is why a lot of Russian propaganda is now turning to trying to undermine that coherence, that unity. Russia has partners in China and Iran which do amplify their propagandistic messages. I believe information warfare has played more of a role in this war than in any other war to date. Russians do have success with information warfare.

On the NATO side, there's been a lot of good work done to negate some of the Russian talking points. One Western campaign has been to alleviate the problems of the economic crisis, the gas crisis in Europe to sustain the war in Ukraine. The debate about the economic crisis is basically never connected to Russia anymore. And Russia is never discussed as a kind of solution to the economic crisis. Separating those two things is important for helping Ukraine in the long run.

Amazingly, Europe's infrastructure has already been built to bring in liquefied natural gas. Other suppliers have been found. This is perhaps Putin's biggest strategic gamble and his biggest failure. He thought that this energy blackmail would really push the West to the negotiating table and force them to give him concessions. That hasn't happened. And he's probably played his strongest card.

Apparently, all through the course of this year, sales of a Russian translation of the novel *1984*, have rocketed in Russia—Big Brother using perpetual conflict to create a tyrannical structure. North Korea is probably the classic example. The education system in Russia is being transformed from kindergarten upwards, entrenching the idea that Russia is a militaristic state, and that its survival is dependent on struggle. You see images of toddlers being shown how to strip down Kalashnikovs.

This isn't just propaganda. You only have to turn on Russian news, and you can see how militarised Russia is compared to Western countries. The transformation is going to be super decisive for generations. Is this going to lead to a Russia bent on revenge? A Russia that is militarised for generations? Or is this going to be a national trauma? The Russian men in the trenches are going to go home and they're going to have families, and that is going to change Russian society.

Russians will have to deal with this trauma. It's something that could fester, psychologically, socially and culturally. Eastern Europeans—people from the Nordic countries, Finland, the Baltics and any country (apart from Hungary) occupied by the Russians during the Soviet period—they instinctively understand what's going on. They are prepared to do everything not to fall under the influence of Russia again. That understanding doesn't seem to be quite as prevalent the further west you move.

The fact is that this war has united the West in a way that we haven't seen for a very long time. We're also gradually getting to the point where there is a realisation in the broader West that Russia must lose this war on the battlefield. The war has basically become about where the new Iron Curtain is going to be, and we need to help Ukraine be on the western side of that Iron Curtain.

13. THE REAL STORY OF NATO ENLARGEMENT

John Lough

John Lough began his career at NATO and was the first NATO representative to be based in Moscow (1995-98). He later gained experience of the Russian oil and gas industry at TNK-BP, Russia's third largest oil producer, in the company's international affairs team (2003-08). He is currently a fellow at Chatham House.[13]

I went to work at NATO headquarters in the autumn of 1993, and the member states had really decided about 18 months to two years before then that the value of the Alliance lay in the fact that it was an extraordinary mechanism for resolving differences between the allies and creating a foundation for security and stability in Europe. We'd seen the dramatic collapse of the Warsaw Pact and of the Soviet Union. It was vital for the purpose of managing the reunification of Germany to have this foundation of stability in Western Europe. The instinct of NATO allies was to broaden this community of like-minded countries, countries who saw the direct value in building relations of trust and partnership, cooperation, all of that, which, of course, became the great mantra after around 1994 when NATO launched its so-called 'Partnership for Peace' initiative.

This was quite clearly an effort to build something that would be inclusive and Europe-wide. There was absolutely no intention or desire or plan to exclude Russia from that process. On the contrary, NATO allies wanted to involve Russia. They saw an opportunity to engage Russia diplomatically. There were most definitely opportunities there. The difficulty on the Russian side was that NATO, of course, was perceived as a Cold War organisation. Many people in Moscow, in important positions, thought that NATO's preservation signalled that the West didn't trust Russia. And these figures were most definitely in the majority. But there was a minority of people, in the policy elite, that saw the value of working together with the West and trying to form some sort of partnership with NATO, and so these conversations rolled on.

Russian President Boris Yeltsin turned up in Warsaw and had a long dinner with the Polish president, Lech Walesa. Yeltsin was probably very well treated at dinner, maybe he had a bit too much to drink, and he said very generously that Russia had no objection to Poland joining NATO. This caused consternation on the Russian side. The Foreign Minister, Andrei Kozyrev, had to try to reel this in and say that the president has misspoken or something of that kind. I remember the reaction among some of my new colleagues at NATO headquarters as well. The reaction of some NATO officials was one of absolute horror that the alliance might expand. Some people were even whispering that perhaps the Russians had found a way to undermine the unity of NATO and that the organisation would not survive the process.

The proposed enlargement of NATO was not driven by the United States, as many people think. In the first instance, it was driven by the Germans and in particular the German defence minister at the time, Volker Rühe, who commissioned the first Rand study about NATO enlargement.

Rühe took a message to President Clinton at the time and persuaded him that this was something the US needed to look at seriously. The point that the German defence minister made was to ask how they could deny Poland and other countries in Central Europe the right to be part of an alliance in the same way that Germany itself was. Of course, the Germans had a vested interest here. They didn't want to be on the front line. In the end, the Russians knew they couldn't stop it. The kind of compromise that was found was the establishment of the NATO-Russia Permanent Joint Council mechanism, then to coordinate actions between NATO and Russia, which in fact, built cooperation in many areas.

At the same time, the Russians sought to limit the nature of NATO enlargement. No nuclear weapons, for example, on the territory of new member states, and no NATO forces permanently stationed there. It was put together in such a way that the Russians felt they could perhaps neutralise the worst elements—as they saw it—of NATO enlargement. It needs stating that the Russian contention that they were somehow deceived over NATO enlargement really doesn't stand scrutiny if you examine what happened closely. If, for example, we'd kept Poland out that would have been a source of instability for the wider region. The same applies to the Czech Republic and to Hungary. Once they came into NATO, investors viewed the region differently because it was seen to be a secure place into which to put your money.

There are still academics, particularly in the United States, who take the view that NATO and Western countries at the time misled Russia and that Russia has a justifiable grievance. I categorically believe it is not founded in fact.

The Russians have centuries of experience of operating in these regions and in shaping those environments to what they regard as their advantage. But there is a very profound contrast here with the way that, for example, West Germany, rebuilt relations with its neighbours, with countries that Germany had invaded, had terrorised and sectors of whose populations it had exterminated. Those relations were still quite difficult. Think about the reconciliation between France and Germany, the effort that went into that.

What I found striking was that at the end of the Cold War, even in the case of, for instance, Poland, the Russians didn't seemingly respect the fact that the Poles had real grievances and that the smart way to deal with them would have been to treat them nicely and to respect them. But instead of that, they very quickly got onto a confrontational track, which means, of course, that you then keep all these historical grievances alive. In the late 1980s, under Mikhail Gorbachev, there prevailed what was really a very liberal Soviet foreign policy, and some clear improvements were made in relations with neighbours. But those advantages were quickly lost.

At the end of the day, building relations of trust with your neighbours—rather than trying to corrupt them or subvert them or apply other tools of pressure—is a very cheap defence investment. When German unification was proceeding at a very rapid pace, Chancellor Kohl reportedly said to his defence minister, don't forget to brief the Luxembourgers. They're neighbours. They may be a very small country, but we still respect them, and we take their sensitivities into account.

Some progress was made under Gorbachev and Yeltsin. Yeltsin's apology to Finland for the behaviour of the Soviet Union was deeply appreciated in Helsinki. Similarly, in the case of the Katyn massacre in Poland, with the Russians recognising that this had been the work of the NKVD (today's FSB), and not the Germans. But many of those benefits have simply been lost. This has coincided, in the case of Ukraine and of some other countries on Russia's periphery, with their growing sense of national identity. Even though Russia may have recognised their independence, it did not regard them as countries that should or could be capable of standing on their own two feet.

It's an attitude that has been present throughout the post-Cold War period, because even those relatively liberal-minded people who were driving Russian foreign policy in the 1990s assumed Russia would continue to play the leading role throughout the territory of the former Soviet Union. Medvedev used a key set of words when he effectively said that Russia was entitled—in his words—to a zone of privileged interests in the region.

That's where we've had this major difference with Russia: over the ways in which security can be built. The Russian assumption is that, as a large country, it has a right to dominate those territories. In other words, the security of Russia comes before the security of its closest neighbours.

You must start with the fact that Ukraine, the Baltic states, Georgia and other countries in the region, even the Central Asians, are countries that have declared their sovereignty. They have a desire as sovereign states to maintain their independence. And they have a right to choose their alliances and to choose who their security partners are. The fact is that Finland, a country that has so carefully managed its relations with Russia, concluded that something had changed in Russian foreign and security policy and it was now a threat to Finland. Once the war started, the Finns flicked the switch and applied to join NATO. Many of us knew the switch was there and that if things got bad, the Finns would exercise that choice, even though they, of all countries, have put the greatest effort into maintaining a stable relationship with Russia, befriending the Russians, and doing business with them.

Putin reportedly very much likes Finland. Yet they feel the need to be under the NATO umbrella. It tells you something about Russia's behaviour and that even those countries that tried very hard have been unable to achieve a satisfactory accommodation with Russia. Despite all the effort they've put into building relations with Russia, they feel that Russia's really left them with no choice because it insists on undermining their security.

What does the future hold?
Putin has developed an extraordinary fixation with Ukraine. It's become this sort of delusional obsession, built on an historical narrative that doesn't have very much to do with reality. The fact is that, at the end of the Cold War, Russia was in a very strong position when it came to Ukraine, because of their cultural relations. I don't think Ukraine was going anywhere rapidly. If the Russians had chosen to be respectful towards Ukrainians, and accepted that, yes, they were going to become more Ukrainian as time went on, but they could find a modus vivendi with them. If they had done that, we would have never got into this war.

The war is creating long-term problems for the development of Russia as a country. The pressure of prosecuting this war in Ukraine is weakening the Russian state from within. And the Prigozhin mutiny, however one looks at it, is a clear example of the processes that have been unleashed. Putin personally, and his system as a whole, have been weakened by the war. As the war continues, I think we will see the cracks in the edifice of power in Russia widen with very unpredictable consequences.

There's not a huge amount of unity in Russia now, even though most opposition figures are now located outside the country. Broadly speaking, the opposition sees the need to remove Putin and his associates from power and to dismantle the system they have created because it is stealing resources from the Russian people. This small group of people has simply usurped the state and turned its resources into an instrument for their own personal advantage. The opposition is looking for some sort of revolutionary upheaval to oust Putin and his associates.

Less radical opposition members, some of those people who are part of the system now but are more moderate, recognise the blind alley into which Putin has led them, and would seek to take action to ensure that he can't continue, and then present themselves as the moderate face of the system.

These people are, in fact, prepared to stop the war in Ukraine. And then, I think, Western countries would find themselves in a difficult position, because we would probably want to talk to these people, and to bring this murderous war to a rapid conclusion. But would we be able to bring it to a conclusion? That's the question. Would this group not, in fact, just be trying to buy time to preserve the system.

The leading thinker about how Russia can be reformed is the former chief executive of the Yukos oil company, Mikhail Khodorkovsky, who Putin put in jail for ten years. Khodorkovsky has written a most remarkable book entitled *How to Slay a Dragon*. His view is that Russia has no future as a hyper-centralised state. The way it must reform itself lies in the regions of Russia, in a reconstruction of their relations with the centre, with Moscow. In his view, the country's future is doomed if they don't undertake those measures. Then ultimately the Russian Federation would face the risk of breakup, not imminently, perhaps, but inevitably. Khodorkovsky is somebody who's got a much longer-term vision.

The health of the regime is intimately tied to those industries and their wealth, because it's got a vast army of *siloviki* and security agents to pay. The moment you can no longer adequately maintain those huge internal resources, it'll have very unpredictable consequences. There are no shock absorbers in the Russian system, there's been no possibility for a successor to position themselves.

I think we're on the cusp of something very significant, and the Ukrainians understand this extremely well. We should not underestimate the fact that they are not just fighting on the battlefield in Ukraine. They are fighting in other spheres. They are conducting psychological warfare in a very, very clever way. Ukrainians are showing that they see Crimea as Russia's

Achilles heel. And if they can achieve some decisive impact there, they recognise it will destabilise the regime in Moscow.

If, after the war, Ukraine is to be rebuilt, it's going to require security guarantees, because investors simply will not put their money there. It's not going to be Western taxpayers who will be financing the reconstruction of Ukraine. The money is very largely going to come from private investors. There is no possibility of rebuilding Ukraine without placing it in an environment where investors believe that whatever money they put into the country will remain safe. That will be the time for NATO member states to take a bolder position and signal the path for Ukraine's entry into NATO.

Section 3
Putin

14. TUNNEL VISION
Fiona Hill

Fiona Hill was deputy assistant to president Donald Trump and senior director for European and Russian affairs on the National Security Council from 2017 to 2019. She is currently Chancellor of Durham University, and external expert on the UK government's Strategic Defence Review, and a senior fellow of the Brookings Institute.[14]

Putin's sense of his own manifest destiny, and its total melding with the destiny of Russia, is very troubling to observe. It's something that's evolved and hardened over time. He certainly had views when he came to power, as everybody does. There was a particular context in which he'd grown up in the post-World War Two Soviet period, which was in many respects the peak of Soviet power. Then he joined the KGB in the 1970s at a time when, based on all kinds of different indices, the Soviet Union was performing well. In fact, it was the height of the Cold War. All that shapes his viewpoint.

He's also been profoundly influenced, not just by the lessons that he's taken from Russian history, as it was taught in the Soviet educational system, but also by his own experience of the Soviet Union. It's very hard for Putin to think of Ukraine, or any of the other former Soviet republics, as not being part of Russia. The geographic map he has in his own mind certainly portrays Russia as including Ukraine and Belarus. They are held to be part of the Russian world, a Slavic, largely Russian-speaking world, and, as we've seen over the last several years, particularly since he returned to the presidency, his gaze has become more and more focused and fixated on Ukraine.

When I speak of the hardening of these views, I think that Covid had a lot to do with this. A lot of other people have spoken about this as well. Vladimir Putin spent a good period of Covid, as we all did, under a kind of house confinement. His house is a bit different from most of ours. I spent a lot of my time in a small office on the edge of my house, while Putin had offices in the Kremlin, and at various dachas out in Valdai and down on the Black Sea. But nonetheless, he was in many respects left to his own devices. The circle around him shrank, and he became much more focused on his view of the world and on his legacy.

Putin's been with us for more than two decades now, and the verticality of power in Russia has become clearer, and more vertical, with a very tight cohort of people around him, fully focused on the view that for him, in this phase, bringing these territories back into Russia's orbit is the imperative.

He's driven by a specific worldview. I'm not sure if everything really hangs together with enough coherence to make it an ideology, but it is a view very much rooted in historic Russian cultural patterns of very centralised governance, with one person at its heart. It's kind of a mish mash of things, a synthesis of all kinds of different viewpoints. There's a heavy emphasis on the old Russian Empire and on imperial culture, and on the Russian imperial heartland, with a smattering of Soviet viewpoints in there as well. But it's certainly a world view which has him at the centre.

Putin wants his story to prevail

Putin has become the history man, in the Orwellian sense that he who controls the past controls the present; that controlling the narrative of the past shapes the future. That's basically what Putin is trying to do right now. He's trying to use his interpretation of the past to define the present and dictate what the future is going to be for Ukraine—and in many respects, for the rest of Europe. He still thinks in terms of spheres of influence. Many of the reactions that we get to the war in Ukraine, the kind of blame that's apportioned to the West and to Europe, is for the West not accepting Russia's sphere of influence.

I think that is where we are to blame, because we fail to fully recognise that worldview and that perspective, where he and the people around him were coming from. So many of the Russians we in the West are familiar with weren't coming from that vantage point either. I mean, while some of them might have been somewhat interested in Russian history, they were living real lives in the real world. This is the catastrophe of it all for Russia, as well as for Ukraine and for the rest of us, in that Putin and the people around Putin have pulled us all back into a different reality. It's not just back to the 20th century, with another great power conflict, as Germany did twice over with World War One and World War Two. We're also getting pulled back to periods of the 19th century. Think about the Crimean War of the 1850s, or even further back to other eras of Russian history. Putin keeps dragging us back to earlier historical times, to demand Russia's primacy and dominance in a particular region. We didn't address this, and we didn't push back on it. We didn't try to counter it or try to draw Russia into a broader European perspective and give them a stake.

War of the Soviet succession

Of course, there were various efforts made, but they weren't very consistent. Ultimately, they didn't really factor in this kind of historical nostalgia. There's a substantial group of people in Russia who still think this way.

It goes back to the early 1990s. A whole host of early documents pertaining to exchanges between Boris Yeltsin and George H.W. Bush, the first Bush, have been declassified by the State Department. They're interesting. A lot of these exchanges go back to the days immediately after the collapse of the Soviet Union. Yeltsin assuring Bush that he wasn't an imperialist, saying that there were still a lot of tensions between Russia and Ukraine because of Ukrainian nationalists who really wanted to pull far away from Russia, just as there were Russian nationalists who wanted to pull Ukraine back into the Russian fold again. Then we have Yegor Gaidar, whom I knew very well, and many others saying that there would never be a Yugoslavia-type war between Russia and Ukraine. Well, 30 years on, there is this war, a war of the Soviet succession. It's taken 30 years to fully manifest itself, although one could argue it began 10 years ago with the annexation of Crimea.

The thing is, that Putin made this decision. When people say Russia was provoked. No, Putin provoked himself. When I was in the government and we would meet with senior Russian officials, they'd say, 'What is Ukraine to you?' and we'd be like, 'What do you mean? What is it to us?'

You can see this was our own misreading of the situation. We kept trying to say, look, we don't want Ukraine. We're not trying to carve the world up like that. But there was still a very strong perception in the group around Putin, and we could never properly explain to them how we were seeing things in a different light, because they kept thinking that we, like them, believed in imperial geopolitics and spheres of influence. They saw how the United States invaded Iraq, how the United States moved into Afghanistan, and how the United States would flex its muscles around the world. But in terms of Europe and Europeans, except for Turkey moving into Northern Cyprus, other European countries weren't going around annexing the territory of their neighbours. Europe had got out of the business of spheres of influence. But Putin believes to this day the United States is an occupying force in Europe.

So we are stuck in this clash of empires, and, to be honest, there are a lot of people around the world who share the view that the United States is still an occupying force in Europe, that Europe has no agency and that NATO is some kind of entity completely controlled by the United States that seeks to expand further and further. But we can see in real time, if people are looking properly, that the United States doesn't control everything in NATO. Turkey is blocking the entry of Sweden and Finland, and the United States can do very little about it. We're stuck in these old patterns of seeing things and it's very hard to shift perspective.

It's a real problem for those of us who studied Russian and who went to live in Russia to see Russia as an aggressor, an invader, when we feel we understand the close links which have existed between the two countries. It's as unthinkable as England invading Scotland. Which, of course, the English did. The English invaded Scotland, and Ireland and Wales. Britain is still an empire, just a mini one, a mini version of its old imperial self. And we've had the Troubles in Northern Ireland with British troops being sent over there. But it seems inconceivable to think of such things on the scale of this invasion of Ukraine. I think most Ukrainians were initially in a state of shock, and so were Russians as well.

Of course, Putin continues to see what he's seen all the way along, from the 1970s onwards, that the United States is the main opponent and that the United States continues to behave just as it did during the Cold War. For him, at some level, this is a clash with the United States, as well as being about Russia and Ukraine. As he's said all along, for him, this is the final showdown with the United States. If Russia was forced to pull out of Europe and the Eastern Bloc as the successor state to the Soviet Union in the 1990s, why did the US not pull out of Europe too?

Equally, there's a huge debate going on in the United States, just as there was at the beginning of World War Two. Remember, the United States didn't have to help Britain in the early 1940s. There was a lot of reluctance to step up and help the United Kingdom, both in the Second World War and in World War One. There are always those tendencies towards isolationism in the United States. And there's always an assumption that the only way to engage with the United States is militarily. We're all going to have to think about the future of the relationship between the United States and Europe, and the whole perspective of European security. But most Europeans, whether they're in the EU or NATO or are separate from those institutions, don't want to be back in a 20th-century style period of conflict over territory and the forcible changes of borders.

A problem of succession

But if we follow the logic that NATO was not a physical threat to Russia, that Russia genuinely would have known that NATO had neither the forces nor the inclination to take any Russian territory, then the crisis comes back to something far simpler—the fact that you've got an incredibly complex post-industrial power that has the political sophistication of a Viking fiefdom. They don't seem to have moved beyond that level. In fact, the Soviet Union was far more sophisticated politically than the vertical of power that Putin has created.

It really does come down to the fact Russia has, unfortunately, over the last 23 years, evolved into a system where only one man counts and we're now in a kind of succession crisis. Every single question is about what's in Vladimir Putin's head. What if he is sick? And who will succeed him? Russia has been, so to speak, hollowed out in many respects over the last 23 years. And some of that is down to our own failures in the West. There were other ways of us engaging with Russia that could have emphasised different pathways. In fact, if we go back to the 1990s, when Boris Yeltsin shelled the Russian White House, we could have dealt with that differently.

The accidental Tsar

The accession of Putin was an extraordinary moment. It was a moment of chance, almost as if it was an accident of Yeltsin's pen, conjuring into existence a kind of nobody. He's the accidental Tzar. So how do we square these contradictions, Zelenskyy saying he's a nobody, but now he's absolutely a somebody? He is the somebody who decides everything, including life or death, literally, and invading another country and creating this enormous tragedy. How do you square all of this?

Putin's living in a different time sequence to the rest of us. He has these larger strategic goals, of making Russia great again. He certainly has the idea of Russia being a modern version of the Empire having dominance in this region, and he still sees the United States as the main adversary, the main imperial opponent. But he was also opportunistic. He saw an opportunity to act, and he grabbed at it. But he completely misread Ukraine and the Ukrainians and Zelenskyy, and everybody else as well. He didn't realise how people would react. He assumed that Ukraine would immediately capitulate and that there would have been some kind of peace process, which would have put Ukraine back into Russia's orbit as a dependency.

That hasn't happened. I think what he was gunning for was a new Slavic Union, with Russia, Belarus and Ukraine, and possibly (northern) Kazakhstan. The Kazakhs worry about that. Then he'd have chosen presidents in each of these, with him the leader of that new Union. That's the kind of drive that we've seen in some circles in Russia since the early 1990s, to kind of bring everything back together again, and those are the people who stand behind Putin.

When Putin starts to be more assertive, beginning in 2007 onwards, Russia starts to have the wherewithal. He thought in 2022 that this was the moment, especially with Chancellor Merkel gone. The United States was involved in the shambolic withdrawal from Afghanistan. Britain is divided, having fights with France and the EU. As far as Putin was concerned, the time was the most propitious it was ever going to be.

I still do believe that diplomacy is crucial in constraining this. I mean, how can anybody be supportive of this mass carnage? But, as one Ukrainian said to me, sometimes a war must be fought, whether you like it or not. And many Finns have told Ukrainians, look, we had to fight in 1941. We didn't want the Winter War, but it's the only way to get their attention, which is a terrible thing to say, but that's basically where we are. Of course, the Finns lost. I mean, they lost all of Karelia and huge swathes of territory around Saint Petersburg, but they also won. They won their independence.

Ukraine's path out of the Soviet mess

To some extent, Ukraine has provided a template for moving out of the post-Soviet mire of corruption and nepotism. Of course, they've still got a lot of cleaning up to do. Ukraine had a terrible reputation for corruption. If you look back to World War Two in the United Kingdom, there were plenty of people engaged in the black market and profiteering and all sorts. Sadly, it's a fact of life that, during wartime, somebody is going to make money out of it. That's something we will have to address in the future in the reconstruction of Ukraine.

As for Ukraine finding a way out from the post-Soviet mess, that is where NATO, the European Union and everyone else comes in. Russia didn't want Ukraine to have any kind of alternative. When it talked about neutralisation of Ukraine, it meant a Ukraine that had nowhere to go other than still being utterly dependent on Russia. But a lot of Ukrainians, going right back to the early 1990s, had different ideas, and it wasn't just about language or ethnic identities—it was about Ukrainian independence.

As we know, there are many settings in Europe where language isn't the only bearer of identity, including in Scotland, for example, where most people speak English or Scots variants of English, but English, nonetheless. The same in the United States and Canada and Australia and New Zealand. All these identities are not driven by language, but by a sense of wanting something different, a different kind of civic or political configuration. And that's where Ukraine is.

We really are in an enormous catastrophe and tragedy at this juncture, but it won't be solved by simply writing off large swathes of Ukrainian territory and not addressing the other problems that have emerged in Russia. This is not Russia of 2023, of 1993, or 2003, or 2013. This is a Russia that has evolved into Putinism, into something much darker and grimmer in all respects worse than we could ever have envisaged before.

15. OPPORTUNISM
Mark Galeotti

Professor Mark Galeotti is one of the 29 Brits declared persona non grata by the Russian Federation on 14 June 2022. He is an Honorary Professor at UCL and a fellow at the RUSI, and has authored many books on Russia's state security, organised crime and history, most recently: Downfall: Prigozhin, Putin, and the New Fight for the Future of Russia with Anna Arutunyan (2024); Putin's Wars: From Chechnya to Ukraine (2022); A Short History of Russia: From the Pagans to Putin (2021); We Need to Talk About Putin: How the West gets him wrong (2019); The Vory: Russia's Super Mafia (2018).[15]

Former Soviet Leader Mikhail Gorbachev and Vladimir Putin
Gorbachev was an old man, and his death was not a particular surprise, though obviously, it was also a moment of great sadness for many. More interesting, though, was the way in which it really brought home the extent to which Putin is, in some ways, the anti-Gorbachev. Gorbachev was ultimately someone who believed in ideals, and he was willing to sacrifice his country in the name of his ideals. Putin can also be said to be willing to sacrifice his country in the name of his ideals—the difference is that his ideals are very much centred on himself.

Putin is a very old-fashioned kind of nationalist. And from Putin's point of view, one of Gorbachev's main flaws—and this is one of the many reasons why the men did not get on particularly well—is that Gorbachev ultimately would not use violence; he would not use force to preserve the state. And that was a crucial weakness as far as Putin is concerned, whereas we would regard it more as a sign of moral strength than anything else.

In terms of preserving the greater Russian world, perhaps there wasn't such a difference between Putin and Gorbachev. Gorbachev didn't want the Soviet Union to collapse. He didn't necessarily want all the countries like the Baltic states and Ukraine to secede, but I would say his Russian imperialism was of an unconscious kind, whereas Putin's is extremely self-conscious. The other thing is that we know Putin has absolutely no respect for the rule of law. In fact, he's eroded and destroyed the rule of law almost entirely in the 22 years he's been in power. Gorbachev, on the other hand, did have a strong, almost idealistic belief in law and truth.

Gorbachev wanted to preserve the Soviet Union, which he ultimately thought was worthy of being preserved, but only if it could be reformed. He was trying to hold something together, but he was ultimately willing to allow portions of it to secede if it was clear that they wanted to. It wasn't something that had to be held together at all costs. Whereas Putin is trying to reassert control over territories that are no longer parts of the Russian Federation and clearly do not want to be part of the Russian Federation, in defiance of international law, domestic law, and what we might think of as basic human law.

Gorbachev was a man who started out as a very conventional Soviet apparatchik. A member of the Party and so forth, who in due course would turn against the Communist Party in the name of a wider cause, ultimately driven by a belief that there was something bigger than himself. Whereas it's clear that, as far as Putin is concerned, nothing is bigger than himself.

Unlike Putin, Gorbachev was never in the KGB. He was a party functionary who simply rose through the ranks. It is quite extraordinary that someone like Gorbachev could rise within the system. But even early on, there were signs that he was unusual for a party hack. Of course, he was ambitious and knew how to get where he wanted. But Gorbachev and his wife were the only Soviet party officials who travelled in the West independently as tourists. They didn't go simply on an official delegation, but they wandered around Italy and so forth. They got to see what the West was really like. The fact they were interested in doing so was an early sign that this was someone who was a little bit more open minded than your standard stolid Soviet apparatchik.

Putin was rather different. It's not as if, before he went into the KGB, Putin was some wide-eyed, innocent or naive idealist. Quite the opposite. We know that even during his rather disreputable childhood, he ran with street gangs, he got involved in fights and it seems that he joined the KGB, not because he wanted to be the sword and shield of the Communist Party, but because it was basically the biggest gang in town. A lot of the people who joined the KGB did so precisely because they reckoned it was a good way to make money, gain power and work your way into what was almost a social elite, especially if you happened to have been born as an outsider. One could say that, working in the Leningrad and Saint Petersburg mayor's office in the 1990s, dealing with all kinds of disreputable businesspeople, gangsters and the like, what that did was simply hone those characteristics of Putin that were already there.

Putin's instinct is to escalate. For him, this is an existential struggle. It's not simply about Russia. It's about his own political future. We should also realize that Putin is a deeply unpleasant but nonetheless rational actor. Some people say, he's mad, he's a sociopath or whatever. For me, saying that is a cop out. It's no good claiming that we can't possibly try and predict what he's going to do because he's crazy. As we saw with his very first drive to try and seize Kyiv, this was clearly a serious operation. We had the flower of Russian special forces pretty much decimated, their major military convoys destroyed. The initial sudden onslaught on Kyiv didn't work. So, Putin realises this isn't going to be the pushover that he thought it would be. He pulls back, reformulates his strategy, and focuses instead on the Donbas and the southeast. This is a man who sees alternatives, and rationally works things out. But all the time, he will be thinking how can I push the situation to my advantage?

Putin doesn't really have much scope to escalate the war in conventional military terms. He doesn't have any scope to escalate it in terms of the economic war with the West. And although people sometimes talk about the risk that he might turn to tactical nuclear weapons, I see no signs the Russians are contemplating that. I think they realise that that would be a real game changer. That's the kind of thing that would stop the West from simply thinking of this as about helping Ukraine win and would start getting the West thinking seriously about regime change.

From his point of view, all Putin can do now is dig in. Again, this came out in his very bullish comments recently in Vladivostok, where he was saying, look, Western sanctions are entirely pointless and meaningless. They're doing no harm at all. They're making Russia stronger and so forth. Obviously, that is nonsense. Sanctions are having a serious impact, but they're long term; they're a slow burn weapon. Another factor influencing Putin now must be that the Ukrainian economy is essentially on life support and is being kept afloat by Western financial assistance. From Putin's point of view, he's hoping that a hard winter gets Europe in particular thinking, is this all worth it?

There is one topic which doesn't get an awful lot of attention and where you still get a great deal of sloppy phraseology in the media, and that is DNR and LNR, the so-called Luhansk and Donetsk people's republics. A lot of people still use language that somehow suggests the insurrections in those territories were organic, that they came from the local population and that maybe Russia was involved, but it wasn't a central player. It's important to realise that there's a key difference between what happened in these regions and what happened in Crimea.

As far as Crimea was concerned, Putin basically told his henchmen, it's time to take back Crimea, and a major, multifaceted operation that involved everything from special forces to subversion to military intelligence to criminality, was deployed for that purpose. Originally that was going to be the end of it. It was just about taking back the Crimean Peninsula. It was strategically vital to the Russians because it was where the Black Sea Fleet was based, but also an area that pretty much every Russian regards as rightfully Russian. Even people who were deeply opposed to Putin still thought that the move on Crimea was right.

However, in the first place, I think that the annexation of Crimea happened so easily that it almost created a sense of forward momentum. In the second place, the Russians used a lot of nationalists and volunteers in their Crimean operation, often simply to mask the presence of actual Russian forces. But then once they'd consolidated their grip on the peninsula, they had no real use for these people. A handful of the more efficient ones got hired into the police or the military, but basically it was, thanks very much, guys, now just go away. So, you had a bunch of disgruntled nationalists with guns and a certain number of them were looking over the frontier because in south-eastern Ukraine there was a genuine mood of dissatisfaction and concern about what was happening in the country.

Overall, these were not people who wanted independence from Ukraine, but they were concerned about suddenly feeling they were going to become second class citizens. And then, on top of that sense of anxiety, you added this mix of volunteer Russian nationalists who simply went over the border thinking that they were going to help their brothers, whether their brothers wanted it or not. Local opportunists, many of whom were indeed gangsters themselves, saw an opportunity to turn what we think of as street power into real political and economic power.

This is a classic Putin move—I'm not going to commit myself so that I can simply deny any role if need be. But on the other hand, something interesting may come of it. Not only that, but it was also seen as a way of putting pressure on Kyiv. Moscow was trying to force the Ukrainians not to tear themselves away from Russia's sphere of influence, but what happened is that the whole thing escalated. And after a certain point, the Russians thought, we don't want our supporters to be totally wiped out, so we better give them some weapons.

Then you had the terrible disaster of the Malaysian Airlines MH17, when a civilian airliner was shot down by a Russian-supplied surface-to-air missile fired by separatists. Then it's almost like Russia got sucked into it and thought, like it or not, we're involved in this, so let's get committed. In the summer of 2014, they started sending in serious numbers of regular troops to support the separatists who otherwise were going to be annihilated by the authorities.

In those early days, no one had a grand plan. It was just a bunch of different opportunists from the Kremlin down to the back streets of Donetsk, who were each just seeing what they could make out of it. In due course, because Putin didn't have the guts to pull out and say, no, this isn't going in the direction I want, he let himself get sucked into it. The rest is history. It's a war that was generated by a whole mix of different actors, including gangsters. Criminality was baked into these structures. It was also a way of keeping them funded. To a degree, turning a blind eye to organised crime, or even on occasions facilitating it, as a way of keeping the DNR's and LNR's economies going.

If we go back to 2014 or 2015, there was not a clear majority in these regions for either joining Russia or declaring full independence. That's precisely one of the reasons why they never held any such referendum. They held 'elections', but they never gave people that kind of straightforward choice. For those on the ground, you just did not dare raise any questions because the local authorities were essentially vicious, collections of thugs more than anything else. People did disappear into the infamous basement of the administration building in Donetsk. In those circumstances, most people just got the hell out. There was quite a marked demographic shift, with particularly younger, fitter people getting out, leaving a much older, more pensioner-age population who didn't feel they could just up sticks, and leave. We should have a lot of sympathy for the people of Donetsk and Luhansk regions, because fundamentally they are the victims of this process.

There were concerns about the rights of Russian speakers in Donbas, but it's all very well when this is a useful political posture, and quite different when Russia is saying 'Russia will assert its power in the region.' If they had been faced with a real choice, to be a citizen of the Russian Federation or a citizen of a dynamic, democratic, liberal European Union, then they knew exactly which side they wanted. There are a lot of people working for the government of the LNR and DNR, not because of any ideological belief, but because people need to eat and people need to look after their families.

Russians have been faced with this barrage of toxic propaganda. Frankly, Russians themselves have been living within propaganda states for more than a century. They are aware of the need to maintain two sets of thoughts—the official set of thoughts and what you believe. If we look at how quickly the Soviet era fell apart, we shouldn't assume that this is something they are genuinely inculcated in.

I always find it interesting that Putin tends to have these sky-high approval ratings from the 60s up into the 80s. It's the sort of approval ratings any Western politician would perfectly happily sell their own grandmother to have. Yet his trust ratings are usually down in the 30 somethings. On one level that implies there's a large portion of Russians who approve of Putin but don't trust him.

This sounds a bit strange, but what it reflects is that the approval rating is because Putin has become an icon of Russia and there is no alternative. His approval ratings are in the 30% because that also tracks very closely to United Russia, which is the main pro-Putin political bloc. It says something that the elections have to be so heavily rigged, that the last vestiges of independent media have been squeezed out, that you can't just simply log on and see the BBC or hear Radio Free Europe or Radio Liberty without using a VPN to bypass the state's information controls. If you are genuinely popular, you don't have to do any of that stuff. Russia is not in any way a genuine democracy.

The Kremlin is the most assiduous user of opinion polling within the Russian Federation. They knew that this would not be a popular war. Russians did not care about the Donbas. Now, of course, there is a large proportion of Russians who, when asked, are willing to say, yes, I support the special military operation. Some of them genuinely do. Some of them do because they're basing it on what they see on the television, where they're told it's a very limited surgical operation to stop a neo-Nazi regime from committing pogroms. As for others, they just know what's the safe answer to give when someone with a clipboard asks you this highly fraught political question.

A lot of the propaganda is based on NATO being an 'aggressive' rather than defensive alliance. Putin and his elite knew objectively that NATO was not going to invade, that it had a minimal force in Europe, that it did not represent a huge threat. But it's very convenient, to be able to use a so-called threat like that for internal repression, coercion and control. But there's also a sense that Russia has been disrespected. There is this belief, you can argue whether it's accurate or not, but it's a belief amongst Putin and his circle, that promises were made to Russia that NATO would not expand. And then NATO did. It's not just simply about whether this represents a threat. It's more about how the world is willing to 'challenge' Russia, to 'demean Russia'. If one looks at Putin's speeches, this is very much how he frames it. There's a strong message of victimhood here. It also represents the kind of corrosive sense of insecurity and dissatisfaction which is at the heart of Putin's message.

At the end of his second term as president, 2008, when Putin to some extent handed over power to his prime minister Medvedev to satisfy constitutional term limits, it's clear that he was toying with the idea of leaving power. History would have been relatively kind to him. He's an unpleasant man who did unpleasant things, particularly in Chechnya, but on the other hand, someone who brought Russia back from the brink of anarchy.

Ultimately, though, he could not let go. He fell afoul of the classic dictator's hubris of thinking himself irreplaceable. In some ways it's part of this merging of his identity with Russia itself. I think Putin genuinely feels that his career, his future, his legacy are on the line. Everything is dependent on the arithmetic of the battlefield and on the West maintaining will and unity sufficiently to keep supporting Ukraine. Any peace deal would mean some degree of sanctions relief because the Russians will demand it. But we're not going to go back to business as usual. There's not going to be some reset. Realistically, we are in a cold war with Russia so long as Putin is in the Kremlin.

It is highly unlikely his successor will be a liberal. If one looks at the younger political generation, men in their late 50s, early 60s—they are basically ruthless, pragmatic kleptocrats. They don't seem to be informed by the same kind of bitterness of the true *Homo Sovieticus* generation like Putin, the people who were at the centre of events when the Soviet Union collapsed. And they feel they need to claw back some of that position. These are people who want to be able to steal at home, bank the proceeds and spend the profits abroad. These are people who will have a very sound pragmatic interest in improving relations with the West, because that's where the money is. That's where the opportunities are. They are not going to be democrats at home. They will essentially scapegoat Putin, when he dies or is incapacitated.

In essence, Putin's made the same mistake as Tsar Nicholas II, where he's visibly taken charge and therefore will be associated with all the failings and catastrophes. If we're going to play the historical parallel, rather than 1917, this feels more like 1904, when Russia got caught in the Russo-Japanese War. They thought it was just going to be a nice, victorious little war, which clearly Putin thought about Ukraine, and where not just failure, but humiliating, embarrassing failure and the huge costs thereof created this nationwide spate of local risings that was called the 1905 revolution. But it wasn't really a coherent revolution. There was still enough unity within the apparatus, and particularly there was Prime Minister Pyotr Stolypin to bring in a combination of tough repression and genuine reforms. One big difference between Putin and Tsar Nicholas II is Putin is not going to allow a new Stolypin to have as much power as Stolypin did, and Putin doesn't have it in him to be a new Stolypin himself.

The Russian Federation is getting more brittle all the time. So long as there's no real shock it can survive for quite a long time. But when there is a shock, I'm not quite so sure how much resilience it'll have. Up until 2012 there was a certain level of consensus with liberal economists, maybe not liberal politically, but liberal economists. But then the security forces, the *siloviki*, the strongmen, began to be overrepresented in government and they're very unlikely to go back prior to what happened in 2012. A handful of the *siloviki* are genuinely ideological, but a lot of them are simply in the security apparatus because there are massive opportunities for embezzlement and corruption. So, there's unlikely to be a revolution, even an incoherent one. Rather we can look forward to a palace coup. One strong man out, another one in.

16. THE GODFATHER
Luke Harding

Luke Harding was based in Moscow as the Guardian's correspondent from 2007 until February 2011, the year he published Mafia State, when he was refused re-entry to Russia and deported. His name was also included on the June 2022 list of banned people. He is the author of Invasion (2022), Shadow State (2020), Collusion (2017), A Very Expensive Poison (2016), The Snowden Files (2014), Expelled (2012).[16]

There was a time when those calling Russia a mafia state, and Putin a terrorist, were in the minority. They were even thought of as extreme voices. I've been following Russia for a long time now. I concluded from my four years there (2007-2011), before I was thrown out, that this was not just a regime that was domestically oppressive. We've seen plenty of evidence of protesters being beaten up and put into vans in the centre of Moscow and in other cities. We've seen the opposition, the movement of Alexei Navalny being rolled up, Navalny himself poisoned and then jailed. We've seen a return to Soviet methods of control and intimidation. That much was clear.

I always strongly believed that Russia was also internationally dangerous. There was plenty of evidence of that, including the war in Georgia, when in August of 2008, Russian tanks were rolling towards Tbilisi, the Georgian capital. It was an attempt to stop Georgia from joining NATO and integrating with the European Union and the West. And as such it was a brutal lesson in neighbourhood realpolitik from Vladimir Putin.

I was in Ukraine in 2014 when Putin annexed Crimea and artificially created military conflict in the east of the country. In the autumn of 2021, Putin sent tanks and armoured vehicles to Ukraine's borders, to Belarus, over the bridge he had constructed into occupied Crimea. I did not read this as a bluff. With Putin, if you have a bad option and a worse option, he will always pick the worse option. There was scepticism in Kyiv, including from the government of Vladimir Zelenskyy, which didn't believe it, or didn't want to believe it. Meanwhile, we had grim intelligence assessments and warnings from Washington and from London saying, this is for real. It was clear that this was a turning point in history. The biggest European war for 80 years.

Through the conflict, we have started to look back and reinterpret the past. What happened in Georgia is a Ukraine conflict in miniature, with staged provocations. Russia already occupied part of Georgian territory and behind the scenes they engineered that crisis, managing to make it look like Georgia was to blame.

Medvedev was Russia's president and Putin was prime minister. It was Medvedev who articulated this doctrine or pseudo-doctrine, that Russia had privileged interests in the former Soviet backyard, that they could call the shots. Putin's been very clear that he regards the collapse of the Soviet Union as a geopolitical catastrophe. He never really accepted the idea that these states were independent, that they had a sovereign identity and could make their own foreign policy and political choices, whether that was joining NATO or not. Putin and Medvedev felt that Moscow should still control these as satellites.

When there was someone like president Viktor Yanukovych in power in Ukraine, that was okay, because he would not do anything antithetical to Moscow's interests. The reason this whole crisis started eight years ago was because Yanukovych tore up an association agreement with the European Union, which would have put Ukraine on a pro-Western course. He accepted a financial bailout from Russia, in other words, a large bribe.

There were street protests in freezing weather with people spending weeks protesting in the Maidan, the main central square of Kyiv, in subzero temperatures. For a long time, these demonstrations were peaceful. Then Yanukovych, acting under pressure from Russia, decided to get nasty. People started being beaten up, taken away, disappearing, turning up dead. This culminated with his security forces opening fire and shooting dead about 100 unarmed protesters in the centre of Kyiv, and him fleeing to Russia. An episode which Putin characterises as an American coup. Of course, it was nothing of the kind. Ultimately it was about the future of Ukraine and what you might characterise as an anti-colonial movement; that anti-colonial movement is still going on now. That is why Ukraine is fighting.

What you might call late-stage Putinism reveals how he has become increasingly lost in a sort of historical fantasy. Putin dreams about Peter the Great, Ivan the Terrible, Stalin. It's a mash-up of Imperial, Soviet and Tsarist history. He published this extraordinary essay arguing that Ukrainians and Russians were one people, and that Ukraine was never a thing. Putin decided that he is the person who is going to make Russia great again. There's a kind of religious component to Putin's vision, with a drive to restore Russian Orthodoxy in Ukraine.

Putin expected to be able to seize Kyiv in a matter of days and install some kind of pro-Russian puppet administration. He completely underestimated the Ukrainians. He thought they were just kind of rural Russians, led by a corrupt, pro-Western elite. He's ended up fighting a country of 40 million plus people.

There are several things going on. One is a serial failure by Western countries to understand how the KGB-trained Russian government thinks. They believe that they're involved in a war with the West. Yes, they're fighting in Ukraine, but essentially the enemy is America and NATO and its allies. That's not the case, but that's how they perceive it. Up until February the 24th, Putin would do egregious things, whether it's murdering dissidents like Alexander Litvinenko, invading Georgia, annexing Crimea, trying to poison Sergei Skripal, and the Western reaction was always feeble and conventional.

The Ukraine project is breathtaking and genocidal. This is Zelenskyy's contention and it's hard to disagree when you see what's been happening. In Putin's head, there's an idea that you can make Ukrainians into good Russians, and, if you can't, you kill them.

Belarus provides an interesting template. The Belarus language over the last 30 years has seen a significant decline. You can now only find it in provincial villages. It tends to be the older generation who speak it. The erosion of the Belarus language is one of the reasons why Russian propaganda has proved to be quite effective in helping to suppress the Belarus independence movement.

What's interesting now is just how many Ukrainians are dumping Russian, and switching to Ukrainian. Everybody is bilingual in Ukraine. And despite what Russian propaganda says, it's perfectly okay to speak Russian in Kyiv and elsewhere, in cities like Kharkiv and Kherson and Kryvyi Rih, President Zelenskyy's hometown. Zelenskyy is a native Russian speaker. They're rejecting the idea that if you speak Russian, you should be under Russian control, you should be a Russian citizen.

In the 90s Russia was in a parlous state. Nonetheless, Russia did not bear the taint of the Soviet Union's crimes. What Putin seems to have done by turning the clock back, and through this war, is to put a stain on Russian culture, Russian history, the Russian language. He has forced a reinterpretation, not just of recent history, but also of longer-term history. Pushkin's work has been utterly instrumentalised in all this, and Tolstoy's, and so on.

In the meantime, Russian soldiers have been destroying Ukrainian monuments, and, are, bizarrely, putting up statues of Lenin again—Putin blames Lenin for creating Ukraine, yet there he is being celebrated. The unifying idea here is of Russia as a great power, with great power privileges. That is what's happening in Ukraine; a classic attempt to crush a rebellious former colony and to reabsorb it. Ukraine is necessary for Russia to be an empire.

Russia in 2000 was a semi-democracy. Boris Yeltsin could be criticised and mocked on Russian TV. What we've seen under Putin is the state growing darker. When I was there, I would describe it as authoritarian. Now I would say it's totalitarian. It's close to being a full-blown dictatorship, where any form of dissent is a crime, where opponents of the regime are locked up on spurious charges and given extraordinarily long jail sentences, where critics are routinely murdered, where businessmen mysteriously fall out of windows. It's a place of arbitrary power. A lot of young Russians who don't fancy fighting and dying in the war have voted with their feet and have fled to the Baltics, to Armenia, to Georgia. Russia has become a gloomy and chilling place, where propaganda gets louder.

There are two projects in contemporary Russia. One is the ultra-nationalistic project which led to this terrible war. The other predates the invasion: a mafia fiefdom and deep corruption.

Through corruption, Putin and his circle have accumulated billions of dollars, just because power is money. Putin arguably is the richest man in the world. Maybe he's not formally the richest, as this money is not formally his—it's held by a series of proxies and by oligarchs, some of whom have been recently sanctioned, some of whom haven't. Putin can instrumentalise this wealth. He can use it for personal pleasure, whether it's a yacht or that ludicrous, overblown palace he had built in Sochi, or he can use it for political projects, for subversion, for sabotage, for throwing elections, for funding far-right parties in Europe and elsewhere, and, of course, for backing the hard left.

If you want to understand Putin, forget about reading scholarly research, just pick up a copy of Mario Puzo's *The Godfather*. What he's managed to build up is the façade of a democratic, pluralistic system. But if you have a public voice, if you're a politician, if you were to go off script in any way, you couldn't have a public role. You're looking at an entire Potemkin village, an entire façade of a hybrid democratic system. Behind the scenes, almost everybody in public life has made their peace with the regime or in some way been bought. No-one has the capacity to act independently. Those pluralistic elements are entirely fake. It is a species of post-modern authoritarian system, and the great tragedy is that most Russians support the war.

Ukraine must win the war, and the West must continue to supply Ukraine with weapons, so that it can liberate more of its territory. We must acknowledge the kind of Russia we're dealing with now, which is aggressive, violent, revisionist, and that if it's not stopped in Ukraine, will keep going.

Putin is now 70 years old. I wouldn't predict that his regime is about to fall. I don't know what the ending will be, whether it ends with a bang or a whimper, I'm not sure. But I think the curtain is coming down. Unfortunately, it's unlikely that a kind of Democratic leader will take over anytime soon. When Putin goes, there will probably be a pause of some kind or tactical realignment in the war against Ukraine. Putin's always been a gambler. He's always sought to escalate rather than step back. With this invasion, he's overreached.

17. PETRO-TYRANNY
Alexander Etkind

Professor Alexander Etkind was born in 1955 in Leningrad (now St Petersburg), Russia, and studied at the University of Leningrad. He was a fellow of King's College, Cambridge, and is currently a professor at the Central European University, Vienna. He recently published Russia Against Modernity (2023), Rethinking the Gulag (2022) and Nature's Evil: A Cultural History of Natural Resources (2021).[17]

It's important to draw a distinction between the first half of Putin's regime, where there seems to have been a concerted effort to try and catch up with at least some aspects of consumerism, and the latter part of his regime—post the 2012 Bolotnaya protests when intellectuals, IT workers and relatively enlightened Muscovites took to the streets to protest against political manipulation. The protests were suppressed, and something changed.

Having a former KGB officer at the top of the government was something that made me uneasy from 2001 onwards. I emigrated from Russia, from Saint Petersburg in 2004. As time went by, I increasingly felt like a political émigré. There was a first stirring in 2014 with the invasion of Crimea; a sense that there had been a lurch towards a dangerous political environment. Most people simply made their peace with what was happening. They kept their heads down and carried on working. They withdrew from politics, or maybe not that many were involved in politics in the first place.

In retrospect, you can see that there was a schizophrenic political division, splitting the population into two parts. One part was to be kept wealthy and ignorant about the occupation of the Crimea, or the current war in Ukraine, or the war in Syria. All these geopolitical, hugely expensive (of course), political and military experiments—that the regime had been carrying out for decades—were abroad, on the periphery of the fragile post-imperial Russian Federation.

Centres like Moscow, Saint Petersburg, and several other major cities were kept in the dark. There was a concerted effort to keep their salaries high and growing, and to introduce all kinds of new financial products such as mortgages. People could buy apartments and cars and so on. Money was earned, not by the labour of all these people, but by natural resources that were traded—mostly to Europe.

So, you've got the middle class, the proto-middle class, that is being kept isolated from real issues and plied with money. But you also have the *siloviki* class, the huge layer of secret state organisations, whether it be the *Rosgvardiya*, which is a sort of paramilitary police force, or the secret service layer, both incredibly expensive to maintain.

What happens when the profit margin on Russia's natural resources dwindle? When Russia's equipment, which is largely supplied by the West, starts breaking down, becoming less efficient? The costs of extraction are going up, and so are the costs of transportation. The costs are huge. Oil goes around the world in tankers, through the Suez Canal or around Africa, but the transportation costs have increased by 20% to 30%. The Kremlin talks about exporting Russian oil and gas and metals to the East, rather than to the West. It will take vast expenditure, redirecting this trade, and building new pipelines across Siberia to China. They will never do it. It's impossible, not only technically, but also financially. A substantial amount of gas will cease to be traded at all. It makes trading in fossil fuel, once fabulously profitable for Russia, increasingly precarious.

The war Putin is conducting seems to have no real economic benefit. People have talked about access to the Black Sea and grain, but when you compare it to the revenues being earned from gas and oil, there's very little economic merit. Places like Crimea and Donbas don't make strategic sense. They have no economic significance either.

Ukraine is potentially a prosperous country, but its wealth depends on the labour of people rather than on natural resources. Its massive metallurgical plants and mines have been destroyed. Given the climate crisis, coal mining and metallurgical plants will never be rebuilt at the same scale.

Ukraine's environment has been hugely polluted by the war. There are mines in the fields, bullets, shells, bombs. There's a great danger that they may explode, and after they explode, they leave lead and other toxic substances in the soil. Contaminated land will have to be cleaned, and water filtered. That will take decades for the Ukrainians to do. The land, waterways, all sorts of natural systems that previously would have been generating wealth are now poisoned. Russian propaganda makes a great play about Ukraine's supposed use of depleted uranium, but compared to lead poisoning that is perhaps something of a sideshow.

I have always been struck by the contrast between Finland and Russia. Finland—and to a certain extent the Baltic states—didn't have much in the way of natural resources. They have had to be relatively inventive to make the most of a harsh environment and what meagre resources they have. Russia suffers from a kind of post-imperial syndrome and can loosely be termed a Petro-tyranny. These two things together create a particularly dangerous combination. It is also a rare combination, because most petrostates such as Saudi Arabia, Norway, Brazil or Nigeria are post-colonial rather than post-imperial. That provides an entirely different historical, social and psychological structure.

If you compare Ukraine and Russia, in Ukraine, you have value placed on the individual, on individual life, on the intellect and abilities of an individual. Russia's rulers have a total contempt for the value of the individual, to human life not only in wartime, but also in times of peace.

This indifference has economic foundations, because the prosperity of the state didn't come from the people, from their labour, their creativity and knowledge, or their ability to combine economically to do things in innovative ways. This enormous prosperity came from natural resources, from holes in the dirt somewhere in the marshes of Western Siberia. It's a question of political geography.

The other element in all this, which is especially pernicious, is that the bulk of those natural resources, whether heavy metals or hydrocarbons, does not come from areas which are ethnically Russian. The parasitism of the Moscow elite requires imperial brainwashing because these resources are not ethnically Russian.

You need only look at the budget of the Russian Federation. There are two districts, located in West Siberia—one is called Khanty-Mansi, the other is called Yamalo-Nenets. These two counties, even though they appear vast on the geographical map, are underpopulated. Their oil is responsible for about half of the Russian budget. The peoples who once lived in those areas have been made extinct; many had to change their names and alter their ethnicity. They became Russian in the Soviet period, or even later, in the post-Soviet decades. They have been removed from any ownership. It's all managed and drilled, transported and budgeted by Moscow. There are many oilmen who come from western Russia working there.

Of course, this population is employed—they provide services, they teach in the universities, they are doctors in the hospitals, barbers in the barber shops. They all are earning their money. But the coffers of the state are filled not by the taxes of these people, professors or barbers, but by fees from the exported oil and gas.

That export wealth doesn't trickle back down to those local communities. A parasitic structure, Moscow, siphons off most of that wealth, as well as most of the trickle-down wealth from services. A chunk of that wealth gets siphoned off by the elite. We don't know the exact figures, but Putin takes a cut of it all. What you have is Industrial activity trickles down mainly to the benefit of Moscow. And there is yet another level of parasitism—capital flight. Over the decades of Putin's rule, it is estimated that more than $1 trillion have been exported legally or illegally from Russia to Western countries, mostly to Europe, to places like Switzerland, Italy, Germany. Some of this wealth went to America. Some of this wealth also went east to Hong Kong or China. It does trickle down but seeps away through Russia's borders.

Assassinated opposition leader Boris Nemtsov predicted that Putin was taking the country in the direction of becoming a vassal of China, an asset to be stripped. It would have nothing to offer the world except raw natural resources, no value after the extraction of those resources.

This prediction has largely been made good, given these plans for redirecting the fossil fuel trade to China and India. China has a great deal of freedom in planning and organising its energy supply. There is LNG, coal, and nuclear power. There is a huge growth in renewable production of energy in China. China will trade with Russia but is in no way dependent on this trade. Russia, however, is dependent on it.

The Soviet Union organised a huge military presence on the Chinese border and in the Pacific. It is a very long border indeed. Old tanks have now been transported from this border to Ukraine. This transfer of military power was going on from the very start of the war in Ukraine in 2022. They were bringing military equipment, armour and soldiers from the Far East, from along the Chinese border, to Ukraine. That military presence had been there for a reason, deterring China and keeping a military balance between Russia and China on the eastern border. That deterrent is gone.

It's up to the Chinese government to decide whether to retake big territories of northern China appropriated by the Russian Empire in the middle 19th century during the Opium Wars with the British Empire, the most predatory war ever waged against China. The settlement (the Treaty of Peking) was mediated by Russian diplomats. Nikolai Ignatieff, who was the Russian Minister of Foreign Affairs, mediated the whole arrangement and, because China was weakened after these two Opium Wars, the Russian Empire received huge chunks of Manchuria—the delta of Amur and the Pacific coast, where Vladivostok and Khabarovsk are now major Russian cities and naval harbours.

Whether the Chinese would like to exact historical revenge and reappropriation of the lost lands is an open question. China is watching Russia exhaust itself against Ukraine. The mystique of Russian power, the mystique behind Russian military equipment, has completely exploded. It's been shown to be merely a sort of Potemkin façade of strength. These huge, unexpected turns have been all triggered by Putin's invasion of Ukraine.

These tanks were dug in along the whole Russian Chinese border, together with parts of the Russia-Mongolia border. They were dug into the dirt. They had supplies of shells created over the decades of Soviet power. They probably would have worked where they were. Would they work against modern Chinese weapons? We don't know. But being dug out, partially restored and then unloaded in Ukraine—there they are proving to be entirely ineffective. This is what we are seeing.

There is an extraordinary shallowness in the critiques by some Western experts about the war. One of those positions that we hear repeatedly in Western media is the anticipation of some kind of revolution in Russia. There is also an expectation that some kind of Western liberalism will emerge from Russian oppositionists. Then they're horrified when these oppositionists don't say the things we expect them to say.

It's hard for the Russian opposition to take a decolonisation point of view. It would go against decades of brainwashing, against decades of cultural values and mindsets. Any opposition who puts forward a view the Russian Empire needs to be dismantled is not going to get much popular backing if there ever were to be free and fair elections in Russia. Current leaders of the opposition, those who are in Russia, are all in jail. Some of them are fantastically brave and gifted and heroic people. They still believe in democratic elections.

However, a free, united, democratic Russia, I think, will not be there after the war. Either Russia will collapse, or it will be partitioned, or it will break into its constituent parts. Some of those parts could indeed be democratic, but probably not all of them. A great reconfiguration of the fundamental values of this country is coming. But the current opposition is behind the curve. They don't see it, nor do Western pundits. There is no way back.

Most Western analysts missed the big events of recent Russian history. They failed to predict the dramatic collapse of the Soviet Union. They failed to predict the democratisation of Eastern Europe. They failed to predict the re-emergence of the *siloviki* and the merger of the security state with the Mafia state.

Even that is not particularly well understood. Until recently, Putin was still seen as a statesman in many quarters, rather than as being a KGB thug. Western pundits and the Russian opposition underestimate how difficult it will be to root out the parasitic class that's taken hold of Russia over many decades and which really emerged very strongly during the Soviet period.

These pundits also failed to predict Putin's war in Ukraine. There were very few voices writing in 2021 that took the American and British intelligence warnings seriously. What is more, even if the intelligence was quite accurate, they got something else horrifically wrong, and that was underestimating the ability of Ukraine to self-organise and to resist the Russian invasion. Throughout this war, the Ukrainians have been extraordinarily innovative. They've been able to take the best of Western weaponry and techniques and convert them to fight a much larger and theoretically better supplied enemy.

There are two sides to this coin. One side is underestimating Ukrainian power, the other side is overestimating Russian power. This second part played a big role because analysts knew very little about Ukraine. Ukraine did have major problems with corruption, which had been unremittingly emphasised. But of course, Russian problems with corruption and the inefficiency of the state were much worse. Alexei Navalny managed to make a breakthrough in our global understanding of the Russian state, how it works, and why it does not work. But the pundits and the experts didn't take it seriously. Everyone watched but did not see.

Putin, however, did take Maidan and the Ukrainian revolution seriously. He grossly misunderstood them and misinterpreted the Maidan protests, but he did recognise them as powerful. In the West we saw them as a local phenomenon, not as the struggle of an emerging democracy against the forces of authoritarianism. Putin understood very well how dynamic and powerful and destructive the forces unleashed in Ukraine could be. He felt extremely threatened by what was happening, though not by the idea of Maidan happening in Russia. The Russian Federation had lots of interests in Ukraine, economic interests, pipelines that go through Ukraine pumping Russian gas.

When the money runs out, when there is not enough money to keep Chechnya, Tuva, Komi and the *siloviki* class living in the standard to which they've become accustomed, when that money starts to get thin on the ground, what's going to happen? What does Russian history tell us about an elite that can no longer pay its bodyguards? The *siloviki* are cynical. They work for money, for good money. We know their salaries. We know the corruption levels. We know where this money comes from.

Putin's regime is built on a host of mythologies, a fetishist attitude to the Second World War and Russia's revolution. There's a focus on authoritarian, statist attitudes. But the local elites of the regions and republics and districts have some rudimentary power—although seriously eroded by Putin throughout the decades. The best scenario is that they will take power, claim independence and start trading amongst themselves, and with the West and the East and the South. Tatarstan has a huge historical tradition. So does neighbouring Bashkortostan, which is similar but different. There are traditions in the Urals. Then there is Siberia. There is even Saint Petersburg. Imagine Saint Petersburg as an independent city state—it would be entirely, economically viable with all its creative industries and universities. There are so many potential futures, and they all hinge on whether Ukraine is victorious. If Ukraine can eject the Russian military from the entirety of its territory, including Crimea, that's going to set off change within Russia.or of *Russian Nationalism and the Russian Ukrainian War* (2022), published prior to the 2022 Russian invasion of Ukraine.[18]

Is this Putin's war or is this a war of the Russian people against Ukraine? To me, it's both. The major difference between the 2014 crisis, when Russia occupied Crimea and launched the hybrid war against eastern Ukraine, and the invasion of 2022, is that in 2014 Ukrainians differentiated between Russian leaders and the Russian people. They very quickly became antagonistic to all Russian leaders—the State Duma, the government, and of course, Putin. We're talking about a stable 80% negative, but there wasn't really any negativity towards the Russian people as such. They kind of separated the two. That's no longer the case with this invasion, and that's a very radical departure.

What Putin has achieved is a final and irrevocable divorce between Ukrainians and Russians. Opinion polls show that this won't go away. What he has done is made the views of western Ukrainians, the views that were very typical amongst the Ukrainian community living in Britain that I grew up in, views that echoed those in the Baltic states, i.e. anti-Russian leaders, those views have now become dominant in eastern Ukraine. It's hardly surprising. After the destruction of Mariupol, after the war crimes, it's Russian speakers who have borne the brunt of this aggression, not West Ukrainians. Which is ironic, because Putin is supposed to be protecting Russian speakers. He allegedly intervened or invaded Ukraine to stop a genocide of Russian speakers. In fact, it's his forces that are doing the genocide.

There's been a lot of writing in the Western press about the 700,000 who have fled Russia, but more people stayed than fled. Occasionally they protest, when they're mobilised, because they don't have any good uniforms, or they don't have anywhere to sleep. Their equipment is lousy, their officers are lousy, their food is stolen, but they still go and fight, and they're still dying. In huge numbers. They're willing to die. They're willing to be cannon fodder.

If you ask them, why didn't you protest inside Russia, the answer is always the same, we can't. Russia's a dictatorship. But now you're living in Georgia and Armenia, democratic countries. Why are you not protesting there? There's something much deeper going on. I think it's partly a consequence of 20 years of the re-Sovietisation of Russian society under Putin. Putin has rebuilt the Soviet Union that he pines for and which he grew up in, and that is the Brezhnev-era Soviet Union, of the 60s and 70s.

That's Putin's era when, as a young man in the mid-70s, he joined the KGB. At a time when most people were becoming less committed to communism, he, coming from a poor background, was fully committed. He's rebuilt Russia to reflect that. Russian people don't feel they have any ability to change anything. That's a marked difference to the feeling in Ukraine, which has had three revolutions since 1993—people's revolutions. Ukrainians do have agency, they are citizens. Hence this very large volunteer movement and large civil society, and where you have a very different army to the Russian army, an army which has flexibility and autonomy.

In Kyiv on the 1st of December 2013, there were a million people on the streets. If you had a million people on the streets in Moscow, Putin and the Kremlin would be dead, they'd be finished. But that's never happened. Belarusians came out in huge numbers in 2020 when the elections were falsified. But, unfortunately, it's very difficult to have any kind of a people's revolution under an authoritarian system. In Ukraine during the three revolutions, there was a semi-authoritarian system, and there was still a lot of freedom. But the Russians have not come out in huge numbers, even compared to the Belarusians, never mind the Ukrainians. This has impacted the way Ukrainians think of Russia and Russians. If Russians had adopted a clear moral stance, if more Russians had come out in protest, I don't think Ukrainians would have turned against them as they have.

There's a debate now in academia whether Ukrainian studies need to be moved from Russian and Eurasian study centres to the schools of East European studies, because there's nothing in common between the two countries. Simply nothing. What we have is a bottom-up de-russification in Ukraine.

In academia, Ukraine, Belarus and Russia were some sort of single entity, and Ukraine an appendage to Russia. Now academics must completely rethink themselves. They're finding it extremely difficult to do so, because they can't explain where all this bitterness and the war crimes and this military aggression is coming from—because they've had their heads in the sand for so long. The reality is that Russia as a great influence on Ukraine is finished.

Russians in general take the view that, if you're a Russian expert, you're somehow an expert on the entire former USSR. That is as ridiculous as saying that, because I'm an expert on Japan, I am also an expert on India or the Philippines. If I'm an expert on Brazil, why would I be an expert on Chile? But no, if you're an expert on Russia, you can make a commentary, you can do blogs, podcasts, write articles, whatever, about the entire former USSR. They get everything wrong, including Ukraine.

If you've fallen in love with Russian culture, you're always going to give it a pass. You're always going to accept excuses. There's the problem that a lot of ambassadors and journalists in Moscow have become Russophiles. They aren't necessarily actively conscious of it, but it's inevitable that they're going to be filtering the Ukrainian war through Russian eyes. All these Western experts got the invasion wrong. They had the same view as the leadership in Moscow, that Ukraine would fail, that Ukraine would be occupied within three days, that Kyiv would fall very quickly, that Zelenskyy would run away, and the Russian army was just the second-best army in the world.

This also shows how much more powerful Russia's informational arsenal was than its military one. They were winning the information war. They were changing people's mindset and how Russia was viewed as a great power. The Baltic republics and elsewhere have always been slapped down as Russophobes.

One of the ironies of this war is that the centre of NATO has shifted from France and Germany towards the east. The Germans were convinced that through trade, energy relations, and economics that they would be able to influence Russia. They've admitted they were wrong. You need to look at Russia realistically, which is something that a lot of the people who say that they are experts on Russia are unable or unwilling to do.

We in the West have been sending signals to Russia, which led Russia to believe that, in 2022, when it invaded Ukraine, it would again just get a slap on the wrist. When we talk about 2022 in the future, we'll be talking about Russia making two major mistakes. It underestimated Ukrainians, because it thought there is no Ukraine, there are no Ukrainians. These little Russians are simply going to welcome the Russian army as liberators. It got that wrong, and they also got the Western reaction wrong. The reason why it got the Western reaction wrong is because the West had been sending weak signals for 20 years prior to the invasion.

The thing to remember is that Russia's main export was never gas or oil. It was corruption. Russia strategically used corruption as a way of influencing Western elites. Russian leaders are very cynical. This cynicism began to grow in the latter days of the Soviet Union. They believe anybody can be bought, it's just a question of negotiating the price. Oligarchs who were living in the West were not independent actors. What Putin did as soon as he came into power in 2000, was to tell the oligarchs that you are now working for me. You can keep everything you've stolen. And if you don't like working for me, then you either must run abroad like Boris Berezovsky (who moved to London), or you can go to jail like Khodorkovsky.

We ignored that until the invasion. Oligarchs were welcomed in London and elsewhere, and their money was not seen as dirty. We kept pointing the finger at corruption in places like Ukraine, Russia, Kazakhstan, elsewhere. It's not surprising that Transparency International said, a couple of years ago, that London is the biggest money laundering centre in the world. Corruption has two sides - where the money is stolen and where the money is banked. Why was it that countries like Ukraine, Russia, Kazakhstan got low rankings in terms of their very high levels of corruption and then countries that took their dirty money got good rankings?

The way to understand Vladimir Putin is to see that he's a composite of three influences.

First there is his KGB past. It is true when they say there's no such thing as a former agent of any secret service. Second, he's a Russian Imperialist, because, in the Soviet Union, Russia and the USSR were one and the same thing. Russia had its own republic. It was one of the 15 republics of the Soviet Union. But the Russian Soviet Republic did not have any institutions in Moscow. The only institutions in Moscow were Soviet. The other 14 republics, like Ukraine in the Soviet Union, had their own Communist party, their own Communist Youth League, their own Academy of Sciences, their own government. Russia did not, because the Russian and Soviet identities were one and the same. When we talk about Russian Imperialism, this is also Soviet Imperialism. Putin never got over the disintegration of the USSR. So that's the second factor.

The third factor is that he is a mafioso. He's a kleptocrat. Russia began to be called a mafia state as long ago as 2010. Now there's a difference between a mafia state and corruption. When you have a mafia state, there's no difference between organised crime and the state. It's one and the same thing. Not only did Putin co-opt the oligarchs, but he also co-opted organised crime. Organised crime is allowed to do exactly what it wants. But occasionally the FSB will knock on their door and say, we have a little task for you, whether it be hacking or some such shady task.

So, he's three things: KGB, post-Russian Soviet Imperialist and kleptocratic mafioso. If you put all those three together, you have a very dangerous person who's living in the past, who's angry, who's nostalgic, who hasn't accepted the collapse of the Soviet Union and who believes he's fighting the West in Ukraine. He's not fighting just Ukraine. He wants to go down in history as the person who defeated the West and gathered all the so-called 'Russian lands', by which he means Ukraine, Russia, and Belarus.

In no way should it be the responsibility of the Ukrainians to reform Russia. When you see this infrastructure of the *siloviki*, this extraordinary blend of KGB and the Mafia, how on earth do you rip this toxic weed out of the body politic of Russia? The liberal opposition, although they are extremely effective communicators and manipulators of the media, do not have any kind of activist edge, or even the ruthlessness that would be required to rip out this toxic weed from Russian society. I simply do not see how pro-Western liberal political forces, which barely exist anyway, could ever come to power in Russia, at least in the foreseeable future.

In late 1991, Yeltsin co-opted the Soviet institutions in Moscow, so Russian state building, from 1992 onwards, was top down, not bottom up. In the other 14 republics, including Ukraine, the state building was bottom up. They didn't have any of the institutions that you need for an independent state. Those institutions had to be built in the 1990s. Institutions such as foreign ministries, ministries of defence, intelligence services, Russia just took over all the Soviet ones in Moscow. And you don't just take over buildings and people. You take over mentalities. It's not that surprising, therefore, that these former security forces came to power. They were angry about the loss of their status, the loss of Russian power. They felt the West wasn't treating them with respect, so they conspired to regain power. It wasn't just Putin in 2000.

The first sign of this regaining of power was Yevgeny Primakov in 1996. He replaced Kozyrev, the pro-Western foreign minister. Primakov was former KGB and had headed one of the two successors of the KGB. One of the first things he said is that Russia is not part of the common European home, it's nothing to do with Europe. Russia is the centre of Eurasia, a civilisation which is superior to the West and in competition with the West. That's a very different emphasis.

It all began in 1996. In the same year, there were elections in Russia where

Yeltsin himself moved towards a Pan-Slavic position because he supported a new union of Russia and Belarus. Yeltsin and Lukashenko, a very odd combination. When they had the apartment bombings in 1999 and 300 Russians were killed, nobody amongst the Russian experts in the West wanted to believe the FSB and Putin were behind it.

The problem is, if you build a mafia state, you're not going to have a great army. Putin has created a mafia state in which he's allowed officers to steal in return for loyalty. You can steal what you want, but we'll keep a file on you. And if you step out of line and don't show loyalty, the file comes out and you're charged with corruption. The Russian army is a disaster zone in terms of logistics, in terms of stolen equipment, in terms of inability to field soldiers properly. These are all things that are interconnected, but it doesn't seem to have sunk in amongst experts in the West, or amongst Russian leaders. The Russian army now is far weaker than the Soviet army was at the collapse of the Soviet Union or the Soviet army that entered Afghanistan. Far from reforming the military, it seems to have been degraded under Putin.

It's back to the Kursk (nuclear submarine disaster) mentality in Putin and not just him, potentially in his successors as well. It's a completely different mindset; it's a win-lose mindset. There's no concept of win-win. There's no concept here that our submarine goes down, we collaborate with the West, and our guys get saved. There's no concept here of partnership. It must be a win-lose. Therefore, whatever comes next, there won't be, and cannot be a normalisation of relations with Russia because they're playing an entirely different game from us.

This was the problem behind the negotiations from 2014, under the so-called Minsk peace agreements. Zelenskyy was ideologically a centrist, and Poroshenko was more centre-right. Zelenskyy was very interested in some kind of compromise deal when he was elected in 2019. But the very term compromise is a dirty word for people like Putin from that Russian Imperialist KGB background. Ukraine must capitulate. You must show your obedience. You're below me. No Ukrainian leader is ever going to do that. If you do that, as Lukashenko did, then you're just a puppet.

There are a couple of things which must be grasped properly. Firstly, the war will continue for as long as Putin is Russian president. There will not be an end to war and conflict and destruction until Putin is gone. He's going to continue. He's obsessed. He believes that any sign of defeat or weakness will work against him. And then, who succeeds him? It'll be another strongman.

Like other historical psychopaths, he probably loathes his own people. He probably has no respect for them at all. He comes from that kind of background, which combines all those factors, mafioso cynicism, corruption, Russian imperialist disdain for the people, looking down on them, seeing them basically as meat, as the Russians say, not cannon fodder, but meat. Those attitudes have a long, long history. If you're in a system like Putin's, which has supported a cult of Stalin for the last twenty years, what do you expect? Because you're promoting a cult of Stalin to back up your religious cult of the Great Patriotic War. Stalin was a great guy because he won the war. He built a nuclear superpower. The West feared it. And he built the new empire.

But at the same time as you're doing that, you must marginalise, deny and downplay Stalin's crimes. You have no respect for human life. Stalin didn't just kill Ukrainians. He killed Russians as well. When Ukraine wins the war, the Russians are going to wake up to a massive nightmare when they're eventually told what is being done in their name.

The analogy I use is, can you imagine Germany, three decades after World War two, and a former Gestapo officer comes to power as the new Chancellor and launches a cult of Adolf Hitler. It's the same. A former KGB officer becomes Russian president and launches a cult of Stalin.

We don't want to see the comparison, the similarity. But that's basically what it is. We do have a bias in the West against Nazism and not really to the same degree against communism, which was seen as a great idea, but mistakenly implemented. Nazism and Communism in Europe of the 20th century were two equal evils. It's about time we listened to the views of the countries that suffered from both. And if you are the leader of a country and you are trying to rehabilitate one of those evils, then you are a dangerous person, because foreign policy is always an outgrowth of your domestic policy.

18. A HUNDRED-YEAR-OLD ZOMBIE
Yuri Felshtinsky

Yuri Felshtinsky is a former Hoover Institution Fellow and co-author of Blowing Up Russia with Alexander Litvinenko, the former FSB colonel who was poisoned with radioactive polonium 210 in London in 2006. He recently published From Red Terror to Terrorist State: Russia's Secret Intelligence Services and Their Fight for World Domination from Felix Dzerzhinsky to Vladimir Putin (2023) and Blowing up Ukraine (2022).[19]

The FSB's meteoric rise to power

In 1994, prior to the election of President Yeltsin in 1996, the First Chechen War was started. It was started as a provocation by the FSB. No one really understood why the Chechens were fighting, no one really understood what was happening. It only became clear later that they needed the war in order to cancel or postpone the elections of 1996, just in case Yeltsin, who was at that point the Kremlin candidate for power, might lose. There were small terrorist attacks—a bus exploded, somebody tried to blow up a railway bridge—local police investigated the crimes and arrested all those involved in these terrorist attacks. And all of these terrorists were from the special services. All of them. They were sentenced for something like 2 or 3 years. Minimum sentences for something else, not for the terrorist acts, but for illegal possession of weapons, or for forging documents, or some such.

In September 1999, a major terrorist act took place. 300 plus people were killed. This was the first major terrorist attack. It was claimed by the Russian government that this attack was carried out by Chechens, as a retaliation for the events that had led to the First Chechen War, and almost immediately the government once again declared war and started offensives against the Chechen Republic. And once again the war was started in case Putin, who by that time was preparing to become president himself, might lose the election or would appear to lose the election. Surprisingly enough, Putin went through with the election and won. It was 51% to 49%.

In 1999, Putin became acting prime minister, and then acting president on 31st of December 1999. Putin was director of the FSB. Yeltsin had three candidates to choose from. One was Putin, who was director of the FSB. The second one was Sergei Stepashin, who was a former director of the FSB. And the third one was Yevgeny Primakov, who was former director of the SVR (Foreign Intelligence Service), which is the main directorate of the KGB for foreign intelligence. Yeltsin agreed to name a former FSB officer as the president of Russia. That's not really a great democracy. Russia never was a democracy. Prior to 1917 it was a monarchy. Between 1917 and 1991, it was communist dictatorship. Once a person is acting president, the government officials or governors all know that this is the person who is in charge. And you better not confront him. You better not oppose him. It was a very easy, pre-programmed victory for Putin. It was, of course, a manipulation of the system. Many people thought that he came to power on behalf of the oligarchs. And there was some truth in that; all the oligarchs were behind Putin, except Gusinsky, who was against Putin because he was hoping to help another group of people come to power.

Oligarchs lined up behind FSB candidate, Putin

Berezovsky actively helped Putin. We had this major conversation with him, in which we tried to explain that the oligarchs should not make a lieutenant-colonel of the FSB the president. There were many other people in Russia—it's after all a huge country—and they should look for somebody else. I told Berezovsky, 'Look, Boris, if Putin becomes president, he will put you in prison. You will end your life in prison'. He said I was crazy. 'He's my friend,' he said. 'My friend is becoming president of Russia. And all you've got to say to me is that he will put me in prison?' 'Boris, that's precisely what I'm trying to explain to you. Find another candidate.' But they did not. And we know where Berezovsky ended up.

Primakov, Stepashin and Putin had major support in addition to Yeltsin. They had this major structure behind them, and this structure was the FSB, the state security apparatus, the former KGB. That's why I never see Putin as a dictator. Belarus's president, Lukashenko, is a classical dictator. If you take him out tomorrow, then Belarus would become a normal country the day after tomorrow.

That's not the case with Russia. I do not believe, even now, that if you somehow got rid of Putin, you would get rid of all problems we have in Russia. Russia's problem is much bigger, and that problem is the state security apparatus. The state security apparatus has been after power, believe it or not, since December of 1917 when it was first formed. The relationship between the Party and the state security apparatus has a very bloody history. The party needed the state security apparatus to fight against all the enemies of the Soviet government. But at the same time, the security apparatus was fighting for power, because they wanted to have absolute power in the state without any political control.

The Red Terror—a civil war between organs of the state

Being a security officer was one of the most dangerous jobs in the Soviet Union. Dozens of thousands of high-ranking state security officers were executed by the Communist Party. The last executions only ended in 1956. There was a settlement that they would not kill each other anymore. There were times when state security would grab the reins. Then they would start killing party officials. But the goal was always the same. To reach a level of absolute control of the state in the Soviet Union. The first time they came close to this was when Andropov, a former KGB chairman, became first General Secretary of the Communist Party and then Chairman of the Supreme Soviet of the Soviet Union. But Andropov only ruled for a year and a half. He died, the KGB lost the initiative, and the Communist Party, of course, took back control.

It came to an end with Gorbachev and his reforms. The KGB hated him very much. They wanted to get rid of him in August of 1991. They tried. They failed. It backfired. The Soviet Union collapsed, but it collapsed, not because of Gorbachev's reforms but because, in August of 1991, hardliner Chairman of the KGB Vladimir Kryuchkov was trying to return Russia to the old Soviet Union. At that time Russia was reforming; it had free elections for the first time, absolute freedom of press, a market economy, and had started to develop open borders which had never been open before. This all happened under Gorbachev. When the coup d'état happened, the Soviet Union was probably the most free it had ever been in the whole history of Russia. The coup d'état failed and Yeltsin came to power. The problem was that there was one institution which was not touched by the August 1991 revolution. It was the only institution which survived the collapse of the Soviet Union. There were no other Soviet institutions which survived this collapse. That institution was the KGB. There were several attempts to take power. One was when a communist parliament, heavily infiltrated by KGB personnel, tried to overthrow Yeltsin and force him to resign.

Putin became Acting President, and then, in early 2000, President. This is, in historical terms, a very, very short period. In less than ten years, the FSB finally reached its objective. They installed their person as President of Russia and very quickly took control of the entire country.

Putin in control—everything is FSB

Putin immediately started to promote FSB officers to major government and political positions. It's worth remembering that, in addition to all those KGB/FSB officers who were serving the country as state security officers, there was also the group of 'active reserve officers.' Under this system, a person who started by working for the FSB (or previously the KGB) never leaves their department but is sent to work undercover in some other part of Russian society.

Under this programme undercover KGB officers were initially sent to parts of Warsaw Pact and USSR and then subsequently into Russia itself. When Putin was working in Dresden, for example, he was not there as a KGB officer. He was there as Director of the Soviet-German Society, but, of course, he was really there as a KGB officer. The KGB were doing the exact same thing inside Russia. They were angling for the best positions, the highest positions possible in the newspapers, in publishing houses, in banks, and in all the major oil and gas companies for their active reserve officers.

Two photos which are widely known demonstrate that the famous August revolution of 1991 had no chance of winning. On the very first day of the revolution, when Yeltsin was standing on a tank giving his first major speech, even then KGB general Aleksandr Kerzhakov was standing by his side. Not only that, but the person next to him was KGB body guard Viktor Zolotov (who in 2016 became Chief of the *Rosgvardiya*, the national guard that reports directly to the president). On the same day, in Saint Petersburg, its mayor Sobchak was giving a similar revolutionary speech, and there was the St Petersburg KGB chief Vladimir Putin standing behind him.

The revolution had only just begun, but all those KGB people were already in place at the highest level as 'democrats'. The Chief of the *Rosgvardiya* under Yegor Gaidar, the first Russian Democratic Prime Minister, was Andrei Lugovoi. He, of course, became later better known as the person who killed Alexander Litvinenko. Behind every conceivable movement you would find that it had already been infiltrated by a high-ranking KGB officer. Whichever revolution won, the result was always black.

The only structure to survive more than a century

Democracy never had a chance in Russia from 1991. For that the KGB would have had to have been disbanded and dispersed. And that was never done. It's an acutely serious problem. The problem is that it would not be enough to get rid of Putin. The FSB is over a hundred years old now and more solid and unassailable than ever. Every other Russian institution, including the USSR and Communist Party, has either collapsed or withered into insignificance over the same period. The result is that for the first time in human history, we have a state controlled by the intelligence services.

In the Soviet Union, the State Security apparatus was under the political control of the Communist Party, but the State Security apparatus wanted to get rid of that political control, because they had this long-held, fervent belief that the only reason the Soviet Union was not winning the war against the United States and against the West was because the security services were hamstrung by the political control of this stupid Communist Party. As soon as they could get rid of political control, then they'd know how to win. And that's why we see what we see now. We see the first attempt of the State Security of the Russian Federation to finally be released from any political control, so that at last finally they can begin to achieve their programme. And that programme is very simple. They plan to rule the world through force, starting with Europe.

Putin doesn't believe in democracy. This was no surprise to us. We kind of understood this. But our hope was that he would be a practical, rational man. We thought and hoped that he's also corrupt, that he is interested in money. If a person is interested in money, it's easy to deal with him. You will always be able to buy him. I talked about this with Berezovsky as well. He said to me, 'Why? Why should I be afraid of Putin? I will buy him. I have money, we have money'. He was referring to the oligarchs. And I told him, 'Boris, they will take your money. They do not want you to give them money. They will take your money.'

Putin unleashed—the FSB goes global

In 2007, in Munich, Putin gave that speech about nostalgia for the Soviet Union. He declared how this was a major personal tragedy for him and a major geopolitical catastrophe for Russia and for the Russian people. And then he invaded Georgia. After the invasion of Georgia, nothing happened. People had a problem finding Georgia on the map or understanding the nature of the conflict. There were no sanctions. No repercussions. This was the moment when Putin knew that he was allowed to do whatever he wanted. But then, of course, 2014 started rather unexpectedly for him because he did not expect Yanukovych to lose power. This was all Putin's fault. He had forced Yanukovych to go back on his word, to renege on the pledge he had given to his country. There is a reason why Ukrainians wanted to be part of the European Union. They wanted the ability to work in Europe. They wanted the European Union to help them to rebuild the economy, and to finance the economy in Ukraine.

Putin forced him to take back his word in exchange for a $15 billion loan to Ukraine. And that's when the revolution started. It was provoked by Putin. He lost the ability to install a pro-Russian government, because prior to this it had always been 50/50. But when Yanukovych lost power, that was the moment when it became clear that Ukrainians would never choose a pro-Russian candidate again. That was the moment when Putin decided that it was time to start dealing with Ukraine. The idea was very simple. He would invade Crimea and seize it quickly. That was straightforward, because the Black Sea Fleet had a major base in Sevastopol, so Russian troops were already there.

Not fighting for Crimea in 2014 was a mistake
The Ukrainians made a mistake, they should have fought for Crimea. They did not. And so then, of course, Putin thought that, well, if that was so easy, shouldn't I try to take more? And he started the invasion of Donbas. This was done through a so-called referendum. There wasn't an organic, ground-up separatist movement. The Russians engineered a 'resistance' movement. We'd already seen the same thing in Georgia.

Even now, Western analysts are not really able to understand what is happening, who started the fight, who was killing whom. Soviet special forces and Russian special forces were superb at organising partisan movements and revolts in places like Africa. It's even easier to organise them in Ukraine, where you speak the native language and you look similar to the local population. The GRU has specially trained military units whose profession is to organise disturbances in places like Africa or Latin America. It was very easy to do the same in Ukraine.

Girkin called for general mobilisation from day one. He was one of the people who organised this 'revolt' or bogus separatist movement.

Belarus—the invasion by stealth
He quietly took Belarus in 2021. This is very interesting, because no one actually noticed. So the troops were now concentrated along the Ukrainian border, not just on Russian territory, but also from Belarus. Why is that important? Because if you want to attack Kyiv, you need to start from Belarus. There is no way you could do it from Russia. It's just far too far. The idea was that they will take Ukraine very quickly.

Yanukovych had already moved to Minsk. He was waiting for the 'invitation' to come proclaim himself the lawful President again. Then the idea was to use the Ukrainian army and the Belarusian army, combine it with the Russian army, and advance into Eastern Europe, probably starting with the Baltic states. This plan failed when the Russians could not take Kyiv.

Back in the day, Stalin put former prisoners of war returning from German concentration camps into prison. He considered them traitors and put them into labour camps in Russia. There was no law which allowed the government to do this. Stalin did it because he was a dictator. Putin has now introduced a law where you are considered to be a traitor if you are taken prisoner. This is something new. Stalin released prisoners from labour camps to send them to the front during the German invasion of Russia. But these were mainly political prisoners. Now Putin is releasing real criminals to be sent to fight in Ukraine. This is so ugly. This is so unlawful. No one pretends there is the rule of law anymore.

19. MOSCOW RULES
Keir Giles

Keir Giles is a Senior Consulting Fellow at the UK's Royal Institute of International Affairs (Chatham House) and works with the Conflict Studies Research Centre (CSRC), a group of deep subject matter experts on Eurasian security formerly attached to the British Ministry of Defence. His books on Russia include Moscow Rules (2019) and Who Will Defend Europe? (2025).[20]

The central argument of my book *Moscow Rules* was that we need to recognise what Russia wants is completely incompatible with what we think is normal or natural or even acceptable. And if that's not resolved, then sooner or later we will be in a deeper crisis and in an open conflict involving Russia and the West.

Here we are, because those differences were not resolved. Russia felt it was strong enough to push for what it wanted, by invading Ukraine. The key question is why exactly Russia thinks it is both entitled to do this and has a duty to do this. In fact, it is operating in an entirely different environment mentally to what we take for granted as normal and natural in the West. It is simply because Russia hasn't gone through the kind of national or societal transformations that other countries have. If you think of Russia's behaviour now, and what they write about other countries and how they acted in the past, it's perfectly normal for other countries, if you go back several centuries.

The Russian threat is not just something that's external to Europe. It's also external to the time we're in. It's not something that comes from the 21st century. Both the attitudes that Russia is acting on, the idea that Russia is entitled to a land empire, and all these small, independent countries around its periphery don't really have any right to exist. They should be governed from Moscow. But also, when Russia does roll its tanks across the borders, the way Russia behaves and the way its individual soldiers behave, it is something from a far older and far more brutal age.

We've had Russian missile strikes, completely random terror strikes on civilians, on cities across Ukraine for no better purpose than sowing terror and death and destruction. And that is not the behaviour of a state that we recognise as a part of the international community. But there's a problem with the so-called geopolitical interpretations of events, in terms of game theory and through a Cold War lens. What they're doing is equating Russia's rationality and methodologies with our own. Those geopolitical arguments really aren't capturing the depth or nature of the problem.

There are several different aspects to that problem. The issue of trying to ascribe Russian behaviours to some theory of international relations is damaging for our understanding of what it is that Russia thinks about the world and how it might react to the world around it. The problem is that if you have people whose entire careers have been built around putting forward a theory of how countries work, they are so invested by the time they reach the end of their careers that they must ignore facts, and reality, to pretend that that still works. Mearsheimer is the classic example. He has now become so detached from what is happening in the real world in his explanations of current events. It is irrelevant, but harmful, because people are still publishing him, and referencing him.

A failure of realism

In general, trying to categorise Russia's behaviour according to some framework of how countries behave as a template, as a pattern tends not to work. Because countries like Russia don't subscribe to the same ideas that drive so much of the theory in Western countries. This is not to say that Russia is completely exceptional, and no rules apply to it. There are some very fundamental, basic, atavistic, visceral behaviours that drive Russian actions. But to try and pretend that they will be rational in the way other countries would be, is to completely misunderstand what Russia is, and to completely ignore what it does, but crucially also what it says about its own behaviour. Comparing it to templates of Western liberal democracies, countries that follow the rules based on international order, is just not realistic or helpful.

If an academic has built their entire career and credibility around presenting facts in the world in a certain way, they have a vested interest in those models, and it's extremely hard for them to go back on that or admit they were wrong. It would destroy their career and undermine the whole point of their existence. But these narratives have a ready audience, especially in countries that think they are protected by distance from the Russian threat. They count the costs of rearmament and deterrence, without understanding the risks of not investing those costs. The countries that would prefer Ukraine to sign a ceasefire agreement with Russia as rapidly as possible, possibly don't realise, or don't care, that by rewarding Russia with control of Ukrainian territories, makes further Russian armed aggression more likely, and confirms for Moscow that that is the best way to behave, to get what it wants.

One of the things that we've benefited from during this crisis, is that Putin and those around him have been entirely more honest about what it is they want from the world, and how they intend to go about getting it. That has completely torpedoed all the arguments that we heard over decades that Russia is just responding to NATO enlargement, NATO accepting membership applications from those countries that wanted protection from Russia. That pretence has been completely discarded by Moscow. It is now engaged in open aggression. It has an open hankering for a return to empire; to bring more countries under Russia's control and they are prepared to resort to brutality to achieve it.

We can go back before the full-scale war was declared, and an accelerating clampdown on the media, civil society was in full swing in 2021. Then Putin published the pseudo academic paper, 'On the Historical Unity of Russians and Ukrainians', which sought to lay the ground for the absorption of Ukraine into a reconstituted Russian imperial project. That's when we saw that Russia had changed gear. Russia was suddenly abandoning all the things that it previously thought were important, like its relationships with the West and pushing for what it wanted, regardless of the damage.

As part of that, we had Putin laying out his vision for where he wanted things to go. And yes, people laughed at it, saying it was nothing like what a Western historian would have written, ignoring the fact that he was presenting a policy manifesto and preparing to follow through on it.

Russia isn't thinking in terms of election cycles. It's not thinking in terms of short-term benefit or needing to justify policies to its people. Many commentators and policy experts fail to understand how the imperial process works and worked since Muscovy came to the fore several hundred years ago. Once it conquers a territory and it's able to subjugate that population, then it will use that population to attack the next chunk of land, and so on. By awarding it Donbas, you get the weaponisation of its population. They're forced into the meat grinder to fight against their fellow Ukrainians.

If you are sitting in the Kremlin, you don't count the costs in terms of numbers of young Russians who have died or the amount of material your ground forces have expended in throwing themselves against the Ukrainian defences. The benefits will be counted in terms of whether this was a success or not. The process that we've seen in the east of Ukraine is the same as we saw, for example, in one of Moscow's previous campaigns of expansion when it was rolling forward across Eastern Europe, after the Second World

War, conscripting the populations of territories that it took over and sending them forward to fight for Russia, as part of the Warsaw Pact.

If we take this process of weaponising a country's population against its neighbours, Chechnya is a classic example. It was implacably opposed to being taken over by Moscow. Many of its cities were razed to the ground and their populations decimated and tortured. Then a warlord was placed to rule over them and terrorise them. Now we see brigades of Chechen fighters being used as part of their shock troops. This is a classic example of that imperial process at work.

The longer time span is crucial, not just because Putin plans further ahead, but if there is a pause in the conflict, it will represent a resolution to it. It will just be a temporary breathing space for Russia to gather strength again for the next effort to subjugate Ukraine. People who have looked at Russia for any length of time understand this. Too many people in the West got used to the idea of Russia as they saw it during the 1990s and early 2000s as weak, incapable, but also, they thought well-disposed towards the West and interested in international relations.

They took that as the norm, as something that would persist from then on. But if you're looking at it from Moscow, that was abnormal. That was the temporary interruption to the normal situation. Now Russia is moving back at an accelerating pace towards its historical comfort zone.

That means repression at home, and it means hostility abroad. Politicians and the media in 2022 couldn't figure out if this was a Putin problem or if it was a Russia problem. That conversation mercifully has moved on. Putin is not inventing all the ideas he comes up with. Instead, he's enacting them. And they are very deeply rooted within Russian society. It's also become much clearer to people that there is no alternative to Putin, primarily because he's made very sure that there's no alternative. If you're looking for a liberal Democratic opposition to replace Putin, as so many people were hoping for, there simply is none to be found.

Which means that if Putin disappears tomorrow, one of his coterie will take over; they are all like-minded, but also the depth of support Putin gets from the Russian populace, for what he is doing, means there's no impetus for change. And there will not be any seeds of change unless and until the comprehensive defeat of Russian forces in Ukraine.

There are fundamental misunderstandings of how this system works. Putin is an inheritor of it and will pass the mantle on to somebody else. This dictatorship is not imposed on the Russian people against their will. It's largely with the acquiescence, and in many cases the sort of tacit support, of the direction of travel. What Russians dislike is losing. What they disliked about Gorbachev was the fact he lost the Empire, not that he brought peace. What they dislike or may turn out to dislike about Putin, is not the war in Crimea and Ukraine, but the fact he is losing that war in an embarrassing fashion.

There was a belief that if people within Russia could be made to understand what was being done in their name in Ukraine, that they would turn against it. But instead, they approve of it, and they urge the Russian forces on to commit more and better genocide, even now. You had people leaving Russia because of the war in two waves. The first, after February 2022, were people who did recognise what Russia had become and wanted nothing to do with it. They emigrated because they did not want to be associated with a war that was being waged against their neighbour, and that was the smaller wave.

Then in September 2022, you had people who were perhaps ambivalent about the war, possibly even in favour of it, but didn't want to be involved in it personally. When Putin declared a partial mobilisation of the Russian population, people fled that. It's interesting looking at the attitudes within those diasporas, within those waves of emigration, because there's an assumption, again a lazy one, that if people have left Russia, it means they are not in favour of Putin's policies. But that turns out to be far from the truth. People who may be opposed to the conduct of the war may in fact approve of Putin in general, and vice versa.

It is a great deal more complex than simply assuming that because somebody is outside Russia, they will not still mentally be located within Russia or existing on a diet of Russian information. It is dangerous to assume all these populations that left Russia are positively disposed towards their adoptive countries. It also means that those left behind within Russia, on average, are likely to be even more supportive of this war or colonial reconquest, or completely passive in the face of the invasion. A lot of the people fleeing mobilisation will be self-selecting. That'll be people who are likely to be subject to mobilisation, which is males under 40. It's a specific sector of the population that disappears.

Myth of the Soviet Golden Age
But it's a mistake to think that it's only the older generation that has a rosy view of the Soviet Union. We also have the problem within Russia that time has passed, and new generations have come along without a clear picture of what the Soviet Union was really like. There is a generation that will remember just how grim and unpleasant life in the USSR was, but a couple

more generations coming after that only have propaganda and old Soviet movies to go by. There's nothing to stop them believing what they are told by the current leadership, that the Soviet Union was a golden age.

It's much more fragmented and layered in terms of opinions about what Russia is doing and what Russia was previously than simply a generational divide. It's not even as simple as a divide between people that get their information from state television and those that get their information from the internet. The overall strong belief across society does seem to be that it is normal and natural for Russia to be a great power, and a great power in a very 19th century sense. An essential attribute of this imperial model is having other countries which are subjugated to itself.

To understand Russia, you need to suspend disbelief. Jade McGlynn's book called *Russia's War* gets to the heart of this. She specifically called it Russia's War, because people tend to erroneously think of it as Putin's war. She looks at patterns of support, how they came about, why it is that Russians exist in this alternative reality with tragic consequences. At the beginning of the full-scale invasion you had Ukrainians calling their friends, their family members in Russia to explain what was happening. They were not believed, because their information jarred with and contradicted the propaganda.

I have been saying for many years that to understand what Russia might be willing to do, you need to put aside any preconceptions about what makes sense. That's the reason why my book, Russia's War on Everybody, is dedicated to Vladimir Putin. Because again, he's made our work so much easier. Now Putin has proven what Russia is ready to do, and on grounds that are completely unrecognisable from Western motivations for state action. Before the war, we had to put in so much work to establish the basics, the fundamentals of dealing with Russia. And to demolish the ideas that Russia would conform to normal and natural behaviours as we see them in the West. A lot of those conversations can be short circuited because some of the basics have been established for us.

The 1990s was the period where there was a cosy belief in the West that the Russia problem was resolved and we could all now be friends. This didn't align with what Russia was saying about itself and its place in the world, nor the kind of relationship it wanted with the West. The ideas of reconstituting the Soviet Union, of bringing all those countries back under Russia's control. These never went away. The key difference was that for an extended period, Russia couldn't do anything about it. Then President Putin arrived and put in place his 20-year program of getting Russia back in a position so that it could.

What came together in the second half of 2021 were two key factors. First, Russia's strength; what it thought, mistakenly, was sufficient conventional military strength to push for what it wanted. Second, the confidence Putin had been given that he could act without costs or consequences being imposed by the West. He was under the impression, based on all previous patterns of Western behaviour, that if he did push forward, and make a move for Russia's long-term, strategic goals, he'd be able to do it without damaging his country.

This brings us to one of the metaphors for Russian influence that comes back time and again, not only over recent decades, but over centuries. It's been called a gas. It's been called a liquid, something that seeps forward, following the path of least resistance. If you're a soft target for Russia, then you will be exploited by Russia. What that means is that Russia's campaign for global influence over the last few years has been most successful, where there has been a vacuum to move into. That can be a vacuum of Western interest. It can be a vacuum of disengagement by a former colonial power. If we're talking about countries in Africa, it can be a vacuum of rule of law. If you look at patterns of Russian engagement in sub-Saharan Africa, for example, they are most successful where there are fewest remaining safeguards against corruption and subversion of government. By contrast, where rule of law remains relatively strong, Russia doesn't make inroads. But the consistent pattern is the same. Lack of resistance invites Russian intervention.

We're facing challenges at different levels. There are specific national pathologies which tend to predetermine attitudes towards Russia and whether you can or cannot work with Moscow. There's also an overarching problem of the general tone and attitude of Western diplomacy being completely unsuited to dealing with Russia overall. Every country in and around Europe has its own problems in dealing with Moscow. They are self-inflicted problems. They're national pathologies. They're reasons why there are specific interests or specific attitudes within that country, or embodied by their leader, that mean they're not going to make headway with Putin.

That's France under Macron, with his messianic vision for France striking out on its own and trying to broker peace deals wherever possible to make France relevant. It's Germany under Scholz, with his absolute reluctance to do anything. It's the UK under a succession of prime ministers who absolutely did not want to look at the problem of Russian influence here, because it was deeply inconvenient for their political careers and their party funding, etc.

That's what led to this procession of senior leaders from Western countries going to Moscow in the days, weeks and months leading up to the full-scale invasion in February 2022. Saying to Moscow, look, we think this is a terribly bad idea. So come on, Putin, old chap, please don't do that. Unfortunately, it had the opposite effect to what was intended. Because it was expressed in words, and words won't do any damage to Moscow. Therefore, they will not be taken seriously.

In the latter stages, when it became completely clear to Western powers, particularly the US and UK, that Putin was going to launch the invasion, these senior figures, these diplomats, these espionage chiefs were going to Moscow armed with that knowledge, confronting Russia with it, saying, we know that you are going to invade. But then not promising any consequences for doing it. So, Russia heard the same old words that they'd heard so many times before. That there would be a serious response, and they knew from historic experience this was something they needn't take seriously.

The absence of consequences

At the same time, they heard people like Biden saying there would not be a military response to support Ukraine. What this convinced Russia of, was that it was all right to go ahead. It was a green light for President Putin because the West was saying, on the one hand, we know exactly what you're going to do. On the other hand, we're not going to do anything that you take seriously to stop it. So go right ahead. That is a fundamental problem. We were trying to deal with Moscow armed with completely the wrong set of tools and weapons when we entered those negotiations with Putin.

There's a wilful disregard of history on one side, and weaponisation of it on the other. Thinking of German war guilt, seems to be a substantial motivation for some of the restraint Germany has shown. It's entirely misplaced. Germany is compensating for having invaded Ukraine in the 1940s by not protecting Ukraine against invasion in this decade. There is another historical myth being exploited, that the West abandoned Russia in the 1990s. Rather, the West helped Russia, pouring in billions in direct financial aid, delivering food aid when Russia was incapable of distributing food to its own population. Then there was the effort to draw Russia into the international community through a dense network of links at all levels, from state-level down to local, and by default, giving Russia the seat at the UN Security Council that it was not entitled to, with devastating consequences.

Now, all these methods to help Russia, are being presented as ways in which the West 'humiliated' Russia during the 1990s. It's a complete reversal of history. For Putin everything is material he can throw on the fire, whether it be people, whether it be the economy, infrastructure, or Russia's cultural reputation, which he's trashing for generations to come. We're not fully there yet, because of this myth of the good Russian. The idea that Russians are just frustrated Liberal Democrats, who are just waiting for Putin to disappear, and then they'll turn into Sweden.

It will not die, regardless of how much support we see from the Russian population for carrying out these atrocities and these acts of aggression. Still, you have the myth that there is a viable opposition somewhere within Russia. It's a problem that occurs with many people who have studied Russia and lived in Russia, have friends in Russia, maybe had liberal conversations, over many years. For a start, that's a very small sample size and it's very distorted. It also presumes people tell you exactly who they are and aren't presenting to you a face they think you want to see, words you want to hear. It does not even consider the idea that they may not be telling you everything that they believe.

Unfortunately, a large proportion of people who are presented as knowing Russia, have only been to Moscow and Saint Petersburg, and have only interacted with people whose conversation made sense to them because it's a self-selecting set. You understand the people who are comprehensible to you. This applies especially to liberal elites or even illiberal elites; the cosmopolitan people, the people who have some understanding of the outside world. There is a very different Russia beyond the conversations that you have with the democratically inclined urbanites. This only scratches the surface of Russia and gives no idea of how different that is. This is especially true now that the democratically inclined urbanites tend to have been either jailed, exiled, or are dead.

There's a reason why this fiction of a Russian liberal opposition has persisted for so long. It's twofold. People who hope for a better future for Russia, want to cling on to this idea, regardless of all the times over decades it's been disappointed and thwarted. Because it seems a normal and natural thing, you emphasise the evidence in support of it, and disregard all the vastly greater counterevidence, that Russia is heading in the opposite direction of liberalisation. But also, Ukrainians have a phrase, that Russian liberalism ends at the Ukrainian border. You can be a liberal in a domestic context, but many Russians might have a deep-seated hankering after a so-called 'big Russia'. You can be liberal in almost every aspect of your life, and yet you can still be an imperialist, whether you're fully conscious of it, or only partly conscious.

It's a commonplace among people who watch Russia and interact with sections of Russian society, that it doesn't matter how much you believe there is a potential democratic future for Russia, that democratic future also includes Russia being an empire and other countries being trampled underfoot. Those two ideas are not irreconcilable to a Russian 'liberal'. It's just one of the ways that familiar language used to describe Russian political views, hides things that are much more complex and sometimes very alien, even though they use the same terminology we do.

Myths of encirclement and the Second World War

But Russians do have a deep-seated sense of being encircled and threatened. But that is entirely abused and utilised by the regime to control their behaviour. It is a central part of Russian national mythology. There are two key aspects to this. There is the way in which the approved version of history is very different from what happened. Russia has returned to all the Soviet myths about the Second World War, according to which it started in 1941, with an unprovoked assault by Nazi Germany on Russia. According to this version, absolutely nothing was happening before then. But Russia's behaviour during and after the war has been twisted beyond all recognition.

The idea that this was a crusade to liberate Eastern Europe from Nazi Germany, as opposed to Russia following through on its initial plan of taking control of Eastern Europe, in collaboration with Nazi Germany. The way in which the war started is completely erased from Russian history books now and it is a criminal offence to refer to it. People get prosecuted for pointing out the real events of 1939 and 1940. This revived Soviet version of war history is now the foundational myth of Putin's power as well.

It's not just the mythology we saw in the late Soviet Union, it's also giving context to the current war against Ukraine. The conflation of these two conflicts means that Ukrainians who believe in their country, who believe that their country has a right to exist, are being equated with Nazis. The myths propose that it's a normal and natural situation for Ukrainians to be dominated and governed by Russia. But instead, they fell into the hands of a neo-Nazi clique that is taking them to the West.

Instead, anybody that agrees with this neo-Nazi clique and resists Russia, must be a Nazi themselves. And this is what lies behind that language. The mythology of the Second World War is giving excuses for what Russia wants to achieve now. It gives it a semi-religious gloss to justify so many of the things that are happening. It makes it easier and more palatable for Russia to understand and to simplify these processes that are happening in the world. Because if you present Kyiv as a new Nazi Germany, it makes it easy to categorise the conflict as one of good versus evil, where Russians think they're on the opposite side to the one they actually find themselves on.

Deceived by unfounded optimism

We hear far too much optimism about what will happen once the active phase of fighting in Ukraine is over. There are far too many perfectly sensible, rational, intelligent people thinking there will then be a better relationship with Russia when the war is finished. A lot of the ideas they have are based on the mental image of Germany, or indeed Japan after the Second World War. But it glosses over that vital stage of a decades-long process of uprooting the Constitution, the education system, changing social attitudes and so on, as well as physical occupation of the defeated nations.

Whatever happens in Russia, it must happen organically, which means it is going to take a vastly longer timeframe. The key ingredient for it to even start, of course, is going to be defeat in Ukraine. Without a defeat, without a setback to Russian imperial aims, that is sufficiently resounding that it's completely undeniable within Russian society, it will not even begin. Russian society will need to look for somebody to blame, and not external enemies. Without that, there will not be that initial seed that might eventually lead to change.

Unfortunately, we are going to be facing precisely the same Russia problem into the foreseeable future. That is the key reason why so many calls for a negotiated settlement in Ukraine, or for freezing the conflict instead of resolving it, are fraught with disaster. I am hopeful, but not optimistic, if that makes sense. I fear that the self-imposed restraint of countries like Germany and the US in terms of not giving Ukraine the weapons systems, equipment and support they need to win the war, mean that they will not be able to make the gains to liberate occupied territories that they need to. Therefore, it is likely to drag on further. Therefore, the calls for a ceasefire and negotiated settlement will grow stronger. My fear is that the opportunity to defeat Russia may have been missed because of Western countries subscribing to this idea that you cannot defeat Russia, that it's too dangerous.

On the other hand, will Ukraine continue to be on the front line? Will it continue to defend Europe? Absolutely, yes. But if Russia finds there is a softer target elsewhere along its western periphery, it will go for the softer target, as it always has done.

Section 4
Action

20. USEFUL IDIOTS
John Sweeney

John Sweeney worked for the Observer, and the BBC's Panorama and Newsnight. In Kyiv, he created a daily war diary of the beginning of Russia's attack on Ukraine and released a documentary Under Deadly Skies (2023). He is the author of Murder in the Gulag (2025), Killer in the Kremlin (2024) and Putin's Prisoner (2023) with Aiden Aslin.[21]

We were filming in February 2023 and our car, which is a big old kind of SUV, it's pretty good off road, but it's not good enough for this deep, deep mud. We got stuck in the mud and then this artillery barrage dials up. 'That's outgoing,' I say. 'That's okay. It's one sound and it's okay. Incoming, it's a longer sound because you hear first the explosion and then the thing landing. If you're lucky, you can feel it through your boots. If you're unlucky, that's entirely different.'

We've got three big stories. The first is the Russian use of terror against civilians. There's a big block of flats in Dnipro that was hit in January, and they killed 50 people, including six kids. It was a massive working-class block of flats, ten storeys high. You put a big rocket the size of a large minibus into that, and you're going to kill people. And Russia has done this again and again. While we were in Dnipro, we happened to bump into the two mums with their little kids. One of the mums was filming her kids when the rocket hit. Her children had friends who were killed; when the Russians say they don't target civilians, they're lying.

Then we do a story about white phosphorus, which is an incendiary bomb which burns at about 3,500°C. There is a military use for it—it's used for masking troop movements at night. But it's against the Geneva Convention to use these kinds of weapons against civilians. We documented the use of white phosphorus bombs in Kherson.

Third, we interviewed a torture victim who went back to where he was tortured in Kherson. This was horrible for him, but he was a brave man. When he returned to the place where he was tortured, you can see his distress. In a separate location we found gas masks. This type of gas mask is called 'the elephant' (*slon* in Russian)—the old Soviet gas mask's corrugated nozzle looks like an elephant's trunk. In this awful place, there were lots of gas masks. The filter has been taken off. I first heard about the *slon* when I did a radio documentary for the BBC about the Russian army's use of torture against civilians when I covered the Second Chechen War. Elephant masks, discarded in the basement of the police station in Kherson, implied torture on an industrial scale.

We made the film because there are useful idiots in the West who believe the Kremlin's stupid narrative, their fairy tales, their dark fairy tales. We've made the film simply to say to these people, the Russian propaganda machine, the Russian lie factory is lying to you. It's lying about not targeting civilians. It's lying about not using banned weapons. It's lying about not torturing people.

When I saw the evidence of torture and fuel air bombs, which are banned against civilians, being used in Chechnya, I was viewed as an eccentric nutter. Alexander Litvinenko was a British subject. He was murdered, in the cruellest, most barbaric way. The British government just expels four Russian spies, which means that Putin must print four new diplomatic passports. And then the same thing in 2008 and the same thing in 2014 with the shooting down of MH17.

The Kremlin has useful idiots, quite a few of whom are in Britain. By their timidity and their lack of understanding of Vladimir Putin and his regime they are doing something that Ukrainians are paying for with their blood. Shame on these people when they talk about 'escalation'. Escalating to what?

I first saw my first dead Ukrainian child in early March 2022. This was a five-year old girl who had been blown up by a Russian bomb that missed the Kyiv TV tower. And Russia says they don't target civilians. Ukraine is fighting a war. Like Britain fought a war against Nazi Germany. We didn't have red lines when we were fighting for survival. There were the worst, the hardest decisions. How do you prevent the Nazis from stopping the Normandy invasion? You bomb the hell out of all French railway lines. And that meant that the RAF killed, I don't know, 10,000, 20,000 innocent French civilians. But they did it for a reason. The idea that Ukraine is behaving badly if it knocks out some elderly Russian ironmongery with its air defence, while its own citizens are being murdered pretty much every night is utterly absurd.

It's the same across the whole of the Western world. There is a problem with the F-16s and the Abrams tanks because of American timidity. They aren't arriving in time, and if they must wait, more of their citizens will be tortured, more of their children will be deported, simply because of our lack of speed and urgency.

In addition, there's another calculation which the Ukrainian army must consider, but the Russian army doesn't, and that is being profligate with lives. What's apparent throughout this conflict is that the Ukrainians believe in the sanctity of life, the value of the individual, and they seem to be guiding their military strategies to, as far as possible, preserve the lives of their troops and their scarce resources. The Russians clearly have no such concern.

On day two of the war, I was arrested by this Ukrainian soldier because he thought I was a Russian spy. I said, 'do I look like a Russian spy'? He goes, 'give me your passport'. Then, as I'm led to the little command post and I'm on my own and it's a bit scary. I just said, 'can you just look at my Twitter banner? Can you just Google me?'

Everybody's super paranoid, everybody's super suspicious, but eventually they call the SBU, the Ukrainian intelligence service. Only then does this guy says, 'You've challenged Vladimir Putin'. 'Yes, I've challenged Vladimir Putin. I used to work for BBC Panorama.' 'And you've challenged Donald Trump.' 'Yes, I've challenged Donald Trump.'

And then this guy looks at me and he has a great big broad smile, and he says, I think you have an interesting story. His name is Vlad Demchenko. Vlad went out on a special mission, a mile in no man's land, with huge risk to himself and his team, to bring back the corpse of one of their comrades, so that his poor mother had a body to bury. He's been fighting in the Bakhmut area and we've become great friends.

There is a tremendous humanity about the Ukrainian army. Obviously, there are bad people in any army and sometimes bad situations. But generally, the morale of the Ukrainian army is incredible. I mean, I've been a war reporter since 1988, and I have never, ever been with an army with such self-belief. It is massive. They really, really believe in what they're doing, and they do it with humanity and they look after their own people. I'm sure there are exceptions to this, but by and large, they look after the Russian prisoners because it's better for them. The Russians surrender and then they can trade them. And everybody in the machinery knows that. Ukrainians are fighting for their homes, and they're fighting for their loved ones who are trapped behind enemy lines. That's a powerful motivation. It means they have great morale.

Russians have been lied to by Putin. I'm bitterly disappointed by the failure of Russian civil society to challenge Putin. I knew Anna Politkovskaya and she warned about what Putin was doing in 2003, that he was zombifying Russia. To a horrible extent. Her prophecy has come true, and Putin now is leading a nation of zombies to commit mass murder.

The problem is that Stalin's evil was never properly washed away after the

Nazis were defeated. There was a serious attempt in West Germany to de-nazify the country. Now, it wasn't perfect, and you can have an argument about it. But that did happen in Russia. When Yeltsin took over, there was a flowering of civil society in Russia, but it wasn't a de-Stalinisation. So, people like Putin and Putin's bosses back then in the '70s have been allowed to get away with mass murder. Last time I was in Moscow, one of the older dissidents said it's far worse under Putin than it was under Brezhnev.

Ukrainians understand in a way that many in the West still don't understand, that if a Ukrainian town is occupied, then anybody who has an association with the army, anyone who has a relative in the army, anyone who's been in the civil administration, the intellectual elite, writers, poets, teachers, at best they'll be tortured, at worst, they'll be liquidated. The reason why the Ukrainians want to liberate all of Ukraine is that, if they don't, then there are some of their brothers and sisters who will be subject to torture or rape or liquidation.

What happens next? My view is that we should play tough with Russia until Russia is led by a Willy Brandt figure who has the moral courage to go to Mariupol and the other mass graves and get down on his knees and say, we are sorry. Russia's wealthy elite used to be able to park their ill-gotten gold in Londongrad. That's becoming more difficult, not impossible, but more difficult. They used to send their spawn to Eton and Winchester. They used to park their yachts in the south of France. Rich Russians don't like the fact that they can't go on holiday to Cyprus, to France, or to Italy. If a turbo-nationalist pops up, we'll say, well, listen, okay, the sanctions continue, everything continues until you come up with somebody better than this.

The Russians don't like their tsars to lose wars. And when they do, bad things happen to them. We must support Ukraine as it liberates itself. The simple, clear thing we have to do is help free Ukraine, and then we have to say to the Russians, if you want to come to our countries on holiday, if you want to trade with us, then you have to believe in the rule of law, and you have to say sorry to the Ukrainians, and you have to pay them an awful lot of money for the terrible damage that you've done. And like the Germans after the Nazis, you must be humble.

This is also a message to the Chinese, because the other great thing the Ukrainians have done is they have sent the Chinese a message. China is, I think, far less keen on invading Taiwan because they're worried about sanctions and they're worried about a free Taiwan fighting back like the Ukrainians have.

I also saw what Saddam did to the Kurds. But I now realise that the invasion of Iraq was a mistake. And the reason it was a mistake is because it made Putin's case easier. From now on the policy must be simple. Democracies must not invade other countries. We must show an example of what is acceptable behaviour, for the autocracies to follow, and we must support the liberty of sovereign democracies.

21. SANCTIONS
Timothy Ash

Timothy Ash is an economist and fellow of Chatham House who writes for the Kyiv Post, Financial Times, Politico, Independent, ABC Australia.[22]

Do sanctions work?

Sanctions technocrats spend a huge amount of time trying to figure out how to hit the targets of sanctions more than their home countries. The experience from sanctions on Iran and Iraq and Russia over the years has been that there are always unintended consequences. You don't want oversised impacts on your home countries nor on global markets. In respect of Russia, there's also a real desire to maintain political unity. One of the big positives, in terms of the reaction to Russia's invasion of Ukraine, has been the unity that we've seen in the EU and NATO, which have both presented a very united front. I think Putin didn't expect that. Where sanctions are concerned, there's a very real desire to keep the Western alliance united. Obviously, though, sanctions have different impacts on different countries, so the desire to ensure the costs of imposing sanctions are spread out amongst those countries that are doing the sanctioning does add extra complications. Biden promised the mother of all sanctions, but people didn't really take him seriously. In fact, no one expected the number of Russian banks that were kicked off Swift, no one expected CBR assets to be sanctioned. That was quite extraordinary and really shocked the Russians. They didn't think the US and its allies would do that. Sanctioning $650 billion of Russian central bank assets is remarkable. So far, they've located and frozen about half of them. The Russians have various facilities with the Chinese that they can hide beyond OFAC, but that's still significant.

In addition, beyond what's been done formally in terms of sanctions, one of the new things that we've not seen before is this idea of self-sanctioning. If you think back to the Iran sanctions, several Western banks tried to keep to the letter of the law, but there was not really much effort to keep to the spirit of sanctions. In this instance, the number of Western companies that have been shamed into getting out of Russia is extraordinary. Over 1000 major companies whose activities in Russia are not, for the most, subject to sanctions have nonetheless decided that Russia's behaviour in Ukraine goes so much beyond the pale of what is internationally acceptable, that they don't want to operate in Russia until Russia changes that behaviour. No-one expected the energy sector to be sanctioned at all. But now we've done coal, and the next step is gas.

What are their limits?

Of course, sanctions are just one of the tools of Western, policy. They're not a magic bullet. If we wanted to totally wreck the Russian economy we could do it, but the consequences for our own economies and for the global economy would also be devastating. It's always a question of nuance, of putting sanctions in the context of the broader spectrum of the support the West is giving Ukraine to counter Russia's malign actions. The general aggressiveness of sanctions is creating an image of Russia as a pariah state internationally. It adds to this general feeling that, whether it's European business, or whether it's Asian business, it's just too much hassle to do business with Russia. Ultimately this will deal a hammer blow to the Russian economy.

Bill Browder, formerly chair of Russia's largest Russian asset manager, has done an excellent job in exposing kleptocracy in Russia and in embarrassing the West in terms of our handling and management of Russia. We were too open after the collapse of the Soviet Union. We gave Putin the benefit of the doubt when he took power in '99 and assumed the presidency in 2000. We didn't look enough at his CV or at his subsequent actions. There's been a lot of focus on energy sanctions and the policy mistakes that were made.

Germany, Austria, the Central European countries who were the big appeasers in terms of their relationship with Russia. They thought that appeasement and engagement with Russia would ultimately moderate Putin's and Russia's behaviour. It didn't. All it meant was that they became dependent on Russian energy. They are responsible for the situation they're in and the cost of their own security, the cost of Ukrainian security—which is linked ultimately to their own security—by accelerating the movement away from Russian energy.

The UK is in a similar boat, because the City of London was too open to Russian capital, turning into Londongrad, the London laundromat. Russia, the FSB and Putin's agents corrupted our Western systems from within. We were too eager to accept Russian money, Russian financing, academia, business, the City of London, real estate agents; none of us came out of this particularly well.

Why are the sanctions justified?

Some of us, like myself, people at Chatham House, were warning about this for many years, and we were dismissed as Cold War warriors. But the reality is that Russia didn't change very much after the collapse of the Soviet Union. Nor did Putin. Russia watchers in the West have been trying to get our establishments to wake up to reality. You could go back to the Yukos case, to the Georgian war of 2008. There's a long track record—Crimea, Donbas, Litvinenko, Skripal, Navalny, Transnistria. Some people argue that we were surprised by Putin's actions, but that's nonsense. Putin had form, but some people chose to ignore it because they preferred to take Putin's forty pieces of silver.

There seems to be this craze for blaming the West, for blaming NATO for this intervention in Ukraine. But if you look at it sensibly, it's perfectly understandable that countries which had a history with Russia—the Baltics, Poland, Hungary, the Czech Republic—all wanted to join NATO; they worried about the threat from Russia. And then they were right. This war was not about NATO enlargement.

If you go back to 2014 and Russia's annexation of Crimea and then its intervention in Donbas, at that point in time, Ukraine had no aspirations to join NATO. The opinion polls showed very low support (single digit) for NATO membership in Ukraine at that time. They had a non-aligned status that changed because of the Russian annexation of Crimea and Donbas. Suddenly the Ukrainians thought their non-aligned status didn't really get them anywhere.

Russia's invasion of Ukraine was not about NATO. It was about Putin's views on Ukraine, his lack of acceptance of Ukraine as an independent state. A very strong case can be made against Russia for war crimes and even genocide against Ukraine. Genocide is not just about the targeting of civilians, it's also about the destruction of cultural sites and artifacts. And I think it's now beyond doubt, the Russians are deliberately targeting cultural centres and museums. They are looting cultural sites and seizing cultural artifacts from the museums.

I don't think you could be a significant oligarch in Russia without doing a deal with the Kremlin. It's about the projection of state power and the use of large private entities to push Russian interests. Irrespective of these people's relationships with Putin, you could not have made that much money in Russia in the mid 90s without breaking the law. In fact, I would say that the law was deliberately constructed in an ambiguous way, so that everybody, by default, does break the law. You cannot do any business without infringing the law. And then the Kremlin can pick and choose who to prosecute and who not to. In the '90s it wasn't just incidental chaos. It was chaos by design.

Western governments at that point in time took the view that progress on the Soviet system of law and corporate governance would take some time. There was an understanding that big businesspeople in Russia had to break the law. We forgave them because there was perceived to be a direction of travel. You could argue that, from a Marxist theoretical perspective, during this period of primitive capitalist accumulation, eventually the robber barons would become like JP Morgan and be interested in playing by our rules, and that they'd change the rules in Russia to mirror ours.

That never happened. There was a Wild West scenario in Russia that allowed this massive accumulation of wealth, and our Western systems were quite happy to look the other way and launder their money.

How effective has Russia been?
Russian propaganda makes a huge play, even now, of corruption in Ukraine, and the fact that you have oligarchs competing against each other to control chunks of the political sphere. However, it seems to me that in countries like Ukraine you have a greater distribution of wealth. It's not all in such a small number of hands. There seems to be a parallel development of a civic society. There's a lot more debate in Parliament, a lot more civic culture, which eventually, one hopes, will triumph over the corruption or at least reduce it down to a manageable level. None of that seems to be happening in Russia. Quite the reverse. Russia's gone on a different track, which is to actively eliminate civic society. This is part of the reason why the Russian military got it so wrong.

Russians generally, and certainly the Kremlin and Putin in particular, view Ukrainians as being like Russians. The conduct of the war ignores the fact that Russians and Ukrainians are very different. Ukraine has maintained this pluralistic culture, whereas Russia has a very centralised command-driven structure. Russia has not changed that much since the Soviet period. There was a chance for change in the 1990s, but then Putin came in and recentralised things, so that the power structure in Russia is very vertical and hierarchical. Russians have got used to being commanded, to being told what to do, and Russia's dreadful military performance partially reflects this. The lack of individualistic decisions at company level, the whole prevailing oligarchic system has certainly put a brake on development and has made policymaking difficult.

There's been a lot of focus on Volodymyr Zelenskyy as a war leader, and he's certainly done a remarkable job. But even if the Russians had taken out Zelenskyy early in the conflict, I think there are enough independent-minded Ukrainian politicians who would have taken up the baton. There's been a very decentralised, very individualistic, pluralistic kind of culture that's developed in Ukraine over the last 30 years, which has been a source of enormous strength. Bottom up instead of top down. You could probably take the roots of this approach back to the 1930s and even before that, in terms of Ukraine's smallholder culture. Stalin obviously tried to eradicate it, through the Holodomor (famine, 1932-33) and the drive for collectivisation, but it's still there. There's still an individualistic sense of freedom in Ukraine which has never existed in Russia. It's a huge strength in this war.

There is a wide variety of attitudes to Putin amongst European leaders. There are those who see him as a statesman, others who see him as a terrorist, and a number who would rather see the war ending in a kind of stalemate rather than in a decisive Ukrainian victory. It's helpful to divide Europe into countries that get Putin and countries that don't. The countries that get Putin are typically those which haven't had a great experience in terms of their relatively recent history with Russia.

Germany has a Russia problem. It still feels guilt for the Second World War. Germans, or the German political leadership, seem to think that their debt is owed to Russia, whereas in fact the debt is owed much more broadly across the region; the biggest killing fields were in Belarus and Ukraine (read Timothy Snyder's *Bloodlands*). The Germans shouldn't be kowtowing to Putin and feeling that they owe this overwhelming debt to Russia. Their debt is to the broader region, which is why they should be doing more to support Ukraine. There is also some corruption in Germany's political establishment, and German dependence on Russian energy is particularly damaging. France is different. Unfortunately, Macron is of a generation that has little to no understanding of the Soviet era. I can sympathise with Macron's naivety. But you can't be brought up in East Germany and not understand how the system works, or how the KGB operates.

As for the USA, the Biden administration got it wrong in the first instance in terms of its assessment of the global security risks. Obviously, it put China at the top of the list and Russia some way down. It had this idea that Russia was a declining power, and so there was this effort simply to box Putin in and to contain him. In fact, Russia has proven to be the most immediate threat to Western liberal market democracy. China may be the longer-term hegemonic threat to the US, but there's no chance of countering the threat from China unless you're able to counter the very immediate threat that we now face from Russia.

Turkey, of course, is a key player in this crisis. They're having their cake and eating it with great relish. They are a key regional power. They're a NATO member. They've helped the Ukrainians with the supply of Bayraktar drones. At the same time, the Turks, or rather specifically Erdogan himself, has a problem. His popularity is low. Obviously, he saw great advantage, most recently in Finland and Sweden's decision to join NATO. That gave him some leverage. The Turks are frustrated, with some justification, about their treatment by Europe in recent years. Turkey's been knocking on the door of EU accession for many years, long before the emerging post-communist European countries. And all those countries got stepped up in terms of membership, whereas Turkey has always been treated as a second-class candidate for accession to the EU. The Turkish economy is very weak. It's very vulnerable to higher energy prices. Russian tourists are a key balance of payments earner. Imposing Western-style sanctions on Russia would cause damage to the Turkish economy at a very vulnerable time and could lose Erdogan the next election. So, he's trying to play both sides and balance things out as far as possible.

Russian propaganda around the war is far less successful in most European countries. It still has influence in some, but certainly in the UK it doesn't really wash anymore. But in the Middle East, Africa, India and China, we see that Russian propaganda still seems to be proving quite effective in pushing their twisted narrative and version of events. They have also invested heavily in networks of trolls and bots outside of Europe. I understand the anti-Western feeling in developing countries. They have a history of colonialism. But what is ironic is that the invasion of Ukraine is pure Russian imperialism. It's Russian colonialism. You'd think developing countries would have some sort of fellow feeling for the Ukrainians. That they don't, is a success for Russian propaganda. In practical terms, food prices are elevated because of Russia's invasion of Ukraine. Russia is blockading Ukrainian ports, stopping 20 million tonnes of grain in storage getting out to the international market. You would hope that developing countries would be knocking on Moscow's door telling it to stop the war and unblock those ports to allow critical food supplies to get out. And it's not only the blockades. Russia is also restricting exports of fertiliser, which is key for agricultural production globally. So again, it's Russia that is doing this. Russia is the aggressor. It is sad that so many developing countries don't get it.

There's no way back, or out for Russia for as long as Putin remains in power. I don't think sanctions will be moderated very easily or quickly. Russia has been proven to be an unreliable energy and business partner, which means that Europe will diversify away from Russian energy and commodities. And if it doesn't have commodities, what does it have? It's a very large country with an aging population suffering capital flight and a brain drain.

What is the new vision? I don't see it.

What has Putin achieved? He's unified the Ukrainians like never before. He's militarised Ukraine like never before. He's unified NATO like never before. He's enlarged NATO with Sweden and Finland. He's accelerated the process of diversification away from Russian energy and commodities. The Russian military has been massively degraded in Ukraine. Putin will lack the finance and technology to be able to upgrade their technology and keep the Russian military as a global power. At the moment there's a propaganda and PR machine working hard to kind of sell this as some kind of great victory, but it's actually an utter disaster.

22. GREY-ZONE AGGRESSION
Elizabeth Braw

Elisabeth Braw is a fellow at the Atlantic Council. She is a columnist with Foreign Policy and writes for Politico, the Frankfurter Allgemeine Zeitung, The Times and Wall Street Journal.[23] *She published Goodbye Globalization (2024), The Defender's Dilemma (2022), God's Spies (2019).*[24]

Why is grey-zone aggression so effective?
Grey zone aggression is aggression below the threshold of military violence. It can include military violence, or not. Then there is hybrid aggression, which is the combination of military violence and grey-zone aggression. That's where there's a lot of confusion because people say hybrid when they mean grey-zone. Hybrid warfare is two different kinds of military violence and can include non-armed military or armed military violence combined with grey zone aggression. Unfortunately, people have used these terms so frequently and carelessly that they get applied to all kinds of things that are not hybrid warfare. If we look at the Trojan horse; the act of rolling the horse in with people inside was grey zone aggression. Obviously, they leapt out and engaged in military violence. Then it became hybrid. But that act itself was a grey zone attack because it didn't look like classical armed military violence.

As a concerted campaign against another country, grey zone aggression is relatively new. The reason for that is the world is so interconnected, not least thanks to modern technology and indeed globalisation, and that it's very easy to use grey zone aggression against another country.

You can exploit all those interconnected areas and be very successful in harming another country without using military violence. A good example of that is what Russia did just before it invaded Ukraine. It put all these soldiers at the border. They were just at the border, not inside Ukraine and not using violence. They were just there. It frightened the business community. Investors left Ukraine. Foreign investors started pulling their investments out of Ukraine. The Ukrainian currency slumped. The price of insuring against a Ukrainian sovereign default rose. All of that was because of Russian soldiers being at the border but not doing anything. It's very hard to define when they reach a point where you must act against them.

North Korea certainly is not China. Iran is a different case altogether. Then there is Russia, which obviously is a unique character. But what they have in common is that they use grey zone aggression, and they're very skilled at using it. Iran, for example, uses a lot of cyber aggression but it also uses disinformation to some extent, but not as much as Russia. Whereas China has been focusing primarily on subversive economic activities. That's something Russia would not be very good at. North Korea, of course, is a specialist in cyber aggression for the sake of getting money. What it requires is public awareness that this is real and it could disrupt our daily lives. Everybody has a role in trying to keep their country safe, even if it is just trying to verify information before sharing it.

The great thing for perpetrators of grey zone aggression is that it's cheap. You can unleash disinformation, and don't have to do it in any sort of coordinated fashion. You can try various things, and they may take off and they may not; but it's not very expensive to put falsehoods on the internet. Unfortunately, we as human beings, are somehow wired in a very unhelpful way that we actively look for scandalous content. Ordinary citizens help the perpetrator by sharing content because it's scandalous, because it's juicy, because it's fascinating, without checking it. Western societies are essentially helping other countries harm our own countries because we are so careless in what we share. The 6t January attack on the Capitol in Washington was an example of that. People have been trying to find out whether it was a Russian campaign, and they haven't really been able to ascertain that was the case. There may have been some Russian involvement, but Americans, ordinary Americans, did the bulk of the work because they willingly shared inaccurate information. Whether they knew or didn't know that it was inaccurate. It doesn't matter.

It's laudable that so many people in so many countries are trying to do their part to fight Russian disinformation. Anything we can do as ordinary citizens is valuable and laudable. I do wonder, though, whether in some instances it contributes to the deterioration of the quality in public discourse. In some instances, it's playing a similar game to the Russians. Whereas we should maintain the high ground and let them operate in the gutter. That's where it could lead to this denigration of the public discourse and public debate.

There's been a lot of discussion about the Russian efforts to interfere with the 2016 election campaign, when Donald Trump won, and cyber interference was a malign influence component. People have been trying to establish if it changed the outcome in any way. But it doesn't matter whether those campaigns or those interference attempts changed the number of votes. What does matter is that it changed people's perception about the sanctity of elections in the US. It gave people the impression that American elections are not safe.

This is what makes Russia so different from the Soviet Union. Soviet leaders wanted their country to be seen as respectable. One that was part of global forums of decision making and one that was taken seriously. So, they would engage in nefarious activities, and even though they did invade Czechoslovakia and so forth, they wanted to be seen as respectable. And that's why, for example, they signed the Helsinki Accords even though they desperately wanted not to.

President Lukashenko of Belarus, seems to have decided that he's not going to aspire to be part of any gatherings of global leaders anymore. He will go down this route. Indeed, XI Jinping seems to have decided to go down this route too. And that is a fundamental choice.

On top of that, the West or the global community loses its power to appeal to their sense of propriety and dignity, responsibility, civic mindedness and so forth, because they simply don't care about it. The West can't say to Russia, stop these constant disinformation campaigns because it's not something a respectable country does. Well, that doesn't work if Russia no longer desires to be a respectable country.

Now, having made that decision, they have so many opportunities available to experiment, to use existing grey zone techniques, but also to experiment with new ones. Belarus, for example, with an act of aviation piracy, when it forced a commercial flight travelling from one EU city to another EU city to divert to Belarus and forced it to land there. We all know what happened. The Belarusians arrested a leading opposition journalist. The weaponisation of migration that Belarus has been engaging in, is another example. That's not something a respectable country would do. But if you don't desire to be a respectable country, nobody can appeal to you to come to your senses.

Disinformation leads to disharmony. Countries lose their ability to focus on other things and become wrapped up in themselves. That's what we've seen with the disinformation campaign that was waged by Russia and others against Sweden, over the Koran burning. An Iraqi refugee burned a Koran, and immediately a massive disinformation campaign was launched from Arabic language accounts and Russian language accounts. It included disinformation about Swedish legislation, alleging the Swedish government permits Koran burnings, when in fact, that's not how Sweden operates.

It caused massive harm to Sweden. The government then had to address all these international complaints about it, as well as domestic unhappiness. It meant that Sweden was weakened because it was consumed by this artificial crisis. That's something you can easily inflict on a liberal democracy and open society, because it's so easy to exploit its openness. That is one of the primary ways in which grey zone aggression can be used and is being used as a geopolitical tool. Combined with subversive economic practices, it can be used to strengthen the aggressor.

What is the most destructive type of grey-zoning?
When we look at intellectual-property theft, you can say, it happens all the time, and it's just the way businesses operate by stealing from one another. But when it's a concerted campaign by one country, it is different: as in the case of China, which has for many years been taking Western companies' intellectual property, commercial secrets—either the Chinese state through various intelligence agencies and agents, or Chinese companies. This strategy means China can accelerate its transformation to a global, high-technology manufacturing superpower, off the back of Western companies by stealing. This strengthens China in this race for global power and weakens Western countries.

The assumption the West made when the Cold War ended, and indeed when China started opening up its markets in the 80s, was that if countries introduce market economics, eventually they'll introduce democracy as well. Because these things go hand in hand. They've gone hand in hand in our countries.

Indeed, they did go hand in hand in most of the former Warsaw Pact countries, in virtually every single one of those countries, we have levels of functioning democracy today, with variations, and we have market economies. We saw how democracy maybe wasn't perfect in Russia, but they did have a market economy. We thought that's going to lead to them becoming more like us in setting up a liberal democracy. For some time, it looked like that was the path China was on. It was becoming more and more liberal.

But there was constant concern about IP loss and the fact that Western companies were forced to relinquish IP to Chinese competitors. The West thought, once China joins the World Trade Organization, it will have to obey WTO rules and get better. It never did get better, but it was manageable. But it was only manageable because China was a weaker economy. And China's companies were not as sophisticated as Western companies.

There was a big gap between Chinese companies and Western companies.

So, they could afford to lose some IP, whether through theft or government-imposed agreements. But now Chinese companies are approaching the level of sophistication of some Western companies. The fact that IP loss is happening, IP loss from Western companies to Chinese companies is suddenly not so manageable anymore because the margin between them is too small for Western companies to be able to afford this sort of loss.

We have reached a pivotal moment where Western companies, in addition to governments, are saying, it doesn't work anymore because the rules-based, globalised order that was thought up after the end of the Cold War, is no longer working. If China in particular keeps being so cavalier about the rules, and China is the world's second largest economy, then it's just not going to work.

23. SPLINTERING RUSSIA
James Nixey

James leads the Russia-Eurasia programme at Chatham House, and his principal expertise concerns the relationships between Russia and the other post-Soviet states. He has published papers and articles in books and journals and commented extensively in the national and global media. He has also organised hundreds of private expert roundtables on Russian and Eurasian affairs while at Chatham House. Publications include The Long Goodbye: Waning Russian Influence in The South Caucasus and Central Asia, Putin Again: Implications for Russia and the West, *and many others.*[25]

Is Russia on the verge of collapse?
It is very hard to contemplate a world in which Russia has overrun Ukraine. One thing that seems certain is that Ukraine is not the limit of Vladimir Putin's appetite. Effectively, he wants a cordon sanitaire around Russia, a buffer zone, a grey zone. There is a map in his mind which conforms to what the world looked like in Soviet times.

If we get this right, you can ultimately have a Russia which undergoes a kind of de-Sovietisation, albeit 30 years late. You can have a Russia which comes to terms with the crimes of its recent and less recent past. You can show other areas of a non-democratic world that invasions are the wrong path, and you will be soundly beaten if you attempt them.

Russia as a quarry from which to extract energy—that is a failing proposition. Pessimists would probably say Russia is doomed, that it is too big and with the wrong climatic conditions to prosper as a country. The rest of the world has indeed moved on technologically, culturally, in every sense. It's astonishing, I'm afraid, how little Russia has changed over time. Yes. You can see some gleaming buildings in Moscow, but the reality is, on a very basic level, funding for R&D in Russia has been cut sharply off. So, they simply can't progress in that sense either.

We need to be thinking in terms of Ukraine's role within the EU, NATO and the European defence framework, as well as beefing up our own militaries, which have been wound down. But there's another side to that, and that is what happens to Russia, and whether we could or should have a view on the kind of country that emerges from the present situation. There's a real problem there. I've described Russia, in its current state and with its imperial ambition, as being almost non-viable in the modern world. This implies the only Russia we could deal with is one that is quite possibly fragmented and unrecognisable from its current state. But many shy away from even thinking about that.

It is very unlikely that we will see the breakup of Russia because of this war. There's simply no movement, there are no institutions, there is no momentum for that to happen. For that to happen, you would need to have the stirrings of it in the beginning. Those stirrings have been quelled, or they were non-existent in the first place. At the same time, we shouldn't be afraid of Russia breaking up to the extent that we self-deter. In other words, it would be perverse to worry about instability inside Russia, when Russia is causing such instability outside of Russia.

It has been a key feature of policymakers' worries that you cause a chain reaction from the front line back through to Moscow. Moscow collapses politically, then there's a de facto civil war. And from that follows loose nukes. There are quite a few problems in that chain of logic. I don't think that is a likely possibility. But policymakers will tell you that it would be neglectful if they did not consider it. Whilst that is a reasonable statement, if you follow it reductio ad absurdum, then it would mean you can't do anything at all to Russia because of this, because you're afraid of causing a Russian collapse.

But the only thing that will ultimately cause a Russian collapse, as it has done several times throughout history, is Russia and the Russians themselves. It's not the West. We simply don't have that kind of power. We do have a great deal of power, which we don't use. Russia does not have as much power, which it does use. I wouldn't credit the West with the ability to foment a revolution—a revolution which we don't want—despite Putin warning of that.

The West's weakness, our failure to use our power strategically, is a provocation for Putin. We often take refuge in words. Putin is looking out for actions. Words mean absolutely nothing. It's what you do, and what you show you are willing to do. A lot of Russian narratives are designed to stop the West acting, to stop the West from creating very clear red lines. Words like escalation do not provoke Russia. We're preventing a future peace or we're prejudicing negotiations, they say. None of which has a basis in reality. But they do have a deterrent value on Western action.

Russia has been enormously successful in this over the years. When you think about what Russia has managed to get away with—with only the lightest of responses—from putting chemical weapons and radiological weapons onto UK soil, to manipulating elections in the world's largest democracy, to killing tens of thousands of people in Syria—all this has been done with almost no pushback whatsoever. The truth is that if you are not told, in no uncertain terms, that actions will have consequences, and be willing to follow through on those consequences, then you're not going to be listened to.

Putin is a gambler, quite honestly, and he's thrown the dice several times and he's won. And that's what gamblers do. If they keep winning, then they keep on gambling. One can only hope that this time the West does come to its senses and realises that Russia must be stopped and that dictatorships don't get to have security concerns, and they don't get to have buffer zones or cordons sanitaires.

24. WAR CRIMES
Kateryna Busol

Kateryna Busol is a senior lecturer at the National University of Kyiv-Mohyla Academy and a fellow of Chatham House. She was attached to the Prosecutor's office of the International Criminal Court and has worked with NGOs such as the Clooney Foundation for Justice, UN Women, the Global Survivors Fund and Global Rights Compliance.[26]

How can the many and varied crimes being committed by Russia be prosecuted and proven in courts of law? Most cases will be dependent on capturing the perpetrators of these crimes.

We should start by describing the avenues through which these crimes can be prosecuted and then assess the likelihood of capturing the alleged suspects. First, there are the domestic Ukrainian courts. It's important to stress that since the beginning of Russia's aggression in 2014, namely since the occupation of Crimea and the beginning of the direct and proxy war in Donbas in Eastern Ukraine, it has been developing domestic prosecutions of alleged enforced disappearances, torture, deportation of the civilian population from the occupied territories by Russia and then Russia relocating swathes of its population to the occupied territories to ensure a demographic change.

Ukraine did start domestic investigations and prosecutions concerning these allegations right from the start of the war. Ukraine has also recognised the jurisdiction of the International Criminal Court to try and go after alleged perpetrators of war crimes, crimes against humanity, and possibly genocide. The International Criminal Court, the ICC, has been investigating, which has resulted in two arrest warrants in respect of both Mr Vladimir Putin and of his Commissioner for Children's Rights, Maria Lvova-Belova. And finally, a very important third legal avenue is the so-called universal jurisdiction proceedings. These are domestic proceedings in third countries which are not connected to the war in Ukraine. For instance, Germany, the Netherlands and France can, because of the gravity of the alleged crimes perpetrated amid Russia's aggression, act to ensure that there is no impunity for the gravest crimes under international law. All three of these regimes have different requirements with regard to the presence of the suspects.

Ukraine, ideally, should try the alleged suspects when they are apprehended. But, if a person suspected of the commission of a crime cannot be apprehended, a trial can, of course, be held in absentia, all the while ensuring that there are strong guarantees regarding the quality of the defence, and that there is the right to appeal. Nevertheless, there are so many Russian prisoners of war, many of whom are either alleged perpetrators of war crimes or witnesses to those alleged crimes, and these people can be made to participate in the proceedings, if there are charges against them or, on the other hand, they can be called as witnesses. In Ukraine's domestic proceedings, a question which often arises is whether, if an alleged perpetrator should be exchanged in return for some Ukrainian prisoners of war, or for some civilians unlawfully detained by Russia—whether there is, in effect, any moral or legal justification for doing that. But the public in Ukraine are clear that they want their people back.

The ICC does not hold trials in absentia. In the case of Vladimir Putin or Maria Lvova-Belova, the actual trials could only start once these people are apprehended and taken to The Hague. But that does not mean that an investigation cannot proceed, as the Syrian example has shown. Many perpetrators did travel and did register as refugees in, for instance, Germany. And that gave Germany the opportunity to hold many successful trials into the alleged war crimes and crimes against humanity perpetrated by the Assad regime.

Russia's treatment of prisoners

International law requires the humane treatment of prisoners of war, including ensuring that this treatment is provided in a gendered way, meaning that female prisoners of war are under the care of the female servicewomen of their antagonist. But this doesn't happen in practice and, of course, we know about the very strong allegations made about inhuman treatment and torture regarding the Russian treatment of prisoners of war. So, there is a natural urge to ensure these prisoner exchanges take place. Additionally, Ukraine has enhanced its approach to keeping Russian POWs because this sends a very important message, both to its own people and also to the international community, that despite whatever Russia is doing, Ukraine is trying to act pursuant to what international law requires, meaning that we feed them, we don't maltreat them, we don't exploit them for forced labour or anything of that nature.

Russia is desperate to have their prisoners go back to the front. They're finding it tough to conscript people. So, for them, a prisoner exchange means that they get some of their troops back, and these are people they can then put back on the front line. That said, there could be different rationales at play for Russia regarding prisoner exchanges. Apart from making people participate further in the war, if they're physically and mentally capable of doing so, it's also important for Russia to make sure that people hold their tongues because, whether they are the perpetrators or simply witnesses of the command policy of, for instance, allowing certain criminal atrocities to take place. They do not want these people to speak out.

What's more, some Russian prisoners have asked not to be returned. They do not want to go back to the front and risk their lives anymore. Before any exchange takes place there should initially be an assessment by a third-party humanitarian organisation as to whether there is a threat of torture and inhumane treatment if they are returned to their home country. The truth of the matter is, though, that many of these people will not be alive at the end of this war to be the subjects of criminal proceedings.

The wider truth-telling process

There are several concerns in this regard. Firstly, it may well be the case that the direct perpetrators are killed. In addition, though, these direct perpetrators may well have had more information about their command and about the tolerance to perpetrating war crimes or even endorsing them.

It's significant that there are now so many ways to document a crime. For instance, with Bucha, a very illustrative example would be Russia's claim that it was not involved in the crimes there and that those crimes were perpetrated by the Ukrainian armed forces. Afterwards, an investigation that analysed the satellite imagery proved that the bodies and the graves appeared in Bucha before the Ukrainian forces got there. This is what is called corroborative evidence, when it's not just the actual perpetrator or a witness who provide the evidence. There is also so much information and so many posts put up by the Russian armed forces themselves, especially during the first phase of the full-scale invasion.

Another way to address the fact that many perpetrators may be killed in battle or under other circumstances, as for instance with Mr. Prigozhin, is for Ukraine and its international partners to ensure that the push for justice does not lie only in the criminal justice domain of the courts, but that we speak about the wider truth-telling process. For example, there could be a Truth Commission such as that set up in South Africa, or in several Latin American countries, where survivors could come and tell their stories, and perhaps sometimes the perpetrators as well could share their points of view. These informal processes would allow a more nuanced understanding of the dynamics of the war and of the factors which enabled this war in the first place. They would enable the truth to emerge even if any trials were dragging on or were simply not possible because perpetrators had been killed.

The most documented conflict in history

Russia's war against Ukraine, the full-scale part, which started in 2022, is arguably, for better or worse, the most documented armed conflict in the history of the world. On the one hand, this is because there are so many ways to document atrocities because of technological developments, but also because such amazing domestic human rights organisations like Truth Hounds have been on the ground since the beginning of the war in Eastern Ukraine and the occupation of Crimea. They have extensive experience in documenting and analysing war crimes, strategizing what the courts would find useful in terms of information, and how they present their methodology. They provide an abundance of evidence. The main challenge now is how to strategise the information. Ukrainian civil society has been trying to do so. They have formed major human rights NGOs involved in conflict-related crimes documentation and analysis. They have put together large coalitions such as the Tribunal for Putin Coalition and the 5 a.m. Coalition, which alludes to the timing of the beginning of the so-called military operation. They have really tried to strategise and streamline their efforts, with certain NGOs specialising in particular crimes. For instance, there's the Crimean Institute for Strategic Research, which focuses on crimes affecting cultural heritage, while there are other organisations that focus on alleged attacks on, for instance, hospitals and medical facilities.

There are specific NGOs which work with victims of sexual violence to devise a viable methodology for preserving the evidence in a victim-centred and sensitive manner, to do no harm and to avoid victimisation. They are also trying to urge Ukraine as a state to provide more holistic psychological and medical support for these survivors. The Ukrainian Office of the Prosecutor General already has more than 100,000 cases to consider, so ideally more cases should go to foreign prosecutors' offices to start international proceedings.

Scale and diversity of crimes

Another challenge is not just the scale but the range of crimes being committed. The sheer diversity of these crimes is a real challenge in terms of documentation. There are two aspects to this. On the one hand, there was one pattern to most crimes which occurred during the first phase of the war, in Crimea and Donbas. This consisted of, for instance, the mistreatment and torture of prisoners of war, the unlawful detention of civilians who were deemed to hold a pro-Ukrainian position, the persecution of those who opposed the occupation, such as the Crimean Tatars and ethnic Ukrainian activists in occupied Crimea. Rape and other forms of sexual violence. What has changed with the full-scale invasion is, on the one hand, the scale, the territorial scope of these crimes, which means that many more investigators and prosecutors need to be trained very quickly to deal with these crimes, because previously there were just two officers dealing with Crimea and Donbas issues, and now essentially the criminal justice specialists across the country have to deal with the documenting and analysing of Russia's crimes.

But another challenge which emerged after the full-scale invasion are the new types of crimes which even those criminal justice professionals and human rights lawyers who worked on Crimea and Donbas had not dealt with before. Crimes such as, for instance, numerous instances of sexual violence against children. The UN Commission of Inquiry has confirmed that the age of victims of sexual violence after the full-scale invasion ranges from 4 to 84 years old. These victims require very sensitive, very professional support because they're very deeply traumatised, especially the children.

Then again, there is the shelling and targeting of Ukraine's critical and energy infrastructure—documenting the shelling, assessing whether there was shelling directly at a civilian object, or whether any damage was a result of imprecise weapon control—this is the type of assessment that Ukraine has had to carry out, from scratch, since 2022.

Incitement to genocide

Lawyers are overly cautious about the use of the term 'genocide'. Under international law, it's a crime that requires a very high threshold of proof to determine a special intent to destroy. In the case of Ukraine, one of four specific groups, a national group, whether in whole or in part. Possible evidence of genocidal intent has emerged with the full-scale invasion. And it requires a very cautious legal approach, including a thorough analysis of the historical background of Russia's imperial nature and its neo-colonial attitude towards Ukraine. We are trying to develop, both internationally and domestically, the appropriate charges to be levelled against Russian propaganda. It's clear that, at some points, their hate speech has reached the threshold of incitement to genocide. Once again, this is a totally new species of case that Ukrainian domestic investigators, prosecutors and human rights lawyers are having to deal with, once the full-scale invasion was under way. Both the geographical scope and the unprecedented nature of certain crimes provide major challenges

Incitements to genocide are not a one-off. Several times a week you can hear key figures, such as Russian propagandists, saying things that are clearly genocidal in their intent. And the people who utter these statements are not taken off the air; they are either regular presenters or they are commentators who are invited back repeatedly.

Nothing shocks me anymore. On one occasion, I was watching Russian TV, and there was a priest, a senior priest, in the Russian Orthodox Church under the Moscow patriarch. This priest said that Ukrainians are not Christian, that in fact they are pagans, and that the only remedy is either to convert them, or if they refused to be converted, then he basically called for their liquidation. These comments happen repeatedly, and they form a pattern.

As I've already said, from a formal legal perspective, there is a very high threshold to prove genocide. Lawyers are notoriously overcautious about using the term because they're very concerned about deploying what they would call political or journalistic language. The legal qualification for genocide is different, and very narrow. One problem is that most international lawyers do not speak Russian, and they don't necessarily have an in-depth knowledge of the history of the region, of the Soviet Union and of Russia's imperial policies. That is why we have professionals like Timothy Snyder or my colleagues from Chatham House, who have a profound, multifaceted understanding of the region and of the historical dynamic between Russia and Ukraine, and who have tried to start compiling translations of the hateful statements made by Russia's top officials or propaganda spokesmen. The international law blog Just Security, for instance, contains a compilation of genocidal rhetoric.

It is also important to look at the sources of this rhetoric, as it comes not only from top officials or top military commanders in Russia but is also embedded in the rhetoric that accompanies the commission of crimes on the ground. There are reports on gender-based violence in eastern Ukraine during the first phase of the war. This hateful rhetoric has accompanied Russian atrocities since the beginning of the war. It's important not just to translate these utterances, but also to connect the hateful rhetoric of the perpetrators on the ground with the messages sent by top propaganda figures, state leaders and church leaders. It's clear, unfortunately, that there is a very strong correlation.

If we consider larger strategic crimes such as the shelling of clinics, cultural institutions and so on, there may be many forms of evidence, including satellite evidence. But when it comes to individual crimes, particularly regarding this kind of sexual violence against individuals, there may not be any other witnesses to those crimes.

Under-reporting of crimes

Sexual violence cases are notoriously under-reported and under-prosecuted in all conflict situations, and Ukraine is no exception. There are a multitude of reasons for this, most notable, the stigma about this particular type of violence, the stigma experienced both by women and by men. The stigma is experienced by both, but in very gendered, highly distinctive ways. It's also worth mentioning that many of these victims need strong psychological and medical support before they are willing and able to participate in criminal proceedings. And it's important not to pressure them. It's important to show that the state and civil society are there to provide this primary foundational support, which, again, should be about promoting a sense of security and providing the appropriate support for the mental and physical well-being of the victims.

There is very strong evidence already that sexual violence has been perpetrated during house-to-house raids in the occupied territories, as well as in the context of detention. We know from human rights NGOs, from organisations such as Truth Hounds, as well as from international human rights NGOs such as Human Rights Watch, for instance, that Russia does seem to have a policy and to have instituted the infrastructure of so-called torture chambers. When Russian troops retreat, the paraphernalia of torture are frequently discovered—for instance, electric leads for electrocuting genitalia are often found in these torture chambers. This evidence corroborates statements made by victims and witnesses. The weaponisation of sexualised torture in such torture chambers is well established. The UN Commission of Inquiry says that Russia even has names for this type of sexualised torture. It's called 'a call to Putin' or 'a call to Lenin' when they connect these leads to a person's genitalia. And again, this applies both to women and to men. It's hard to prosecute sexual violence, but increasingly more dots are being connected and evidence on the ground is being gathered to build and prosecute these cases.

Frequently, both victims and perpetrators can be found on the soil of third countries as refugees. There should be more support, mental health support and medical health support for victims and witnesses, and for the criminal justice professionals. It takes a lot of emotional strength for investigators and prosecutors to constantly deal with the evidence of torture and sexual violence.

Transitional justice and reparations
Transitional justice is a range of both judicial and non-judicial measures, and by non-judicial measures I mean truth-telling initiatives, memorialisation, reparations and institutional reforms, in addition to criminal prosecutions,

which are judicial measures. It's a very holistic set of measures aimed at providing holistic support to victims and also aimed at transforming the state and civil society in a way that makes them more resilient and stable, to prevent any further aggression. Criminal prosecutions are being made effective, as well as institutional reforms, which are a big component of transitional justice. It's also about Ukraine living up to the expectations of its own people, which means finalising the anticorruption reforms, finalising the reforms of the judiciary, making the assets of state officials public, and holding them accountable.

Whereas institutions like journalism were being transformed very early on, after Maidan they were able to clear out the older generations all in one go, removing all those who were trained under the Soviet system, and a new wave of young professionals was able to bring about changes quite rapidly in the field of justice. Zero tolerance for corruption and effective punishment for it should be ensured system-wide, not only within the judiciary. But sacking professionals in the judiciary will not help, firstly because it would incapacitate the proper consideration of legal cases, and secondly, because Ukraine is already short of criminal justice professionals now. So, it's really about transformation.

After the full-scale Russian invasion, professionals in the criminal justice system are very aware that the international community, foreign fellow lawyers are looking very carefully at the way they're considering conflict-related cases. Because of that, they have opened to external consultancy. This is seen in the way they cooperate very closely with the Ukrainian human rights community. They work closely with academics and with foreign lawyers as well. The office of the Prosecutor General also has a separate set of advisors, leading international lawyers who have practiced at international courts across the world and who are trying to bring their expertise and to combine it with that of the young Ukrainian lawyers who also know the Ukrainian context.

This openness, in what was once a very rigid and closed criminal justice sector, to external consultants and to engagement, both with its own Ukrainian young professionals and with foreign consultants, is already a step change. Now it's important to ensure that this change is system-wide at all levels, that it's not just Kyiv and the central offices, and the war crimes unit of the office of the Prosecutor General, but that the courts and investigators across the country have the opportunity to engage with human rights lawyers and civil society in a way that really enhances their quality and the quality of their proceedings. Reparations can be an important part of the healing process.

Reparations for individual victims

In the Ukrainian context, reparations are often understood as interstate payments after the end of the war. Very few people here in Ukraine understand that, under international human rights law, reparations also consist of the support provided to individual victims of the gravest war crimes. And this lack of awareness, of course, has had its impact on the development of appropriate policies. Ukraine had a scheme for victims of torture who had been detained and tortured because of their pro-Ukrainian position. But now, after the full-scale invasion, and the fact that so many more people became involved, the state understood that more holistic support for victims is needed.

There are currently several draft laws on the way to ensure that Ukraine has an electronic registry of victims. This means that people can submit their cases and describe the type of damage that has been inflicted on them by the Russian invasion, and then, based on that, their needs will be assessed, and support will be provided. Ukraine is still considering a system of the so-called urgent interim reparations, which could be small payments while the wider system of reparations is being approved. A couple of draft laws are being considered, and hopefully they will be soon registered with Parliament. Ukraine has also approved a system of registering damage to property and applying for compensation in that regard. But again, we should see just how effective this system is.

Section 5
Ukrainian Views

25. ABSENCE OF A RUSSIAN NATION
Volodymyr Yermolenko

Volodymyr Yermolenko is the president of PEN Ukraine and a senior philosophy lecturer at the Kyiv-Mohyla Academy. In 2020, he and his wife Tetyana, a lecturer and Maidan activist, Yermolenko started the Kult podcast, dedicated to defining epochs in the history of Ukrainian culture and literature.[27]

We travel a lot through Ukrainian territories. We go to de-occupied territories. We go very close to the frontline. We see all those destroyed villages. We talk to people who have lost members of their families. One of the biggest dangers of our time is this virtual world which obscures the real world. We believe in material facts. In something you can see, you can hear, you can smell.

With my wife Tetyana we try to make our podcast as objective as we can. If we doubt ourselves too much, doubt our nation, our neighbours, our soldiers, then this opens the way to despair and defeat. We try to have this critical eye, while still maintaining faith in our struggle.

Russian propaganda tries to foster indifference and apathy amongst people. The word nihilistic is key here. Russian propaganda is about seeding doubt and seeding division, but not just that. Nihilism is only part of the propaganda. This divisiveness and seeding of doubt are only directed at people whom Russia doesn't expect to persuade. But when we are talking about people who Russia does want to persuade—variously its own citizens, Ukrainian citizens at certain moments in time, and people in the non-Western world—there is a clear message very much in line with Soviet propaganda.

Part of the struggle is to reflect upon the cult of violence, which is present in contemporary Russia, but was also present in other periods of Russian history. We describe how Ukrainians come back to destroyed villages, how they cultivate their land, how they cultivate their flowers, even when their houses are destroyed. There is something in this love of life which is very much the opposite of the Russian idea: that you can win the war only by sending hundreds of thousands of people to their deaths, that you need to be cruel not only towards your enemy, but towards your own people. This is a pattern we see not only in this war, but in the way the Soviet Union fought the Second World War. People like General Zhukov were waging war without any consideration for human lives spent in the process.

There are two extremes of attitude in the commemoration of any war. One extreme is to have a cult of victory that forgets about victims—that was the Soviet type of commemoration.

The way Ukraine commemorates the Second World War has diverged from the Soviet world. It's messy and complex—trying to reevaluate it based on evidence and lived experience, stripped of ideology.

In Russia it's been turned into a cult of death that looks backwards rather than forwards. People are not really telling stories about the war. Apart from a few exceptions, literature and films about the war were propaganda.

In Ukraine we'd rather have monuments to the Unknown Soldier than attempts to remember people by name. And the Soviet Union completely erased the history of the Holocaust, just erased the victims.

This is something Ukraine has been struggling with in the past decades. When it aligned itself with the European way of looking at war—rather commemorating the victims, than praising the victory, and considering the war as primarily a huge tragedy—the idea of 'never again' was much more prevalent in Ukraine than in Russia. 'We can do it again' is one of the Russian propaganda slogans. That's what they are doing right now.

There is another danger in how we commemorate the war. From the 1960s and 70s, there was a move in Europe to focus only on victims. But there is a danger that, if you change your discourse from heroism to victimhood, you erode the ability to fight. If Ukraine didn't have its cult of heroes—the word 'hero' is, I think, obsolete in Europe—it would be extremely dangerous. Because if you don't have this idea that at one moment of history, you need to have people who go to the frontline, people who defend your country, people who we call heroes in the ancient Greek sense—if you don't have that, you become defenceless.

It's very important to combine the two, to have the utter belief that you need to fight, but also to understand that war is not a chess game, war is not a football match. There are victims, both civilian and military. It is important to combine the commitment to fighting with compassion. I hope that Ukraine keeps both.

I think a mistake of the 1990s in Europe and in America was that Hegel won over Aristotle. In philosophical terms, Fukuyama won against, let's say, people like Leo Strauss. It's a paradox that in European political philosophy in the 20th century, there was always the idea that we need to return to the Greeks. It's something you see in Hannah Arendt.

It is important because Greeks and Romans understood very well that democracy is fragile. The notion of democracy as the rule of the greatest number, at least in Aristotle's conception at the time, is sound, but such a system will always degenerate over time. There is a long history of European political thought, up until Machiavelli and Montesquieu, which has been totally forgotten.

These classic philosophers describe in detail how democracy fails when people take freedom for granted, they consider political and civic freedom as their right and not their obligation. They consume it instead of promoting and defending it. And then what happens? A society becomes very egoistic. People confuse the idea of common good with the idea of their private good. They become disenchanted and then they vote for a tyrant, for someone who comes and says, I will fix all your problems. That is what happened in the United States with Trump. This is what is happening now in some European countries.

There is kind of a myopia towards Europe's own intellectual tradition. For Ukrainians, liberty is not something which is taken for granted. It is not guaranteed, it's something you need to fight for with rallies, with demonstrations and Euromaidan, and even by taking up arms and fighting a war. It is a big reminder to the democratic world that nothing is inevitable.

I like the theory put forward by French philosopher Rémi Brague of the eccentricity of Europe. He looks at how Rome sought to incorporate Greek culture, seeing it as the European way of life. Every new phase of cultural development, every new phase of civilisation sought to incorporate the previous one, not destroying it, but rather building upon it. So, we have Greek culture taken over by Roman culture, then taken over by Christian culture, which goes much farther north, then taken over by British culture, then by American culture.

Russia is different, because, Russia was trying to annex the past of Kyiv, annexe the past of Crimean Tatar culture, the past of this region of Novorossiya and the new Russia, which has a deep, very interesting culture of Iranian-speaking tribes, the culture of Turkic-speaking tribes, the culture of Ukrainian Cossacks, the culture of Crimean Tatars. All of this is erased in the Russian version of the past, so that the history of this region only starts with Catherine the Great.

One of the causes of the current war is profoundly psychopathic. At a certain moment in Russian history, Russia declared the history of Kyiv to be its own history, appropriating its history as the history of a state which didn't exist at the time.

The key founding Roman myth was the myth of Aeneas; the Roman hero as opposed to the Greek Odysseus. The idea was not to erase the story of Odysseus, but rather to say we have a better story.

First, Aenas overcomes the Trojan defeat. Second, he did not return to the place of that defeat. He founded something new. This is a profound Roman myth.

I have wondered why Russians did not take this myth for themselves, because it would be logical to say that Kyiv is a kind of a Troy, a Troy that was burned down by the Mongols, then transferred to a new Rome, which is Moscow. In fact, though, the Aeneas myth is much more important for Ukrainians (from Kotlyarevsky onwards), than it is for Russians. The Russians did not present this part of Ukrainian culture as a competing story. They simply wanted to say, this is our story. Odysseus did not exist.

If you live in an ancient city, you can't help but be aware of the layers of history that have come before you. It's always struck me that, despite the space race, despite industrialisation, despite all the trappings of modern civilisation, Russian imperialism is different from British imperialism, French imperialism, or Dutch imperialism.

In those versions of imperialism, the idea of difference was the tool of domination. Western imperialism tells colonised cultures: 'You will never be the same as me.' That's why you have racist theories which were born in Britain and France and Belgium and then passed on to Germany.

In Russian imperialism there is the diametrically opposite idea—you will never be different from me. That's what Russians are telling Ukrainians and Belarusians, and other peoples who are ethnically much more different. It's not difference which is a tool of domination, but rather the idea of sameness.

At the root, we have a paradox. There is Russian nationalism, but there is no Russian nation. The idea of the nation is constructed on the level of the relations between citizen and citizen in European countries in the late 18th and early 19th century. But I don't believe that happened in Russia.

It was different for Poles and Ukrainians. They lacked a state, and therefore they defined themselves in terms other than hierarchy. For Ukrainian intellectuals of the 19th century, the key idea was that the future lies within us, because we lack hierarchy, we have established horizontal relations.

Paradoxically, Russian culture is very elitist. It's not populist at all. Take Pushkin and compare him to Ukraine's Taras Shevchenko. They are utterly different writers. Pushkin is very elitist. Pushkin is a product of salon culture; the French Rococo. Pushkin is known by heart primarily by intellectuals, he's cherished in universities and in cities. In Ukraine, Taras Shevchenko people have his portrait in their houses, in villages, in cottages. People know his poems by heart in the same way that they know popular folk songs.

The Russian intelligentsia was too far away from the people. It failed to construct a Russian nation which was distinct from the imperial structures. For a Russian citizen, it is very difficult to imagine him or herself without the state, without Putin, without the Tsar, without hierarchy. Despite urbanisation, there is still this huge gulf between the elite and the people. This makes the people so much crueller and more uncultivated. This explains, on a very profound level, why Russian soldiers are so cruel.

It also explains why the Russian intelligentsia is so helpless. It doesn't have any influence. This explains their silence, why there are no demonstrations against the war, neither inside Russia, nor even outside Russia. For Ukrainians it's very easy to imagine ourselves without hierarchy, without the state.

At a certain moment of time, Russians will have to choose whether they want to be a nation or an empire. The paradox is that the Russian Empire tried to create a Russian nation. A Russian nation which comprised great Russians, White Russians and Little Russians, Ukrainians. Then again, through the idea of the Soviet people in the 20th century. These were both attempts to create a Russian nation through the state, top down. Right now, it's an empire with nationalism, with Russian nationalism, but without a nation.

If one day the Russians do choose to be a community through horizontal ties that will pose big questions for them. For example, size. You cannot really have a democracy when you have a huge territory like that. Let's read Montesquieu, let's read Rousseau, but also Russian thinkers themselves, because Russian thinkers like the Eurasianists primarily developed the idea of an authoritarian Russia.

If you want Russia to be big, then forget about democracy. The idea should be to 'make Russia small again'. That's what Russians need to want if they really seek a Russian state in which there will be much less violence towards them than there is today. They will face a very difficult dilemma, and I don't really see that being faced by Russian émigrés or the Russian intelligentsia.

Nor do I see it being considered in the Western world, in realistic, sober thinking about Russia. Rather I see the hope that things will normalise one day, Putin will die and so on. Navalny and many of the opposition—even if they voiced the idea of being anti-imperial, even if they vocalised the idea of being anti-Putin—the idea of a big Russia still holds a firm grip on most people's minds.

The roots of Ukraine, the roots of Belarus, the roots of the Georgians or the Armenians are much deeper. We look at Eastern Europe through the 19th century, maybe even through the 18th century, and what we see are Peter the Great, Catherine the Great, who destroyed the spirit of Republican Eastern Europe. We need to look deeper to understand the origins of Ukraine. They can be found in the Greek settlements of the Black Sea. They can be found in Khazar culture, in Khazar statehood in the late first millennium, in the interconnection between the North and the South, between the Varangians, the Vikings, and the Byzantines. This is how Kyiv was created as a powerful city.

There are so many interesting stories. There was a very pluralistic political culture around Kyiv in medieval times. Kyiv was closer to the idea of a feudal republic. Then we move towards other statehoods such as the Grand Duchy of Lithuania and the Polish Lithuanian Commonwealth, in which we also see an anti-tyrannical way of thinking, an anti-tyrannical approach to politics.

Then of course there are the Cossacks, the idea of free warriors, a kind of a knightly culture. We can consider Ukrainian Cossacks of the 17th century as a continuation of the medieval knightly culture beyond medieval times in Eastern Europe. There are many, many interesting things to see before the Russian world came here. The Russian world came here to some extent in the mid-17th century, but fully in the early 18th century. We are being asked to look at the history of Eastern Europe through the past three centuries instead of looking at the millennium which came before.

What happened in Europe in the mid-19th century will probably be happening in the 21st century, around the current European Union. I'm not only speaking about Ukraine. I'm speaking about Belarus, I'm speaking about Moldova, I'm speaking about Georgia.

Over the past two decades, starting from early 2000, these countries have seen revolutions against tyranny. Most of them failed, most of them were defeated. In Ukraine too there was the Orange Revolution, then almost immediately, the counter-revolution, with Putin-backed President Yanukovych back in power, and then another revolution.

The Russians tried to foment an internal counter-revolution in Ukraine with Yanukovych several times. They failed. If we take the 1848 revolutions, they were considered by contemporaries as the start of something big, but they were defeated. Europe in the second half of the 19th century was a Europe of authoritarianisms—the Second Empire in France, the Austrian Empire and the Russian Empire and Prussia. Everybody thought that the story of revolution, the story of democracies in Europe was over.

Despite all the defeats in other places, the spirit of freedom can win and can even stay resilient, despite external invasion. There is a great deal of sympathy in Ukraine towards this process, such as with the protests in Hong Kong, such as Taiwan, such as the Iranian protests.

And, of course, there are territories like Georgia which are trying to pull themselves out of post-Soviet imperial influence. Belarus too. Ukraine is currently under attack, but nevertheless, there's an equivalent struggle going on for Belarus. Lukashenko has become much more tyrannical, much crueller, and much more pro-Russian. Ukraine is a key state, for the future of democracy in wider Europe, or even in the Mediterranean space and the Black Sea space.

We used to emphasise the divisions within Ukraine. But things have changed. In the 2010 election of Yanukovych, Ukraine was divided in two. There was a fair election, and the majority of the people, over half of citizens, chose pro-Russian. It took some years for those who voted for him to understand just how bad he was.

If you take the year 2000, the common narrative in Ukraine was, we are so divided. Look at Poland, how united they are. We are so divided about EU membership and NATO membership. Look at the Poles and the Baltic states, the Lithuanians, the Latvians, the Estonians, how united they are as they move towards the EU and NATO. Then look at Ukraine now and look at Poland. Poland is much more divided now than Ukraine is. Britain is much more divided than Ukraine is, but it doesn't mean that it will always be like that.

Nonetheless, Ukraine is going to be a fortress border, against what is bound to be decades of chaos, disorder and violence emanating from our unruly neighbour. Unfortunately, Ukraine is accustomed to being on this border. Something very interesting can come from the borderlands, but equally something very bloody.

On the other hand, one of the elements of history is that a borderland frequently becomes a place in which certain processes have their beginnings. Britain was this borderland country in, let's say, the Elizabethan era. Britain showed how you can turn from being a borderland into becoming something central. We can look forward to the next stages in Ukrainian history with an expectation of seeing something like this. Nonetheless, we should also understand that we can fall back into a repetition of our previous history, when being a borderland meant that Ukraine was caught in this vicious circle of violence.

26. THE INTEREST OF DEMOCRACY
Olena Halushka

Olena Halushka Olena is a contributor to the Atlantic Council, Washington Post, Foreign Policy, and EU Observer and active in Ukrainian civil society reform.[28]

The designation of Russia as a state sponsor of terrorism is an urgent topic. Russians are using terrorism. It is much easier to wage a war against babies, mothers, the elderly, attacking heating and lighting infrastructure, and bombing residential areas, hospitals, schools and kindergartens. According to estimates, Ukraine's losses from the Russian aggression vary between $400 billion and $700 billion. (Western countries are potentially treating this money as leverage over Russia, or part of a future negotiation process.)

It is important to remember, however, that Russia is prepared to play a long game. What Ukraine needs is Western military assistance and sanctions. The Russian calculation is that you cannot go on living with this brutal situation for five, seven, ten years. That is exactly the range of planning which Russia is applying, because time is against Ukraine in this war.

It's very important to move forward with the confiscation of Russian assets, sovereign assets, state assets, and also oligarchs' private assets outside of Russia. They could ensure Ukraine can sufficiently defend itself from Russian aggression.

Russia has been trying to depict Ukraine as a Western colony for at least as long as I myself have been working on Ukrainian reforms. They claim that the 2014 Revolution of Dignity was masterminded in Washington D.C., Brussels, Berlin, wherever. But the Revolution of Dignity expressed the hopes of the Ukrainian people. This is an existential fight for us. Ukraine will carry on fighting, with or without assistance.

At the beginning of the invasion, the Ukrainian economy was growing. The Ukrainian economy grew even during Covid, when most economies were declining. Critically important for us is access to the sea. That is why Russia tried to occupy the south of Ukraine. That's why they targeted Odesa. Most of our exports are transported by sea.

Russia's idea of Novorossiya is taking control of the entire coastline, all the way to Moldova. Controlling the entire southern coast would make the Ukrainian economy unviable and would turn Ukraine into a partially failed state. That was why it was so important that Ukraine managed to prevent it from happening.

After they invaded Crimea in 2014, Russia tried to occupy the southern part of Ukraine as well, but they failed utterly because there was very strong anti-Russian sentiment and resistance locally, including in Kherson, in Mykolaiv, and in Odesa. They never relinquished their plan, however. They merely realised that, back in 2014, they didn't have sufficient military capacity for a full-scale invasion.

There are so many people who are hoping or are pretending to hope that, this time, Russia will act with integrity, this time they will adhere to whatever agreements they sign, agreements not worth the price of the paper they're printed on.

Between 2014 and 2022, Russia constantly violated ceasefires, killing Ukrainians. They tried to use the Minsk Agreements to undermine the Ukrainian state from within, and to prevent our democratic transformation and the reforms we were putting in place. Why should this time be any different?

The Revolution of Dignity (18-23 February 2014) was a turning point in Ukraine. It was the moment when the corruption of the previous president, Yanukovych, peaked. He had built a semi-authoritarian state in Ukraine, almost a family business. His people were everywhere, money flowed to them through all the state-owned enterprises. They controlled law enforcement and the judiciary.

The last straw was when the Yanukovych government rejected the signing of the Association Agreement with the EU. It was a document about bringing Ukrainian legislation in line with European legislation, the introduction of European standards, economic reform. It was a symbol of European values, it stood as a kind of a lighthouse.

As a result of the Revolution, Ukraine has changed dramatically since 2014. There is a new system, with new accountability in all state institutions, an unprecedented system of transparency: an electronic asset declaration system in which all public officials have to report their incomes.

Ukraine still has issues to fix. As an anti-corruption activist, I recognise there is still a problem. But when there is a diagnosis, there is also the possibility of a cure. We understand that we have to improve judicial reform. But if you compare Ukraine as it is today to what it was in, let's say, 2010 or 2013, there are two completely different countries.

In a real democracy you never know for certain who will win the next election, or who will be the next president and what might be the composition of the parliament. A year before the 2019 elections nobody could have predicted that Zelenskyy would be President.

For decades Russia has been using corruption in Ukraine to influence Ukraine. Privatisation failed and oligarchs appeared—many of them with close ties to Russia. The moment Ukraine began turning away from Russia, getting stronger and becoming resilient to Russian influence, the Russians realised that they could not control Ukraine anymore. Or not in the same way that they had during the '90s and beginning of 2000.

As Ukraine advances, gets stronger, develops its own military industrial complex, and becomes more integrated with Europe, it will become proportionately more expensive and even perhaps impossible for Russia to reincorporate it into its imperial vision. As Ukrainians emerge from a Soviet mindset, as they're able to tackle corruption and reform their society, that provides a template for how other states can do the same.

Before the 2022 war began, I thought that a democratic, successful Ukraine was a threat to Putin's regime because it might show the Russian people that you can live decently if you want to. I no longer think so.

It is not just Putin's war—as many would want it to be—it is also a war being waged by Russian society against Ukraine. So many Russians are ready to endure living conditions without indoor toilets and other basic needs. But at the same time, they are celebrating what they are going to do to Ukraine, raping our women, killing our kids, looting our homes. Russian people appear to want others to be living in even worse conditions than they are living in. And from that perspective, Russian society is very much aligned with Putin

I wouldn't say the Ukrainian Revolution inspired others. In 2016, when I was talking a lot to Belarus activists, I kept asking them, did our Maidan inspire you to do something? They said, absolutely not.

There was a feeling that it was better to have stability, and not some kind of revolution because you do not know how that will end. There might be revolution and then some reforms and then some rollbacks. We paid a hefty price in that Revolution, standing up against authoritarianism. And we still are. Many who engaged in the democracy-building process during the Revolution of Dignity were the first ones who joined up to fight. We are losing these inspired people, while Russia is losing thugs and criminals.

There are three things that are fundamental to Ukraine's future security and stability—anti-corruption, EU and NATO membership. This is the only way to prevent future Russian wars against Ukraine.

Anti-corruption and the rule of law, that's part of our internal resilience.

We have to finalise the reforms that we started. Everything is absolutely clear with regards to what still needs to be done. Our experience is already being studied by other countries such as Moldova and other emerging democracies. The question of anti-corruption reforms is very closely related to EU integration.

All of the reforms we built were thanks to tools and instruments like EU Visa Liberalisation Action Plan, or the IMF and European macro financial assistance programmes, conditions set where money was linked to very specific and concrete steps, which Ukraine had to follow.

It is not a complicated principle. If you do not have the foundation of a NATO security umbrella, businesses are unwilling to invest in Ukraine as Russian missiles might arrive in three or five years, killing their employees and destroying their investments. In the same way, many Ukrainian refugee families will return to Ukraine, particularly those who have kids. Ukrainian integration in the EU and NATO is essential to Ukraine's sovereignty and halt Russia's never-ending encroachment towards the West.

27. PLEASURE IN DESTRUCTION
Anna Danylchuk

Anna Danylchuk was linguistics professor at the Lesya Ukrainka Volyn National University, Lutsk, but became a professional Youtube diarist after the 2022 invasion of Ukraine by Russia.[29]

Ukraine in 1917 and Ukraine in 1922 can be seen as two short periods during which Ukraine was independent—after the fall of the Russian Empire, and before being swallowed up by the Bolshevik army and incorporated into the USSR. Sometimes I try to imagine how different my country would have been if we had managed to continue developing in our own way. I read literature from the 1920s, and am surprised at how rich the language is, and how modern the ideas are. A lot of the writers from that period were able to travel. They spent time in London or Paris. They did not know the borders would be closed. At the beginning of the 20th century, Ukraine was a part of Europe. And then it was not.

Ukraine lost 16 million people at the beginning of the 20th century. We had the Holodomor, we had deportations, we had the Red Terror, and many of our intellectuals, writers, and composers disappeared in the Gulag. The best people, the people forming our national cultural identity, were lost.

As the ex-Soviet states, from the Baltics to Eastern Europe to Ukraine, gradually re-emerged and tried to rediscover their identities, they diverged relatively quickly. That process isn't over.

But how did Ukraine retain a connection to its identity as an independent country in the 1920s? How did it reestablish a connection to the 19th century, when it was also struggling under imperial pressure to abandon its language and national identity?

When you look at the past three centuries, you will see we constantly had problems with: Russia, then the Russian Empire, then the Soviet Union, and now the Russian Federation.

Through all of this, there seems to be something built into our DNA. Our history goes back to Kyivan Rus. In the 17th century we had the Cossack state, which was freedom loving, then at the beginning of the 20th century we had a spell of independence.

That long history gave birth to generations of talented thinkers—writers, poets, scientists, politicians. There were rebellions against the USSR right up to the 60s. It is in the Ukrainian spirit. We have never accepted that we are Russian. In fact, it was Ukrainians who founded Moscow. Russians forget you cannot steal the spirit that formed us.

When you look at Ukraine you will see that we don't like politicians. We never worship them. We never let our presidents serve for 22 years. If we feel something is wrong, we start protesting. We understand that politicians are not gods. They are not Tsars. In Russia now, they have the perfect conditions to protest. All their military are in Ukraine. The Russian people don't like this mobilisation. They don't live well. But still, they never protest.

I'm not saying we are perfect. Get two Ukrainians together and you have three *hetmans* (leaders). But if there's something that needs repairing on the streets, we fix it. If the state doesn't have the money or the initiative to improve our schools or hospitals, then we do it ourselves. At protests at Maidan, people were arrested. But the rest of people did not just stand around watching or filming it on their mobile phones. They started shaking police vans, and in the end the people won because there were a million of them and just one thousand policemen.

Russian society is much more traumatised than Ukrainian society. It's a trauma that they don't even notice, and it creates people that are not citizens. Russians emigrating to Georgia and elsewhere don't want to influence their society, they don't want to change anything, they just want to leave. At the same time, many if not most Ukrainians stay put, in dangerous areas, shooting down drones, volunteering, doing everything they can to protect their country.

I feel more optimistic about Belarus because they did protest, they tried to change their president. They demonstrated their dissatisfaction. But the linguistic situation is tragic. Only 5% of people still speak Belarusian. It may change, but most of their discourse revolves around the Second World War. They have forgotten about their connections with the Grand Duchy of Lithuania or Ukraine or elsewhere. And the so-called president, the dictator Lukashenko, has managed to suppress these protests. There are a lot of Belarusians fighting for Ukraine, and not only fighting. They are also collecting important experience that they can apply to their own country in the future. Lukashenko's regime is totally dependent on Putin.

Russians, too, need to take responsibility for the changes in their own society. If the system was being shaken up from both sides, with protests being held inside Russia, that would help to end this war sooner. But the Russians simply stand back and observe because they are afraid. They try explaining that it's too dangerous to protest because you will end up in prison. It's dangerous to live in Ukraine now, with thousands being killed every month. How can I sympathise with them?

After the war, there will be a lot of trauma, both psychological and physical, and sometimes I try to comfort myself by picturing Europe after the Second World War. It seems to me that this was a golden period. A lot of people were optimistic. They had gone through so much that, somehow, they emerged from the experience not as victims, but as winners. That's why I want to believe that my people and my country will be stronger. We'll develop faster. And Putin, with his war in Ukraine, will have achieved precisely the opposite of what he was looking for.

Many people switch to speaking Ukrainian; they dig deeper into their family history to find Ukrainian traditions. Putin has managed to unite East, West, South and North. Ukraine is more united now than it ever was in the last century. People believed that the Russian army was the second greatest army in the world, and now they know that the second greatest army is in Ukraine. After learning so much about weapons, tactics and so on, we have become strong militarily. I like the joke that NATO now needs to apply to join Ukraine and not the other way around.

It is said that one of the French generals during the Napoleonic Wars was astonished to find that the Russians did not value the lives of their soldiers at all. The fact is, there are always more soldiers where they came from. And that means that Russia starts doing things that seem illogical and abnormal to any other military. During the Second World War, so many Soviet soldiers were sacrificed unnecessarily. Millions more could have survived if the Russian leadership cared about individuals. Today, when you see Putin you realise a person can be 100% evil. What Putin does is just pure evil.

In some sections of the population in Ukraine—and elsewhere—there is nostalgia for the Soviet Union. Those who were young in the final years of the USSR conflate the happiness of youth with the life in the Soviet Union. Perhaps, in the same way, lots of people in Germany were happy during the Nazi regime, not because of the Nazi regime, but because they were dating their boyfriend or living a good life in other ways.

Russian missiles smashing into Kharkiv was quite a wake-up call. Destroying infrastructure such as power stations already demonstrates that they know they will never win these territories, because if they had plans to develop the country, they would never wipe everything out. They simply want to ruin our life, then to ruin other countries' lives, then to ruin the world. Russia's mission is to export hatred, poverty, and corruption.

Many Ukrainians work in the EU. When they came back to Ukraine, they tried to bring back with them some of the positive things they'd learned from living in Europe. House construction, for example, or an attitude to the environment. We are never angry with people who live better than we do. We want to learn from them. We want to copy that style. We want to introduce these standards and behaviours and attitudes into Ukraine, not to destroy your houses, your schools or whatever.

But Russians do the opposite. They have so much work to do inside their country, but they don't do it. And then they come to Ukraine. They are surprised that we have better roads, that we have better apartments, that we have better wardrobes. And they loot. It's a tragedy when a Russian soldier comes into your home and steals your sneakers. But it's a tragedy for that country, not for Ukraine. We're not a rich country. But we are trying to work it out. We're trying to learn from others. And we don't hate others for the fact that they live better.

We were a part of the Soviet Union, so we have had problems around private property and private ownership. We are in the process of recovery, and while we recover, we learn. We borrow techniques and standards that have already been developed. We were very close to the epicentre of evil, and so it's undeniable that a lot of problems were imported from the Soviet Union. We are fighting this infection. It is a healthy process, a process of recovery. And, of course, we know Russia better than politicians or commentators in the West do. As Russia has now become a global threat, we can be useful here in explaining the ways in which Russians think and the ways in which they don't. (Russians are happy if you suffer the way they are suffering—everything is fine once you are equally wretched.)

This war is not yet won. But I believe that we will win. In fact, I think that we and our allies already won on the very first day, or on the second or third day of this war, when Putin's blitzkrieg failed, and the world saw his real face. Even if some politicians were ready to close their eyes, the citizens of this country did not. Russia has already lost. We continue fighting and we are losing people, which is a tragedy. But at the same time, we are already the winners in this war.

I don't know how it will end for Russia. Will it entail the fall of Putin's regime, or will he manage to survive? Perhaps, if it's the fall of Putin's regime, then maybe Russia will collapse, because there are lots of indigenous peoples that suffer inside Russia. They were brutally Russified. For example, in Siberia, there are a lot of people who believe they are a different nationality. But it will not be a geopolitical catastrophe. It may be that there will be lots of beautiful new independent states springing up within what was once the Russian Federation. People will be able to return to their cultural identities, to revive their national dances, languages, and so on. Why not? And Moscow will stay as Moscow.

28. HUNDRED PER CENT EVIL
Sasha Dovzhyk

Sasha Dovzhyk is an academic who moved back to Ukraine from Britain after the 2022 invasion. Her writing has appeared in the New York Times, Los Angeles Review of Books, The Guardian, New Lines Magazine.[30]

Lesia Ukrainka, a Ukrainian author, feminist and anti-colonial thinker, warned us in particular about Russian colonialism, and the danger of being mesmerised by the greatness of Russian culture. In her poetic drama 'Boyarynya the Noblewoman', based on Ukrainian history, Ukrainka explores the tragedy of a 17th century woman from Ukraine, where she has agency and is active in public and political life. She moves to Moscow, as a wife, where all her functions are reduced to just that—a wife. Ukrainka makes all these astute observations about the differences between Ukrainian and Russian culture, from a feminist point of view. She wrote it at the beginning of the 20th century, but all her observations are still valid.

I have a quotation from one of her letters, which refers to the vaunted greatness of Russian culture. The passage comes from her essay, published in 1896, in French. It's called 'The Voice of One Prisoner of Russia'. In it, she reacts to the celebration of a visit of Nicholas the Second to France in 1896, and to all these grand celebrations of a Russian emperor. She writes, 'My glorious brothers, do you know what squalor is? The squalor of a country which you call great? This is your favourite word, the squalid word greatness, the taste for which the French are born with. Yes, Russia is huge. One can send a Russian into exile to the end of the world without throwing him outside his country's borders. Yes, Russia is huge. Starvation, ignorance, criminality, hypocrisy and tyranny with no end in sight. And all these great misfortunes are huge, colossal and grand'. These are reflections of a turn of the century Ukrainian author who felt imprisoned inside the Russian Empire. That's extraordinary, isn't it?

The roots of Ukrainian resilience are in its history. We've been dealing with Russian imperialism and with various attempts to make us extinct for at least 300 years. The founder of Ukrainian literature, Ivan Kotlyarevsky, wrote a Cossack retelling of the Roman myth of Aeneas. We have humour as one of our coping strategies. We had literary figures such as Taras Shevchenko.

He too was again warning us about the dangers of imprisonment inside an imperial culture and was fighting with words for Ukrainian liberation.

This continued throughout the 20th century with writers like Lesia Ukrainka, but also with what we now call the executed renaissance of Ukrainian writers. We always have this amazing culture to fall back on.

What Russia is trying to accomplish these days is not only to bomb Ukraine into a waste land, into the barren fields of the 16th century, but also to lay waste to its culture—that there is nothing here. It's just this empty land to be invaded, claim and conquered.

We are fighting for our culture and to protect it. That our ancestors could not accomplish this, was probably because they did not have statehood behind them. Today, Ukraine has a state, and that allows us to fight for our survival. We have no choice. What else is there for us? We either resist this genocidal invasion or we just cease to exist. There isn't, honestly, anything else to be done.

You look back and see Russian imperialism create a culture that transcends all the national cultures. It's a miracle that Ukrainian culture did survive. This process is still going on. The most recent chain of destruction is the murder of Ukrainian writer Victoria Amelina by a Russian missile in Kramatorsk, where she was researching Russian war crimes. Victoria fought for her life for a number of days. Eventually she died, on the birthday of another Ukrainian writer killed by Russians, Volodymyr Vakulenko.

Volodymyr Vakulenko wrote a diary of occupation in Izyum. Victoria Amelina dug out the diary in the backyard of Volodymyr's family house. It was very important for her to actually find that diary. She knew of its existence from his parents, and she left us this testimony that she felt she was unearthing all the buried Ukrainian manuscripts, all the buried and unwritten Ukrainian texts, all the Ukrainian cultural riches that have been erased by Russia for decades, for centuries. Her effort to preserve Ukrainian culture was encapsulated by the uncovering of Volodymyr Vakulenko's occupation diary. This is an instance of Ukrainian perseverance and insistence that we must preserve this culture, and we must pass on the torch.

Victoria seemed to burn with a brilliant intensity. Her words had a kind of cutting edge of truth to them and a fury behind them. It's a horrible irony that she, of all people, was cut down by Russian bombs.

We have seen the home of Polina Raiko destroyed by the Kakhovka dam flood. I'm sure there are many dozens of other names of artists and writers whose works have been destroyed, whose apartments, archives, collections have been damaged and destroyed. This is a terrible, terrible price that

Ukraine is paying. Russian culture is not sending any of its creative people to the front. It's sending its worst people. It's sending people who are either criminals or people who are politically neutered. Meanwhile Russia is killing our cultural producers, our artists, our writers. These are Ukrainian voices; they burn bright and they're very prominent. I know of 19-year-olds who have not yet been able to accomplish much and who have been killed by Russia in this war. The loss to their parents and to us as a people is no less than the loss of prominent Ukrainian artists and writers. There are people that nobody will ever remember because they were just ordinary Ukrainians living in villages, and yet they took up arms and they sacrificed their lives for me and for people like me and for all of us. The challenge here is to remember everyone and try not to single out people whose lives feel more relevant for us because we do similar work. I don't know how we will be able to accomplish this, nor how we will be able to commemorate all these sacrifices.

Russia finds its people disposable. We don't. I'd like us to go back to the point which ruptured Ukrainian history. The Maidan protest, which started in November 2013, when Ukrainian president Viktor Yanukovych decided to turn the country's course from a pro-European alliance and to align the fate of the country with Russia. There were a number of protesters, most of them students, in the centre of Kyiv, in the Maidan square. Then Yanukovych ordered Ukrainian riot police to beat them up.

The footage of that beating of Ukrainian students on the news the next morning was so shocking and so painful that we felt as if we couldn't breathe. It was so enraging that the next day one million people went onto the streets of Kyiv in protest against the police violence. Ukrainians could not allow that to happen in their capital, in their country. It was outrageous. People rose up in response to that. Since then, every Ukrainian loss is mourned, since the first protester was shot down in the centre of Kyiv to the first deaths of Ukrainians during Russia's invasion. We mourn every loss as our own because it is our own. We value those lives that are being sacrificed for our freedom. We cannot allow our freedom to evaporate and to turn into this authoritarian state. In Russia, they've lost how many? The voices raised in protest are so few that they only emphasise the absence of protest in Russia.

I'm not here to offer my thoughts on the state of Russian civic society. I think it's non-existent. At this point, Russian society probably doesn't exist. They are so atomised and their voices are so muted, and that is probably one of the reasons why we don't hear them. How do I say this politely? I don't care. I don't care about the state of Russian civic protest, the absence of their resistance. I just try to concentrate my efforts on preserving this fighting spirit within my community to make sure that I do everything I can for Ukrainian victory.

Russian was my first language. I'm from Zaporizhzhia, a Russian-speaking region in the southeast of Ukraine. I was brought up in a Russophone family. Ukrainian was the language of my schooling, but because of the Russian narratives ingrained when I was growing up in the 1990s and early 2000s, Ukrainian was seen as a kind of provincial language—the language of farmers and peasants, not the language of high culture.

I chose Russian as the language of exploration. The literature that I was interested in was Russian classical literature, Dostoyevsky and Bulgakov and all the imperialist writers who actually denied my culture and my people the right to exist. It took me years and decades to realise that this had been imposed on me by the Russian imperialist project. I started exploring Ukrainian culture through language, later in life, in my 20s. But the definitive point in my switching to Ukrainian was the Maidan revolution and Russia's invasion of my country in 2014, when the land and the language question was used as an excuse or justification for the invasion.

The Russians said that they invaded my country in order to liberate me, a Russian speaking Ukrainian, from Ukrainian neo-Nazis who were staging a coup in Kyiv. I was part of the revolution that took place in Kyiv!

This Russian propaganda made me realise that they could weaponise my first language; but that I would not just voluntarily give them this weapon, and that I had to turn to the Ukrainian language and to start using it as my first language. I had to reject Russian because it was the language that gave them an excuse to come here to kill me. This shift was commonplace in 2014 and it's even more prevalent after 2022. Kyiv today sounds more Ukrainian than Russian to me. Everyone understands Russian, but not too many people will reply in Russian.

My attitude is also grounded in the reality that I witness in Ukraine. As you drive through villages in the Russian-speaking eastern part of the country, the villages that have been razed to the ground by Russian artillery fire. The villages and towns do not exist anymore. They literally erased Russian-speaking villages with their Russian-speaking populations from the face of the earth. This is what it means apparently when Russia liberates Russians.

We should also not discount Russian stupidity and ignorance. Remember the astonishing fact that Russian troops invaded the Chernobyl Exclusion Zone in the north of the country at the start of the full-scale invasion? They were the ones who dug trenches in the Red Forest. Every Ukrainian schoolchild knows it's radioactive, but it was apparently not known to the Russian invaders when they dug those trenches. A number of them got radiation poisoning.

Chernobyl was a nuclear catastrophe that polluted our land, and it was the direct result of Soviet policy. It's a fact of the Ukrainian collective memory. In Russia, these things do not exist because they happened elsewhere. They happened in these colonised territories, so they do not enter the national narrative.

One thing to mention at this point is that, despite sanctions against Russia, one of its largest industries is its atomic industry, and Rosatom is not fully sanctioned. This is a mystery. Why is their nuclear industry allowed to continue, pitching around the world and investing in very substantial infrastructure projects worth many tens of billions? Rosatom was among the first Russian enterprises that should have been sanctioned. After the occupation of the Chernobyl nuclear plant or the Zaporizhzhia nuclear plant, when personnel at the Zaporizhzhia nuclear power plant were tortured, kidnapped and bullied. We still allow them to carry on without any sanctions, without any repercussions.

The destruction and the poisoning of Ukrainian land and of the Ukrainian people were among the reasons why Ukrainians started their ecological movement, which was interlinked with the literary movement and with political activism. Ukrainians simply said that Russian dominance in our country is what will either kill us, or we will put an end to it. And this was one of the reasons why Ukrainians galvanised their political life, which was an element in the dismantling of the Soviet Union in 1991.

Since then, the impact of Chernobyl has been lingering in Ukrainian culture, in Ukrainian literature, even in works that do not discuss the impact of the explosion directly, you can still feel this sense of living next to a huge, indescribable catastrophe. There is an essay by Oksana Zabuzhko, one of the key Ukrainian literary voices, called Planet Wormwood, in which she describes this apocalyptic feeling of the end of the world.

There is gallows humour, which probably derives from the fact that you're always on the side of resistance, not the ones who come here to conquer. You cannot allow yourself to be swallowed up by grief. Nobody talks about whether they were woken up by explosions last night. It's just dull. Like rainfall drips, bombs drop, life goes on. Let's keep going. Let's just not be boring about it. When we buried Victoria Amelina a friend made a joke and I burst out laughing even while I cried.

Humour is a great anaesthetic. I think it's as true for Ukrainian culture as it is for Irish culture. This gallows humour is definitely one of the features of colonised peoples or colonised social groups. It's something that keeps them going.

We are currently the front line of this fight for freedom in the world, and that is felt by everyone here in Ukraine. Part of my job consists in helping foreign journalists who come here to cover the war. The smartest among them tell me that, in Ukraine, they actually feel alive, as opposed to in their native countries, because here you really feel the price paid for freedom. You feel the price and you cherish it. It is cherished here more than in any other part of the world. That is probably why Ukraine is so precious. We will continue making it clear to everyone around us. We will keep on being Ukrainian killjoys, we will keep telling everyone, remember who is fighting for your continued existence.

29. ENVY
Olga Tokariuk

Olga Tokariuk writes from Ukraine for TIME, Washington Post, Daily Beast, NPR, New Lines, Monocle, EFE, Il Foglio, ANSA.[31]

Mikhail Gorbachev is widely despised in Russia for his role in the breakup of the Soviet Union. For Ukrainians he's an ambiguous figure because on the one hand, yes, he contributed to the collapse of the Soviet Union. But, on the other hand, it's not as if his legacy is bloodless. He sent tanks to Vilnius, to Lithuania, to Azerbaijan, to Baku, and to other former Soviet Republics to suppress the drive towards independence in the weeks and months before the Soviet Union actually collapsed.

In Ukraine, he's also seen as controversial because he was in charge when the Chernobyl disaster happened, and he was involved in a cover up of that disaster. Just four days after the blast at the nuclear power plant, people in neighbouring Kyiv were ordered to march in the May Day Parade. So at a time when radiation levels were already very high, people in Kyiv were not told to evacuate or take their children out of the city. Only the party leadership and those close to the Politburo who knew about the catastrophe moved themselves and their families away from the radiation zone. Everyone else, millions of people, stayed in the Ukrainian capital. Many Ukrainians can't forgive Gorbachev for that.

I have my own personal grievance against Gorbachev. In 1985, the year he came to power, my favourite Ukrainian poet, Vasyl Stus, died in a gulag. Despite perestroika and glasnost in the USSR Ukrainian poets back in 1985 were still dying in gulags thousands of kilometres from Ukraine.

Under the Soviets, this was rarely mentioned in public. You could end up in a gulag or in prison, or, at the very least, be kicked out of your job if you brought up prison camps and gulags.

Particularly since Russia first invaded Ukraine in 2014, Soviet repression, the artificial Holodomor famine, the gulags are all discussed more and more in Ukraine. People discovered these pages of Ukrainian history for themselves for the first time, because it had been so taboo, and such a painful and traumatic experience. And now, of course, we are seeing this history repeated in front of our eyes, because it is exactly the same. What the

Russians have been doing since 1914 in the occupied territories in the south of Ukraine, in Donbas, in occupied Crimea since 2014 is following exactly the same playbook of deportations, prison camps, arbitrary detentions without charge, torture, parents being forcibly separated from their children. All are identical to Soviet repressive methods and under the Russian Empire. It's something the Russians have been doing for centuries.

From 2010, human rights defenders from the Memorial Organisation—an organisation labelled as a foreign agent and shut down in Russia in 2022—warned the cult of Stalin was once again alive and well in Russia. The Memorial Organisation was made up of people who were trying to keep the memory of Stalin's repressions alive, by telling the personal stories of those who suffered and died in the gulags, so that these crimes would not be repeated in the future. They were having a very hard time in Russia after the cult of Stalin was revived by governmental diktat. Founded in Soviet times, under Putin the organisation was dismantled.

It's hard to generalise the impact of the war on Ukraine, because Ukraine is a huge country, and different parts of the country have been affected in different ways. All Ukrainians have been affected, but not always in the same way. I'm from the western part of the country. I moved to the west with my husband and my daughter when the 2022 invasion started. It's very different, though, for my journalistic colleagues in other parts of Ukraine, especially those who worked in territories that are now under Russian occupation. They had to flee and start their lives anew, whilst also continuing to work as journalists to keep themselves busy, because that helps you to cope with the horrific nature of what is happening.

My own background is as an international news correspondent and international news editor, and as head of the foreign news desk at Ukrainian TV. That perhaps gives me a broader perspective than many other Ukrainian journalists who've only been covering local news and local politics. I can put events into context and maybe talk about them in a way which is more relatable for an international audience.

When I was asked to do a piece for the BBC, it was an offer I couldn't refuse. For me the BBC has always provided the gold standard for journalism. In that piece I shared my personal story of Ukrainian Independence Day.

It began when I was a six year-old girl, when I went along with my parents who, like 90% of all Ukrainians, voted for Ukraine's independence in the 1991 referendum. I didn't understand at the time what it meant, but I sensed that it was very important to them. As I grew up I felt it was important

Ukraine was independent. But I didn't really understand why, or what had happened in the past. Like many other Ukrainians of my generation, I took independence for granted. It was just there. As a young woman I didn't really celebrate Independence Day. But of course that changed abruptly in 2014 when Russia invaded Ukraine. Suddenly independence started to have a completely different meaning. It had to be defended with Ukrainian lives, sometimes by people younger than me, the generation born after independence. They were going to the frontline and were fighting and were sacrificing their lives to preserve Ukraine. After the 2022 invasion, the significance of independence day has become even more important.

As far as the reasons for the Russian invasion are concerned, I believe that the main factor behind this invasion is very trivial. Putin saw that Ukraine was becoming more democratic and more prosperous. In December 2022, Ukraine's average salary exceeded the average salary in Russia for the first time—despite the war that has been going on since 2014, despite the economic hardships that it entailed. Putin saw Ukraine's success as a threat to his regime. He saw a successful, westernising, democratising, prosperous Ukraine, and this was a threat to him, because, while Russians would turn a blind eye to many things, they wouldn't turn a blind eye to Ukraine becoming richer than Russia.

The transformation of Ukraine has almost gone unnoticed. One of the crucial changes was in the reorganisation of the Ukrainian army. It is a very different army from what it was in 2014, in terms of its capabilities, its flexibility, the potential to learn fast and to adjust and to take situational, tactical decisions at middle level without waiting for approval from above. There's a huge difference between the Ukrainian and the Russian military. And that, of course, is tied to the fundamental character of the Ukrainian people.

Ukrainian history is complex. It was the Vikings from Scandinavia who first came to Kyiv and established this city that became a cradle of Eastern Slavic civilisation. Christianity spread from Kyiv to Moscow, which was founded centuries later than Kyiv. There were ties with the West, with France, with Germany, as well as with Russia, throughout Ukrainian history. While a part of Ukraine fell under the Russian Empire, there was another part of the country that maintained strong ties to the West, to democratic or proto democratic states: the Polish-Lithuanian Commonwealth, the Austro-Hungarian Empire, and so on. It was a monarchy, but there was much more freedom for the expression of Ukrainian culture, literature and language, and also for a democratic tradition of governance at a local level. There was no serfdom as there was in the Russian Empire.

During the three decades of independence from the Soviet Union, Ukraine has faced many problems. It wasn't able to transform itself as quickly as some other countries of the former communist bloc such as the Baltic states or Poland or the Czech Republic. Some parts of Ukrainian society were integrated into the Communist Party and collaborated with the Soviet regime. So the starting point was very different. Nonetheless, there was a strong democratic, grassroots civil society in Ukraine, which has come to prominence when it became clear that the old Soviet-style elite wasn't capable of governing the country: Yanukovych was the last representative of this elite.

Ukraine is a huge and very diverse country. It's an independent country with a free media and a strong civil society. It seems to me that the fundamental difference between the Ukrainian and Russian political systems and the way in which they shape social attitudes is that, in Russia, everything has been tightly controlled from the top down. In Ukraine, that has never been the case. Since independence, there have been attempts by various presidents to establish that kind of control, most notably by Yanukovych. Fundamentally, this was the main reason that he was overthrown, because it was simply impossible to replicate the Russian model in Ukraine. That's what he attempted to do. But he overstretched himself by trying to achieve for himself what Putin achieved in Russia—absolute power.

After Yanukovych escaped and Russian aggression towards Ukraine began in 2014, it became clear to the majority of Ukrainians that this authoritarian model is not Ukrainian. That can sound quite paradoxical today, considering the result of the 2019 elections and the fact that President Zelenskyy and his party have a monopoly. While formally they have absolute power, in fact, it is nothing like the absolute power of Putin or Lukashenko. There remains disagreement within the government, within the governing coalition, and a lot of debates even within Zelenskyy's own party.

At the same time, civil society continues to grow. That has put a lot of pressure on the government and on the president to press forward with reform, particularly of the judiciary. Here progress has been really slow compared to other areas. But the pressure for change is there. It's even there while the war is going on. Society, civil society, NGOs, journalists, the people, are still keeping tabs on the government and using what tools they can to express discontent with some moves that they don't like. Some say this undermines our unity in times of war, but I think it's essential to keep Ukraine independent and to hold the government accountable, even in times of war.

Ukrainian Osint communities have been doing a remarkable job in collecting evidence of Russian war crimes and human rights abuses since 2014. One of these communities, InformNapalm, was founded by people originally from Crimea, who were personally affected by the Russian occupation. They started collecting evidence of what Russian soldiers were doing, then tracing them to military units in the Russian Federation, finding their social media profiles and collecting databases of the Russian chain of command. They are attracting more attention now because the government is leading efforts to document Russian war crimes. The General Prosecutor's Office is asking people to work as Osint researchers and send them the data, verified geolocations, and any images and videos, as testimony of Russian war crimes and human rights abuses.

The propagandists of the Russian state TV networks should also be included in any future trial. They have been inciting hatred against Ukrainians since 2014, describing Ukraine as a Nazi state and spreading all sorts of fake news.

They invent a story from scratch, and a lot of people will believe it and refuse to acknowledge any evidence debunking it. My father told me that he was texting with relatives in Russia, who told him that the Ukrainians were bombing themselves. These are people who are from Ukraine originally, but they have been living in Russia for decades, and they've been so completely brainwashed by this that they do not believe their own relatives in Ukraine, but instead choose to believe genocidal propaganda in order not to feel responsible for what's happening.

My hope is that this propaganda that Russian state media is spewing will finally be seen for what it is. Finally, we are seeing the clips from Russian state TV subtitled into English or into other languages and a lot of people abroad are shocked and surprised at the level of anti-West rhetoric attacking not just the UK and the US, but even Germany, which has been pretty moderate, one could say, towards Russia in the past. I hope there will be a greater understanding of the way in which this propaganda operates.

Of course, Ukrainians living in Ukraine have a much better grasp of the local context, and you don't have to explain things to a Ukrainian audience in the same way as you have for a foreign audience. But I think if you are telling human stories of people who have been affected by the war, whose relatives have died, or who have been witnesses to, or victims of war, then those stories work exactly in the same way for local and international audiences.

It's a good development that Western media outlets are opening their offices in Kyiv and are no longer reporting on Ukraine from their Moscow bureaus: that has been a problem for a long time. When you sit in Moscow, even though you may be anti-Putin and completely pro-democracy, you are still living in this toxic environment and communicating daily with people who are promulgating an imperialist, colonialist vision of Ukraine and Ukrainians. You might see as neutral some things that are not actually neutral, but are factually wrong.

For instance, take the phrase 'Russian-backed separatist', a common phrase describing Russian proxies in Donbas from 2014 onwards. If you say 'Russian-backed separatists', it implies that there was some local grassroots separatist movement that Russia just supports, as if Russia just backs it with money and weapons. In reality, there was never a grassroots separatist movement in Donetsk or in the Luhansk region of Ukraine before Russia invaded in 2014. It was Russian special forces who invaded these areas and paid a number of marginalised Ukrainians to fight with them. But everything was always led, orchestrated and financed by Russia and Russians.

It's a very welcome development that foreign journalists are now based in Kyiv, because it changes their perspective. In order to objectively report on a country, you really have to live there. You have to talk to its people. Maybe these journalists might even have more freedom to report on Russia from Kyiv than if they were still based in Moscow. Because, as far as I understand it, many foreign reporters in Russia are under pressure to keep their reporting, let's say, not too critical of the Kremlin in order not to be expelled from Russia as happened to Sarah Rainsford from the BBC.

Restrictions on the work of international journalists—refrain from criticism or we will kick you out—is the Kremlin's strategy. I don't want to imply that all media outlets are under Russian pressure or being compromised by Russia, but certainly some journalists, such as the Italians, are simply parroting what the Kremlin says. Of course, Italy is one of the countries that has been most compromised in terms of Russian money and Russian oligarchs. We all know about the ties between some Italian political parties and Russia. But that would be a topic for another conversation, I think.

30. THE NOBEL PEACE PRIZE
Oleksandra Romantsova

Oleksandra Romantsova is co-recipient of the Nobel Peace Prize of 2022 as Executive Director of the Centre for Civil Liberties, an organisation that documents war crimes and human rights abuses.[32]

For us the war began in 2014. That's when we started documenting war crimes. Initially we were a mobile group of volunteers, going into Donbas and using photographs and videos to document everything that had happened there in the aftermath of Igor Girkin's seizing of Sloviansk. Over the years since we have grown into a coalition of human rights organisations, all working together to document these thousands of crimes against humanity, this genocide, and to hold Vladimir Putin to account.

One of the things that has become clear through this work is how the most vulnerable are targeted. It's not just a war between armies, with professional soldiers fighting each other—it's the whole of the Russian population against the whole of the Ukrainian population. Finding the victims and witnesses who can testify to what has happened is a huge challenge. Nonetheless, the evidence is stacking up daily. Between 2014 and 2022 we had around 10,000 war crimes cases fully documented. Today, the number is over 36,500. Each week we add another 1000 to the total.

Collecting and collating this information is a way for us to put a halt to Russia's aggression, and to begin the process of bringing those responsible to justice before evidence is destroyed. For instance, the Russians are now going after men with military experience. Over the last nine years, we have had six waves of mobilisation, so there is a whole tranche of civilians, businessmen, taxi drivers, and others, who have fought on the front lines in Donbas, and they experienced things and saw things which we need to document. It's a massive challenge for the whole of Ukrainian society, but Ukrainian society is really flexible and motivated. Putin has said that Ukrainians shouldn't exist, and that has made our choices much easier—we have to fight.

What we can document is just the tip of the iceberg. For instance, after the occupation of a small sector of the Mykolaiv region, there were two men who were missing. The parents of each of the men approached us and asked us to find out what had happened to them. The bodies of both men were found in a basement, but there weren't just two men; there were 27 bodies in that basement. And that demonstrates the gulf between what we know about and what has actually happened.

There are so many instances when incidents remain unseen and unrecorded because they have happened in occupied territory. Occupation is not just a change of flag, or a different language being broadcast on the radio. It's thousands of small towns and villages where war crimes are being carried out every day, crimes which we are seeking to document in every way we can—from witnesses who are still in the occupied territories, who send messages or post on the internet, even sometimes from the photos which Russian soldiers post in open data such as Telegram chats.

The Russian Federation is trying to hide the war crimes being carried out in Mariupol. They are doing it methodically, by destroying every single building in which war crimes have taken place. That's why the Tribunal against Crimes of Aggression is so important. The Tribunal is crucial, because it provides a route to stopping those in authority who have chosen to control and manipulate their people. Without the recording and prosecution of war crimes, such crimes against humanity become normalised.

It's not the totality of the Russian population who are implicated. It's a few who have enriched themselves on Russia's resources, and who see themselves as better, and more valuable than everyone else. They have not invested in their own country, but have turned on their neighbours, and have turned the Russian population against their neighbours. It's abuse. I myself come from a Russian-speaking family. I am familiar with Russian culture, and I can speak to Russians with understanding, showing them how there is a different way of being.

That's why we Ukrainians are so dangerous to Putin and his cronies. We're not only fighting for ourselves, we're fighting for democracy. We chose democracy rather than autocracy, and that is why Russia is punishing us. Ukraine has suffered enormously during the Russian Empire, during the Soviet Union, and now under the Russian Federation.

We are at a point in history where we want to alter the pattern, and part of that is making sure that all the abuses are recorded and prosecuted. Even if the perpetrator is later killed in battle, they can still be prosecuted; the evidence brought against them, and they can be pronounced guilty. That's important. That's enforcing the rule of law.

There are all sorts of different kinds of war crimes being brought into play now. There is military aggression, there is economic warfare, there is information warfare—these are all challenges to be met by our international system. New weapons and new challenges.

One of Russia's ways of carrying out warfare is by attacking the healthcare system. As Russian soldiers have done wherever they have been, not only in Ukraine. They've done the same thing systematically in Chechnya, in Syria, in Mali—wherever the Russian military has been operating. Our database reveals just how systematic these attacks on hospitals have been.

It's really important for us as Ukrainians that we don't become like the Russians. That's why we hold to the principle of justice, and we assiduously, against huge odds, collect all this evidence. With the evidence we seek to draw a straight line between propaganda, between the words uttered in a speech, and individuals dying. It's not straightforward. How can you protect freedom of speech when people are using speech to disseminate propaganda?

In Ukraine we have freedom of speech to express our thoughts. We have freedom of assembly. That's why, in a time of crisis, we have so many volunteers joining up spontaneously, acting together as individuals. After the '90s, Russia turned its back on that kind of freedom. Ukraine is an open society, with the beginnings of democracy. Russia is very far from being an open society. In Russia there is no opportunity for individuals to express themselves, to take responsibility for their lives.

Ukrainians really love managing their own lives, and organise them to express their individuality. That's why Ukraine is a successful multi-ethnic society. The Russian Federation has about 500 different ethnicities under its control, and every one of them is despised and derided, and then dumped into the army to be killed.

It's not just Putin. It's an entire system. Feel uncomfortable? Swallow the Soviet Union pill, and you'll never have to think again. With 20 years of propaganda telling people that they were unfit to manage their own lives, of course they're not able to think for themselves. It will take a lot to change this, and I'm not sure we will manage. But there's a chance. If we freed all our people from the occupied territories, and educated them, and gave them the opportunity to take responsibility for their lives and their communities, that would be a beginning. But it's worth remembering that what is needed is not just a surface, external transformation. It's an internal transformation. And we can help Russian society achieve that. Once the war is over, and Ukraine is in recovery, we can seek reconciliation. Because, in the end, what we really want is to be a healthy society.

NOTES

1. According to some estimates.
2. 1 February, 2026
3. 22nd February 2023.
4. 13th January 2023.
5. 6th January 2023.
6. 5th August 2023.
7. 22 November 2022.
8. 12th July 2023.
9. 25th January 2023.
10. 5th June 2023.
11. 3rd October 2022.
12. 16th January 2023.
13. 6th August 2023.
14. 3rd February 2023.
15. 25th April 2023.
16. 13th December 2022.
17. 23rd February 2023.
18. 28th February 2023.
19. 23rd February 2023.
20. 17 December 2025
21. 22nd November 2023.
22. 1st June 2022.
23. 18th August 2023.
24. 18th August 2023.
25. 1st August 2023.
26. 31st august 2023.
27. 9th May 2023.
28. 12th December 2023.
29. 22nd October 2022.
30. 17th July 2023.
31. 1st September 2022.
32. 9th April 2023.

INDEX

BBC 28, 67, 106, 145, 146, 147, 198, 202
Belarus 25, 73, 80, 95, 99, 109, 111, 121, 124, 125, 128, 132, 154, 159, 179, 180, 181, 184, 187
Berezovsky, Boris 123, 128, 131
Carlson, Tucker 38
Chechnya 17, 36, 53, 72, 101, 107, 119, 136, 146, 205
China 33, 38, 44, 61, 81, 83, 85, 115, 117, 148, 154, 155, 158, 160, 161
Cold War 9, 10, 24, 42, 67, 85, 95, 98, 107, 134, 151, 160, 161
Covid 41, 42, 60, 85, 95, 182
Crimea 7, 15, 17, 41, 51, 52, 63, 75, 77, 81, 97, 103, 104, 109, 111, 114, 115, 120, 131, 132, 137, 152, 165, 168, 169, 183, 198, 201
DNR 103, 105
Donbas 7, 18, 40, 79, 85, 103, 105, 106, 115, 132, 135, 152, 165, 168, 169, 198, 202, 203
Donetsk 40, 41, 103, 105, 202
Dugin 18, 19
Erdogan, President Recep 155
EU 30, 81, 98, 99, 150, 155, 159, 162, 181, 182, 183, 184, 185, 189
Euromaidan 177
Gaidar, Yegor 97, 130
Georgia 17, 24, 28, 42, 43, 51, 67, 72, 81, 109, 110, 111, 112, 121, 131, 132, 180, 181, 187
Gorbachev, Mikhail 101, 102, 129, 137, 197
Gulag 31, 46, 114, 145, 186, 197
HIMARS 77
Holodomor 154, 186, 197
human rights 23, 168, 169, 171, 172, 173, 198, 201, 203
ICC 165, 166
imperialism 8, 19, 32, 101, 123, 155, 178, 191, 192
intelligentsia 179
invasion 7, 15, 17, 28, 37, 38, 40, 42, 43, 60, 74, 81, 84, 85, 98, 109, 112, 113, 114, 118, 119, 120, 122, 123, 131, 132, 137, 138, 140, 146, 149, 150, 152, 155, 167, 169, 172, 173, 180, 182, 183, 186, 191, 192, 193, 194, 198, 199
Kazakhstan 25, 99, 123
KGB 24, 28, 35, 36, 41, 45, 47, 53, 71, 95, 102, 111, 114, 118, 121, 123, 124, 125, 126, 128, 129, 130, 154
Khodorkovsky, Mikhail 22, 27, 28, 36, 123
kleptocratic 12, 16, 124
kleptocracy 13, 69, 151
kleptocrats 12, 107
Litvinenko, Alexander 49, 111, 127, 130, 146, 152
LNR 103, 105
Londongrad 10, 148, 151
Lugovoi, Andrei 130
Luhansk 40, 41, 103, 105, 202
Lukashenko, Alexander 25, 73, 78, 125, 128, 159, 181, 187, 200
MAGA 13
Magnitsky, Sergei 21, 23
Maidan 36, 41, 110, 119, 172, 175, 184, 187, 193, 194
Mein Kampf 84
Moldova 17, 51, 53, 67, 180, 182, 185
Moscow 8, 9, 12, 13, 15, 16, 19, 23, 24, 28, 33, 34, 36, 40, 41, 42, 43, 44, 49, 50, 53, 63, 70, 73, 75, 104, 109, 110, 114, 116, 117, 121, 122, 123, 124, 133, 135, 136, 139, 140, 141, 148, 155, 162, 163, 170, 178, 187, 190, 191, 199, 202
Munich Security Conference 34, 131
myth 10, 75, 137, 140, 141, 142, 177, 178, 191

NATO 16, 32, 37, 38, 40, 42, 43, 44, 58, 62, 63, 64, 65, 67, 68, 70, 72, 73, 75, 81, 84, 86, 97, 98, 100, 106, 109, 110, 111, 122, 135, 150, 152, 154, 155, 156, 162, 181, 184, 185, 188
Navalny, Alexei 27, 34, 35, 43, 46, 47, 109, 119, 152, 179
Nazi 7, 24, 30, 35, 66, 67, 106, 142, 146, 188, 201
Nemtsov, Boris 24, 27, 34, 117
NKVD
Nobel Prize 45, 203
North Korea 42, 76, 85, 86, 158
Novorossiya 177, 182
Occupation 114, 143, 165, 168, 192, 195, 198, 201, 203, 204
Odesa 18, 28, 182, 183
Odysseus 178
Orange Revolution 180
Patrushev, Nikolai 41, 43
Prigozhin, Yevgeny 19, 26, 27, 101, 167
Pushkin, Alexander 32, 111, 178
Revolution of Dignity 182, 183, 184
Saint Petersburg 38, 73, 75, 100, 102, 114, 120, 130, 141
SBU 147
Second World War 7, 11, 24, 35, 80, 98, 119, 135, 142, 143, 154, 175, 176, 187, 188
siloviki 108, 115, 118, 119, 124
Stalin 9, 32, 37, 40, 82, 110, 126, 132, 147, 154, 198
Strauss, Leo 176
Syria 17, 72, 114, 164, 205
Telegram 17, 43, 204
terrorism 182
Turkey 97, 154, 155
victimhood 30, 67, 68, 106, 176
Xi, President 37, 61, 82, 159
Yeltsin, Boris 9, 21, 22, 36, 97, 99, 112, 124, 125, 127, 128, 129, 130, 148
Yukos 15, 22, 152
Zaporizhzhia 82, 194, 195